Ordinary Theology

Looking, listening and learning in theology

JEFF ASTLEY
North of England Institute
for Christian Education

ASHGATE

Published by
Ashgate Publishing Limited
Gower House
Croft Road
Aldershot
Hants GU11 3HR
England

Ashgate Publishing Company
Suite 420
101 Cherry Street
Burlington, VT 05401-4405 USA

Ashgate website: http://www.ashgate.com

British Library Cataloguing in Publication Data
Astley, Jeff
    Ordinary theology : looking, listening and learning in theology. - (Explorations in practical, pastoral and empirical theology)
    1.Theology, Practical
    I.Title
    260

Library of Congress Cataloguing-in-Publication Data
Astley, Jeff
    Ordinary theology : looking, listening and learning in theology/Jeff Astley.
        p.cm. -- (Explorations in practical, pastoral, and empirical theology)
    Includes bibliographical references and indexes.
    ISBN 0-7546-0583-3 -- ISBN 0-7546-0584-1 (pbk.)
    1. Laity. 2. Theology. I. Title. II. Series.

    BV687 .A88 2002
    230'.071--dc21

2002023248

ISBN 0 7546 0583 3 (Hbk)
ISBN 0 7546 0584 1 (Pbk)

Typeset in South Africa by Martingraphix.
Printed and bound in Great Britain by MPG Books Ltd., Bodmin, Cornwall.

ORDINARY THEOLOGY

'Ordinary theology' is Jeff Astley's phrase for the theology and theologising of Christians who have received little or no theological education of a scholarly, academic or systematic kind. Astley argues that an in-depth study of ordinary theology, which should involve both empirical research and theological reflection, can help recover theology as a fundamental dimension of every Christian's vocation.

Ordinary Theology analyses the problems and possibilities of research and reflection in this area. This book explores the philosophical, theological and educational dimensions of the concept of ordinary theology, its significance for the work of the theologian as well as for those engaged in the ministry of the church, and the criticisms that it faces. 'Ordinary theology', Astley writes, 'is the church's front line. Statistically speaking, it *is* the theology of God's church.'

Explorations in Practical, Pastoral and Empirical Theology

Series Editors: Leslie J. Francis, University of Wales, Bangor, UK
and Jeff Astley, University of Durham, UK

This series encourages new developments in pastoral, practical and applied aspects of theology worldwide. Drawing together leading international authors from a range of disciplines, and with a firm footing in academic research as well as ministry or other practical arenas, this cluster of books aims to advance new scholarship and practice across a diverse range of contemporary topics, with the intention of rejuvenating the relevance of theology to the life of the individual and to society.

Contents

Preface

Over the last few years I have been working with the concept of 'ordinary theology', something that has grown out of my concern to take seriously the beliefs of 'non-theologically educated' churchgoers and other Christian believers, and of those outside the churches. This notion also chimes in with my conviction that the genesis of a person's religious belief, understood in terms of her religious *learning*, is also of considerable significance.

Neither of these themes has received much attention from academic theologians, not even from many of those who work in the domain of practical theology. Popular theology is just not very popular in such circles. I hope in this text to present some grounds for a more serious consideration of its nature and origins. It is my belief that the study of ordinary theology can promote a perspective that meets the contention of Edward Farley and others that we should recover theology as a fundamental dimension of piety, an inherent part of *every* Christian's vocation. In this way, theology may be given back to the laity with a vengeance.

This volume does not purport to be any sort of definitive study. It should be thought of as no more than an *essay*, a tentative attempt that has something of the manner of a venture or speculation, intended to provoke discussion. Nor am I presenting here a carefully researched empirical account of the beliefs of any group of 'ordinary Christians'. This book represents more of a plea for the study of ordinary theology than an example of such a study. Nevertheless, I will draw where I can on empirical data, and my thinking throughout will be informed by my own research and particularly by my reading of many transcripts from interview studies of adult lay Christians. It will also draw on my experience over thirty years as an Anglican priest involved in various ways in parish ministry, chaplaincy, consultancy and Christian adult education work, as well as in teaching and research in higher education.

What follows brings together a disparate range of literature, including educational, empirical and philosophical studies, as well as publications from different areas of theology. It seems to me that this is how practical theology and the study of religious learning can best be done, as a multidisciplinary exercise focused on a complex field of practice. Such a procedure is likely to tax severely the depth and range of a single author's knowledge, however, and I can only hope that sympathetic critics will be willing to contribute from their own specialisms to a widening of the debate and a deepening of our understanding of this area.

In reflecting on these topics, I have benefited greatly from conversations with friends who would happily describe themselves as ordinary Christians and who also fall into my category of ordinary theologians. I have also received helpful criticism and insights from discussions that followed presentations of some of this material at the University of Durham; the University of Wales Bangor; Hinde Street Methodist

Church, London (Hugh Price Hughes Lecture Series) and my institute's own Christian Education Seminar.

I am particularly grateful to Professor Ann Loades, CBE, of the University of Durham's Department of Theology, for her encouragement in the early stages of my thinking, and to Mrs Evelyn Jackson for her diligence in typing and retyping the many drafts of this text alongside all her other work as Administrative Secretary at the North of England Institute for Christian Education.

Stylistic Note

I have sometimes written about human beings in the feminine gender and sometimes in the masculine. In nearly all such cases, 'she' implies 'she or he' and 'he' implies 'he or she'. I believe that this shorthand is acceptable provided that it is adopted in both forms.

Acknowledgements

The author and publisher are grateful to the *British Journal of Theological Education* and the *British Journal of Religious Education* for permission to rework previously published material by the author. They also wish to express their gratitude to the following for permission to quote from other material: The Community Religions Project and Professor Kim Knott of the University of Leeds Department of Theology for permission to quote from the Religious Research Papers on Conventional Religion and Common Religion in Leeds; Professor George Pattison and Dr William Kay for permission to quote from their unpublished work.

Chapter 1

The Learning Context of Theology

This book is concerned with two different but closely related things. In the first two chapters it explores the significance of learning for religion, and argues for a recognition of the importance of the learning context of our theology. In the next three chapters it reflects on one of the main products of that learning for the great majority of Christians, a product that I call 'ordinary theology'.

Ordinary theology is my term for the theological beliefs and processes of believing that find expression in the God-talk of those believers who have received no scholarly theological education. Ordinary theology is routinely ignored by academic Christian theology. As John Hull put it at a symposium hosted by the North of England Institute for Christian Education in July 1996, 'If theology is what goes on in people's lives, we know amazingly little about Christian theology.' Precisely so. I believe that we ought to do more to remedy this ignorance. I therefore offer here an analysis and apologia for this concept, together with a justification for the study of ordinary theology, and especially for listening to it and looking for it in the words and lives of ordinary believers. I argue for the relevance of these themes for Christian theology, the Christian religion and Christian learning, and for living theologically in response to our learning of Christ.

My purpose is to offer a 'theology in context'. We should take the preposition 'in' seriously. It expresses 'position within' and is to be distinguished from 'into', which would suggest that the theology that we need to do here lies beyond and flourishes outside all contexts, but may condescend to move or orientate itself towards one of them. 'In' is a preposition of inclusion, not direction. It is used to express the sense that theology needs to be done from inside a particular framework of interests and concerns.

The Centrality of Practical Theology

The phrase 'the theology that we need to do here' suggests that there are different types of theology. The species of theology that I am attempting in this book often carries the rather obscure and slightly embarrassing label of 'practical theology'. Although this phrase is more familiar than it once was and what it refers to is not now considered quite so demeaning an activity, any person or activity described as 'practical' runs the risk of being allowed into polite company only if they can show themselves able to provide some useful service, and then for no longer than it takes to unblock the drains. Once the floorboards are back in place, they will be expected to return to wherever their vans are stationed until the next time the householder notices that something has gone wrong.

'Practical theology' is, indeed, about practice; it is concerned with practical matters, including 'practices' in the more technical sense of co-operative human activities governed by implicit rules. In Christianity such practices encompass a wide range of overtly and implicitly religious activities: pastoral care, counselling and spiritual direction; the forming and maintenance of community; the teaching and learning of religion (and therefore preaching, education, evangelism and other forms of communication); social and political action; prayer, worship and liturgy; responses to moral issues at an individual, interpersonal, communal and global level; and so on. Traditionally these ministries and behaviours have been thought of as *applications* of theology – the points at which 'pure theology', whatever that might be (presumably the discipline of systematic theology), is put to work deductively and applied to the life of the church and the world.

But most of those who confess and call themselves practical theologians today do not see the situation like that at all. For them, the movement at issue is not to be thought of as a slide from theory, principle or tradition down to practice. It involves, rather, a more complicated set of movements, often with the first manoeuvre being some sort of 'inductive' or 'situational' shift from practice to theory, a move which must then be followed by a return to practice. On this account, the starting point and the finishing point are both located in the same place, and practical theology begins and ends with the practice of the Christian faith as its practitioners experience it (cf. Atkinson and Field, 1995: 42). While 'applied theology' might seem to imply that theology is not affected by interaction with practical issues, and has been 'given immunity from having to change in the light of experience', 'practical theology' suggests a more interactive and dialogical process of mutual change (Pattison and Woodward, 2000: 3). The self-critical reflection that is often taken to be an integral part of practice thus 'involves a circular movement from practice to critical reflection and back to corrected practice, or to radically transformed practice' (Kelsey, 1992: 123).

Although practical theology has been variously defined, all such definitions make some reference to the particular territory on which it focuses. As I have indicated, this territory is usually identified with Christian practice or (as it is often put) Christian *praxis*.[1] In more detail, the focus is on 'Christian life and practice within the Church and in relation to wider society' (Ballard and Pritchard, 1996: 1) or, more subtly, 'the mediation of the Christian faith in the praxis of modern society' (Heitink, 1999: 6).

But practical theology is about theology as well as practice. It is always theological, although the ways in which its theological dimension has been understood are many and varied. They include interpreting practical theology itself as a theological *discipline*, and treating it as a *field* which the discipline(s) of theology (along with other disciplines) attempt to understand (cf. Tracy, 1983; Williams, 1985; Ballard and Pritchard, 1996: ch. 5 and 171–7; Wood, 1996a: 312; Heitink, 1999: ch. 7). Different accounts have also been given of the ways in which the reflections of the practical theologian may guide Christian action and being (cf. Fowler, 1983: 154–5; Osmer, 1990b: 227; Browning, 1991: 36; Ballard, 1995;

---

[1]   Praxis is reflective action or 'value-directed and value-laden action' (Graham, 1996: 7).

Heitink, 1999: chs 8, 9 and 11). However this is conceived, practical theology is usually thought of as having some practical use. According to Charles Wood, for example, practical theology is 'that dimension of theological study which pursues the question as to the fittingness of Christian witness [understood as practice] to its context' (Wood, 1996a: 312–13; cf. 1985: 47–9; 1996b: 356–7). This includes reflecting on how Christian practice and church structures help or hinder valid Christian witness. And that, presumably, is a useful thing to do.

Like other theologians, practical theologians do not much enjoy being sidelined. They hold that they have something to contribute to the rest of theology. Some apologists for practical theology go further, arguing that they can offer a way of understanding all theology, for Christian theology *as such* 'should be seen as practical through and through and at its very heart' (Browning, 1991: 7; cf. Osmer, 1990a: 148). One basis for this claim is that our secular and religious practices are themselves 'theory laden'. Our reflective practice, it is said, always has an underlying *theological* dimension that comprises the framework of religious meanings and values which (at least in our culture) is implied even by many of our secular practices. Our practices, and therefore our experiences, are thus undergirded by meaning, in so far as these things are 'meaningful' to us. It is these meanings that shape the questions, concerns and criteria that we bring to our more 'theoretical' discussions about the Bible and Christian doctrine, which have themselves arisen in very specific contexts of human and religious activity. All real theology, it may then be argued, arises in a *dialogue* between 'us' (our lives and experiences) and 'them' (the Christian tradition). This dialogue – or, to use more informal language, this conversation – is between the 'interpretations', the implicit or explicit questions and answers, of Christian Faith, on the one hand, and those of our human experience and life, on the other. In general terms, then, all Christian theology may be thought of as a discipline that attempts to correlate 'the meaning and truth of an interpretation of the Christian fact [its scriptures, doctrines, rituals, witnesses, symbols, etc.] and the meaning and truth of an interpretation of the contemporary situation'; with the sub-disciplines of fundamental, systematic and practical theology only differing in the emphasis which each side of the correlation receives (Tracy, 1983).

When theology is construed in this way, it is *contextual*, as is every conversation. Theology is always set in some context, rooted in some life experience or issue. This context, to deliberately mix the metaphors, may be thought of in terms both of the setting of a dialogue and of a dance. It is the conversation that takes place during the embrace between the dancers of present, contextualized, experienced practice, and their partners from the dancing school of past tradition. The conversation they engage in, as they go backwards and forwards, circles around some concern or another, but always returns to the point from which the dance began. It is a *real* conversation, for both partners speak during their dance; and 'as with all authentic conversation, critical freedom and receptivity are equally important in allowing the subject matter to take over in the back and forth movement between text and interpreter' (Tracy, 1981: 255, cf. 101, 167, 452; cf. also Tracy, 1975: chs 3 and 4; Gadamer, 1982: 325–33).

Such images of movement and conversation often underlie accounts in practical theology of the correlation that is required between experience and tradition. This 'mutual relation' must not be thought of as wholly without controversy. The progress of the talk during this particular dance is not always smooth; questions are asked and explanations sought, both of tradition and of experience. Yet 'the goal is not to attack the tradition, but to befriend it; . . . to make it accessible' (Kinast, 2000: 68). On this interpretation, then, all theology is practical, and all theology is 'in context'.

Learning as the Key Term

I want now to argue that part of the context of Christian theology is its *learning context*. I believe that it is a large part of that context, but it is a part whose significance is frequently hidden or ignored. We need to recognize its importance, for doctrine is 'an aspect . . . of Christian pedagogy' (Lash, 1986: 258) and 'religion itself is a kind of learning' (Holmer, 1978: 145). Its concepts, arguments, attitudes and practices are all learned.

I deliberately use the word 'learning' here rather than 'education', because education is by definition a more narrow thing. This is true in three ways. First, education is usually defined as facilitated learning: that is to say, learning that is intended and engineered, what some have called 'deliberate learning'. But not all learning is promoted by teaching. Some learning is unstructured; it 'just happens'.[2] We may think of the 'hidden curriculum' of our life or our liturgy, which impacts on us and changes our values, dispositions or beliefs. It is a truism, at least on a wide definition, that 'most situations could be regarded as potential learning situations' (Lawson, 1974: 88).

Secondly, 'education' is a word that for many people implies self-conscious critical reflection and explicit cognitive understanding (cf. Astley, 1994b: 37–40). For them, 'education' is always education-with-critical-understanding, what others might call (revealingly) 'real education'. This usage restricts the word to cognitive learning processes by which people learn knowledge and beliefs. Learning, however, in the loose sense that I wish to adopt, is a much wider concept. It labels *any* enduring change brought about by experience.[3] We learn (that is we change in) our values, dispositions, attitudes, feelings and skills, as well as in our beliefs and understanding. I therefore reject the claims of those who flatly assert that 'learning without understanding is not learning' (Barrow and Milburn, 1990: 179; cf. Astley, 1994b: 33–5).[4]

---

[2]   Others allow that teaching may happen without any conscious intention, so that we may be said to be 'taught' by books or environments (Moran, 1997: ch. 2, 175–9). My use of the term learning should also be distinguished from that adopted by those philosophers of education who insist on a definition of learning as '*intentionally* coming to know, or believe, or perform . . . as a result of experience' (Hamm, 1989: 91, my italics).

[3]   Sometimes this change is no more than a *reinforcement* of our existing patterns of knowledge or behaviour (cf. Rogers, 1986: 43).

[4]   Some who have written of growing into a culture have adopted the Greek word *paideia* to label a broader notion of education in character and contemplation (Kelsey, 1992: ch. 3; cf. 1993; Hodgson, 1999: chs 4 and 5). James Fowler advocates using the German word *Bildung* ('formation') for this more comprehensive understanding of intentional

My final reason for focusing on learning rather than education is that education will be assumed by many to be an activity directed solely to children. A related restriction is to treat the word as synonymous with *schooling*, which designates the formal, institutional education of the 5-year-old, the 18-year-old, or those of us who are still stuck in some sort of school beyond our fiftieth year. A great deal of learning does take place in these institutions, of course, but much also takes place outside them. Adults as well as children learn in homes and factories and churches, in streets and on hills. And although the Christian church has its own educational institutions, more is often learned in situations of worship, fellowship, conversation and joint endeavour than in the context of formal classes. To locate Christian learning on this wider canvas, and to include adults within its scope, helps to underscore the claim that (even if we have ourselves moved away from all educational institutions) our learning is not just something that is in the past. And this is itself a significant insight: learning is something that takes place *now*; I learn *whenever* I change my beliefs and attitudes in response to experience. 'Lifelong learning' is not a new invention, then. It is as old as life, as well as being as long-lived as our human inventiveness.

The Means of Christian Learning

I want to say something now about the ways in which Christianity is learned and the significance of these ways for our thinking about its nature. I shall begin by shamelessly purloining a text from Søren Kierkegaard. It is to be found in a collection of material from the end of his life published in translation as *Kierkegaard's Attack upon 'Christendom'*. He writes there about 'the eternal', that about which Christianity is concerned, as being 'not a thing which can be had regardless of the way in which it is acquired' (Kierkegaard, 1968: 100).

Now Kierkegaard insists on this point because he is arguing that Christianity is a 'method' or a 'way': 'the eternal is not really a thing, but is the way in which it is acquired.' As he writes elsewhere, 'Christianly understood, the truth consists not in knowing the truth but in being the truth', because 'truth is, if it is at all, a being, a life'; and 'when the truth itself is the way, the way cannot be shortened or drop out, without the truth being corrupted or dropping out' (Kierkegaard, 1968: 100, 138; 1941b: 201–2). For Kierkegaard, therefore, 'In respect to *God*, the *how* is *what*. He who does not involve himself with God in the mode of absolute devotion does not become involved with God'; and 'eternally speaking, . . . the means and the end are one and the same thing' (Kierkegaard, 1967, Vol. 2, sec. 1405; 1941b: 202). Thus the

---

education, which includes both formal and informal contexts and processes (Fowler, 1983: 155; 1990: 64). However, *Bildung* 'is intended mainly in an intransitive and reflexive, not in a transitive sense' to denote *self-formation* or *self-cultivation* through a process of experience and reflection, best seen (according to some) as 'critical formation' (Nipkow, 1996: 55). Peter Hodgson also insists that *paideia* 'entails a multidimensional critical thinking' (Hodgson, 1999: 115).

'what', the goal or product of religious endeavour, cannot be separated from the 'how', the way in which we reach it.

The point I want to make is at least analogous to Kierkegaard's claim, but I want to press this quotation to serve a rather broader thesis. I steal his text to illustrate my claim that *the nature of our religious faith is partly, but significantly, determined by the way in which it came and comes* (and, indeed, goes). My claim is that the product of learning is specific to the processes of learning, at least sometimes and to some extent.

We can readily think of secular analogies to Kierkegaard's principle. If your doctor, personal trainer or 'life counsellor' has advised a 4-mile walk each day, it is no use taking a 4-mile drive instead, excusing yourself on the grounds that this will take you to the same destination along the same route. It is *the walking* that matters; the walking is everything. But this is because the essential point of this journey is the exercise rather than the destination. I want to argue, however, that the learning may be 'everything' in other circumstances as well. Sometimes our learning can come in no other way; what I have learned here, in this way, is what it is *because* I have learned it here and in this way. This is a claim that cannot be made of all types of learning. I can learn many historical facts about China from reading a book, by talking to Chinese people, or by accessing an educational CD-Rom or Internet web page. In this example, there are many different ways to the same end, and the end is relatively undetermined by the means. But this is in marked contrast to the sort of learning on which I now wish to concentrate.

The examples that come most readily to mind include some processes of learning that are specific by definition. We may learn obedience through suffering (cf. Hebrews 5: 8) and learn to be a servant by experiencing the service of others (cf. Luke 22: 27; John 13: 14–17). In such cases, the learning end may be wedded to its means. Thus I cannot learn obedience-through-suffering – that is, I cannot learn the sort of obedience that one only learns through suffering – without doing the suffering (cf. Kierkegaard, 1941b: 201–2). Similar things may be argued of those occasions in which people learn how to bear failure by failing, or learn how to be joyful by seeking out situations that bring joy.

But there are other examples whose truth does not come in this tautological, analytic way. Many of them are examples of learning through action and of learning through life experience and, particularly, of learning that involves the emotions and results in profound changes in our attitudes and values. In a word, they are all *self-involving* forms of learning. This is the case when we consider the difference it makes to know some person or some place directly, through our experience of or 'acquaintance' with them, as compared with knowing *about* them without ever having met the person or visited the place – knowing them 'in absence', as it were, by means of descriptions reported by others through conversations, lectures, books, pictures, CD-Roms and the like. In self-involving forms of learning, how our knowledge of a person or place comes to us will control to a much greater extent and in a more profound way what it is that we learn about them, and how we think about what we have learned about them. Such learning, I contend, cannot be had 'regardless of the way it is acquired'; for the learning process contributes to what is learned, in a way similar to the manner in which the 'the *how* of a speaker's discourse becomes or shapes the *what*, the thought content' (Manheimer, 1977: 161). Here the medium (of education) is, in some sense, a part or aspect of the message. It somehow informs what is passed on.

Marshall McLuhan famously argued for a profound and intimate interaction between the medium ('process') of communication and the material (the 'product' or message) being communicated – 'the medium is the message' (cf. McLuhan, 1964; Marchand, 1989). McLuhan's dictum, understood more generally in terms of some congruence between the 'what' and the 'how' of learning, may be applied to the learning situation in a range of different ways. In this chapter I shall suggest a number of examples that are particularly relevant to the learning of a religious faith.

The Role of Affect

Specific emotions serve as marks of personal religious understanding (Berntsen, 1996: 239). For this reason, I cannot be said fully – or perhaps even remotely – to understand, say, the doctrine of creation that I purport to embrace, unless I experience the appropriate affective states: feelings of dependence, contingency, gratitude and awe. Nor can I be said to understand the Christian claims about Jesus' relationship with God, unless I positively evaluate Jesus, ascribe supreme worth to him, and come to worship him. 'Without such things as fear, contrition, and increasing love of God', Dean Martin argues, the concept of God has not been fully understood (Martin, 1994: 190). Such a complete religious understanding can only result from an affective (affect-creating, affect-laden) learning. In addition to learning feeling-states, in learning a religion one learns a range of what we may call affective *skills*. These include 'the reordering and redirecting of one's affections' (Martin, 1994: 188): processes that encourage the shift in the learner from a third-person to a first-person expression, which is the most important aspect of the movement from the state of learning about a religion to that of learning the religion (see Chapter 2).

Modelling and Apprenticeship

Secular education has begun to value again the ancient 'apprenticeship' model of learning, which has such an honourable place in the church's traditional understanding of Christian discipleship (cf. Melchert, 1998: 222–5, 252–3, 285). An apprenticeship perspective in education normally includes an understanding of the teacher as *mentor*: one who provides support, sets challenges and offers a vision that includes a map of the tradition being passed on and the language that it uses (Daloz, 1986: 215–35). Under the right circumstances, and with the right person, the teacher-mentor will model the particular skills and knowledge that need to be learned. It is uncontroversial that we learn to be like a master or mistress in the way that they exercise their craft, professional role or scholarly discipline.

But apprenticeship is not just a matter of passing on information or technical skills, nor is it just conduit-learning. Additionally, what teachers are like in their character and demeanour, their character virtues and spirituality, may affect what *we* are like (cf. Bandura, 1969). We learn not only their ideas and their actions; we also learn to *be* as they are, and their attractiveness as models can profoundly influence the effectiveness of this learning (Meye, 1988: 109–14; Melchert, 1998: 239, 256). It should not be thought, however, that such 'transmission', 'nurture' or 'formation' involves any manipulation of the learner or loss of her autonomy in mere submission (cf. Thiessen, 1993; Astley, 1994b: chs 4 and 5; 2000a: 106–7).

In the literature on moral education, the development of moral attitudes in the learner and the transmission of values to her is routinely described as 'character education'. As David Carr argues, this requires some acquaintanceship with individuals and communities that already exemplify the moral virtues. He writes:

> Nothing is more legitimate, indeed urgent, than for teachers and other educationalists to appreciate that the moral education of children, the job of acquainting them with those homely and familiar human excellences called the moral virtues – honesty, tolerance, fairmindedness, courage, persistence, consideration, patience and so forth – is the highest and most important task of education. The schools which best provide this firm foundation for living well are . . . those in which children are taught by teachers who are themselves clearly committed to integrity, truth and justice and who have sought to transform the school and the classroom into the kinds of communities where a love of what is right, decent and good is exhibited as often as possible in the conduct of those into whose care they have been given.
>
> (Carr, 1991: 269)[5]

Such a learning of character is surely key to any convincing account of Christian learning. And here again the way of learning can profoundly influence what is learned.

But Christian education requires the learning of Christian practices also. 'Christian education is that particular work which the church does to teach the historical, communal, difficult, countercultural practices of the church so that the church may learn to participate in them ever more fully and deeply' (Dykstra, 1996: 117). How might this best be done? Again, the teacher-mentors will model the practice into which the learner is to be inducted. The role of language is highly significant here. Lave and Wenger argue that in secular industries the apprentice's learning does not come by way of replicating the performances of others or acquiring knowledge that has been transmitted by instruction, but through what they call 'centripetal participation' in the learning curriculum of the industry's practice. This process involves 'learning to speak as a full member of a community of practice'. They hold that apprentices do not learn much from talk *about* a practice, for this does not help them to learn to talk *within* the practice. Talking within the practice fulfils not only the obvious functions of exchanging information and focusing attention, but also that of 'supporting communal forms of memory and reflection, as well as signalling membership' (Lave and Wenger, 1999: 25, 29–30). (Talking about the practice comes later, as the apprentices share anecdotes of past or paradigmatic practice.) I shall argue for a parallel situation in Christian learning.

---

[5]   For a detailed description and analysis of how this works out in practice in schooling, see the excellent study *The Moral Life of Schools* (Jackson *et al.*, 1993: 44, 286–94 and *passim*).

Collateral Learning

People rail against the educationalist who takes an hour and 50 minutes to inform his audience that most people these days cannot cope with more than 20 minutes of continuous speaking (Craig, 1994: 39). The teacher-educator who lectures on the importance of student discussion while preventing his students from getting a word in edgeways is also held up to scorn. In such examples, we fear that the medium may prove to be a stronger message than the one that the teacher intended to convey. John Dewey used the term 'collateral learning' for much of the 'formation of enduring attitudes' in educational situations. He wrote, 'Perhaps the greatest of all pedagogical fallacies is the notion that a person learns only the particular thing he is studying at the time' (Dewey, 1963: 48).

Part of this collateral learning arises from what educationalists call the 'hidden curriculum': a set of experiences through which people learn very effectively, but which are not explicitly labelled as *learning* experiences, and which normally are not consciously intended as such. There is a marked analogy between the hidden curriculum that underlies all the manifest curricula of education, and the non-verbal communication that results from the tone of voice, gestures, and facial expressions that accompany a speaker's explicit verbal communication. In the latter case, there is strong evidence that these implicit messages are often communicated more effectively than the explicit ones (cf. Argyle, 1983: ch. 2).

The character formation considered in the previous section provides a good example of the effectiveness of a hidden moral curriculum. In the religious context, everything from behaviour in the pews prior to a service, through ritual, music and church architecture, to reading church noticeboards and budget decisions may be said to serve as a medium of implicit Christian learning.

> All Christians, and all Christian activities, operate as sources of Christian learning whether they intend (or are intentionally-designed) to teach us Christianity or not. . . . [Through its hidden curriculum,] worship is arguably the most important medium of implicit Christian learning.
>
> (Astley, 1992: 143, 149)

These experiences provide a powerful message, partly because they are so ubiquitous and partly because we are unconscious that we are learning through them. Unfortunately such messages are often at odds with the explicit message that those who control these media intend to convey through them.

The Bible as a Teacher of Style

Writers on the role of the Bible in religious communication have offered some convincing arguments for the influence of the biblical medium on the message of the Christian gospel. For example, E. A. Judge argues that Paul's unwillingness to be a boastful teacher who praised himself was an 'unprecedented atrocity' in his age. His unboasting teaching was a shocking thing, and was itself intended to communicate a gospel that threw over the contemporary structures of privilege. The way that Paul taught the gospel, therefore, conveyed a message that he saw as part of the gospel.

> Paul regards boasting as folly. Yet his argument with his competitors draws him inexorably into it ('you forced me to it' [2 Corinthians 12: 11]) and he launches himself into a formal and long-sustained recital of his credentials [2 Corinthians 11: 22–3]. . . . But Paul, in an appalling parody, inverts the contents of his self-eulogy, in order to boast of his weaknesses. . . . Why did he do it? Because he had learned from the case of Christ the paradox that weakness and humiliation put one in the position where God's power prevails [2 Corinthians 12: 9–10].
>
> (Judge, 1996: 86)

One might argue that this reverse-boasting is a matter of explicit content, rather than implicit process or 'style'. But at another level, Paul's failure to fulfil the expectations of his readers (his failure to boast properly) conveys his radical message better than anything he actually does say. This is an example of the silence of the 'null curriculum' (that which is not explicitly taught) speaking volumes.

Jesus is master of the processes of religious communication. The style and method of Jesus' teaching was consonant with, and perhaps the only way to convey, his good news. John Tinsley illuminates this claim in his thoughtful reflection on Emily Dickinson's poem, 'Tell all the Truth but tell it slant – Success in Circuit lies' (Dickinson, 1970: 506). Tinsley emphasizes the importance here of what Kierkegaard called *indirect communication*. This method of pedagogic humility, which is the opposite of didactic teaching, is an attempt to engage a person by means of ambiguity and contradiction. The communicator approaches people and awakens their subjectivity 'from behind': 'manoeuvring them into a position from which they themselves, as a result of interior reflection, could step back and make a radical choice between remaining where they were and opting for a fundamental change' (Gardiner, 1988: 38; Pattison, 1997: 4–5, 27–8, 89). For Kierkegaard, God's revelation in Christ was necessarily indirect, both so as to protect our freedom and responsibility and also because 'the nature of God is such that it is impossible to recognise him directly' (Rose, 2001: 117). Kierkegaard explains indirect communication through the telling analogy of saying something 'to a passer-by in passing', without stopping him to discuss it and 'without attempting to persuade him to go the same way, but giving him instead an impulse to go precisely his own way' (Kierkegaard, 1941a: 247).

As we might expect, indirect communication involves the communication of abilities, capacities and skills of how to do something or how to become someone. 'The key word for indicating indirect communication is "How"' (McPherson, 2001: 165). According to Kierkegaard, the gospel message is not to be objectified but responded to. 'The difference between direct (naïve) and indirect (reflective) communication is that the latter is symbolic and requires interpretation and therefore an "appropriation process"' (Manheimer, 1977: 202, cf. 149–51, 159, 161, 189). Maria Harris comments: 'The intention of the teacher is to manifest content in such a way that the content escapes attempts to make it fixed, secured, ordered, understood, and tolerable. At the same time, this content *seduces* into rapt attention' (Harris, 1991: 70).

Tinsley agrees that the proper communication of the gospel must be a self-effacing and indirect communication, for 'the gospel is not only *what* is said, but *how* it is said' and therefore learned. Jesus is a 'prophet of indirect communication': '"Telling it slant" is more than an appropriate form of the gospel; it is its essential content, a manner incumbent upon the Christian communicator by the very nature of the gospel' (Tinsley, 1996: 88, cf. 92). Hence Jesus is indirect about himself ('Let me ask you a question'), about the kingdom ('It does not come with observation') and about the nature and intentions of the God who, in the Synoptic tradition, is described in parable, paradox, ambiguity and irony – as a God of hiddenness, spoken of in a provisional, incomplete revelation (Tinsley, 1996: 93; cf. Melchert, 1998: 245–51). As indirect communication oriented towards response, Jesus' teaching method itself may be interpreted as a catalyst for salvation. By 'engaging people in conversation and forcing them to reflect on the deeper meaning of their convictions', and by providing resources through which they can break the hold of the powers that constrain them, Jesus' teaching 'continues to work salvifically' (Hodgson, 1999: 140).

The theme of indirection is also taken up by Kenneth Cragg in his discussion of the biblical revelation and its informal, *human* medium. Cragg distinguishes this chancy process from the model of revelation in Islam, in which the 'text does not in any way participate in the texture of its reception' (Cragg, 1981: 24). The New Testament literature could not have come about on this Islamic principle of verbal, direct revelation. It is, rather, indirect and incarnational, in a way that is appropriate to the 'hazardous' form, context and mechanics of Jesus' teaching ministry and its reception, mediation and dissemination. Infallibilism is an impossible position to hold with respect to a revelation that is so rooted in the human and to a specific earthly time and place. As Cragg insists, 'One cannot well infallibilize what does not come that way' (25).

Learning Attitudes

The central argument of this chapter is perhaps most clearly shown not in any factual beliefs, but in our attitudes and values and the orientations of life that incorporate them. We may consider as an example the attitude-disposition of 'trust'. In so far as we 'learn to trust', our trust has some source; our *trustfulness* derives from the trustworthy relationships that we have experienced in the past. I am concerned here, however, not with the past but with how we are *now*. Part of my point (although it is only a part) is that the engine that drives our current attitudes and virtues is powered by the memories, images and emotional aftertastes of their origination that still lie deep within us. Thus a *complete* description of your trust for others and for God would include some description of how you learned, and how you continue to learn, so to trust.

The psychologist James Day has emphasized the 'embodied' or 'incarnational' aspect even of our most cognitive and secular learning. He writes:

> When we talk about educational experience we feel something physical. We see faces and hear voices as we speak. The notion of education as the imparting of a truth apart from the way we experience it is false, dangerous and corrupting.

> (Day, 1999: 277)

It is in the area of attitude learning that these maxims are most convincing. Day tells the story from his research interviews of 'Sharon', her passion for algebra (!) and the signal influence in shaping this passion of Mr Norton, her teacher. Sharon confesses:

> I had a teacher who *loved* algebra, and made me feel it meant the world to him that I could love it too. . . . When I do algebra, I think of him. I see his face, I hear his voice, and when I get stuck on a problem in mathematics, or maybe even a problem, you know, in life, I think of how it was he talked with me. I hear his voice as I think the problem through, it's like I talk with him about it. . . . To me, algebra is what it felt like to learn it with Mr Norton, and though I know the subject well, I can use it to my personal benefit and teach it to others as a subject, I can't say that my thinking about it or my sense of its importance are at all independent of him.

> (Day, 1999: 267–8)

Her father had retorted that all this meant was that she had a crush on her algebra teacher, but Sharon sternly denies this. She admits, however, that there is a form of love here: 'When you care for something, when you believe in it as I have come to feel about algebra, there is a kind of love involved.' Mr Norton had certainly been a catalyst for this different sort of attraction and response. He had helped her to fall in love with algebra.

There are significant parallels here with a great deal of our religious learning, which at its deeper levels is closely related to falling in love.

Process as Content

Many of these examples are illustrations of the general educational claim that 'instructional practice' (broadly speaking, educational approaches, methods and techniques) may properly be regarded as an educational *content*: that is, as a subject matter in its own right. Indeed, some have called it 'structural content' or 'process content' (Lee, 1985: 8, 79; 1973: 28).[6] Theologians, by contrast, often assume a merely instrumental view of the processes whereby the Christian religion is learned, conceiving it 'as some sort of formless entity, without structure or substance of its own'. Process is then conceived as equivalent to nothing more substantial than the grease on the track along which theological goods are conveyed 'intact and unaffected to the mind and heart of the learner'. But the instructional process, for good or ill, is much more than that. It is 'a dynamic substantive in its own right which exercises significant impact on the shape and form and even product content of learning' (Lee, 1971: 238–9). Thus educational practice is itself a content; indeed 'everything which occurs in the concrete teaching-learning situation is content' (Lee, 1973: 29).

---

6   In educational jargon, content is 'the name given to that which the teacher teaches and the student learns' (Lee, 1985: 13): that is, subject matter. The situation is complicated by the fact that in any given educational process (what goes on in the teaching-learning situation), the substantive content that is taught and learned may be a process in *its* own right – for example the acts, performances or operations of thinking, loving, reflecting, believing, feeling, valuing, trusting, experiencing, living, and loving – as well as a 'product' in the

James Michael Lee castigates those whose approach to Christian education encapsulates a wholly inadequate understanding of what it is to be Christian. This is the case in the traditional method of memorizing a catechism, particularly in any repressive atmosphere that frowns on discussion and debate. Readers of Frank McCourt's *Angela's Ashes* will perhaps recall in this context the schoolmaster's response to young Brendan Quigley's question about 'Sanctifying Grace':

> Never mind what's Sanctifying Grace, Quigley. That's none of your business. You're here to learn the catechism and do what you're told. You're not here to be asking questions. There are too many people wandering the world asking questions and that's what has us in the state we're in and if I find any boy in this class asking questions I won't be responsible for what happens.
>
> (McCourt, 1997: 130)

Lee comments on this type of traditional, limited education into Christianity:

> It is assumed that a learner becomes religious primarily by acquiring a set of doctrinal propositions or by receiving from another some key insights into the intellectual understanding of these doctrines, to be followed up by conative acts faithful to these doctrinal propositions. But the process by which the learner accomplishes this all too frequently squeezes out of him the vital juices of religious awaring and valuing and living.
>
> (Lee, 1971: 38)

Implications for Theology

It is for reasons such as these that *a complete description of our learned faith must include some reference to its genesis.* It will thus be rather messy and in places fairly obscure. It is natural, therefore, to want to sluice it down and spruce it up; removing these marks of origination so as to reveal the naked, clear and timeless cognitions that are embodied within our wind-blown, lived-in and learned beliefs, attitudes, values and dispositions. Sometimes, of course, this is exactly what we should do, not least in academic theology. But if we *always* operate in this way when we do theology, we shall never know the full truth about the nature of the central structures, concepts and dynamics of our own, or other people's, concrete and distinctive lives of faith. The subjective meaning that a particular idea or belief has for someone depends on a range of connotations and associations, both cognitive and affective, that are peculiar to his or her life experience and past learning. This sort of learning can never be plucked out of its context and picked clean; it always carries with it some of the soil in which it was nurtured (cf. Lee, 1973: ch. 6). If we ignore the learning context of a person's Christian theology, we shall not be able adequately to understand or describe it.

---

sense of an outcome of *these* processes (for example thoughts, beliefs, knowledge, values and other achieved states, orientations or dispositions). See Lee, 1971: 56; 1985: chs 2 and 3. On the 'process-product paradigm' more generally, see Gage, 1978: 69–74.

How can we give a full account of such theology? When I used to teach an introductory course on Christian doctrine within a programme of theological and ministerial education, I would begin by asking the students about the 'formative factors' that had shaped, and were now shaping, their own Christian beliefs, attitudes and practices. I had at hand a checklist against which to compare their answers, ultimately derived from John Macquarrie's *Principles of Christian Theology* (Macquarrie, 1977: 4–18). Armed with this crib, I invited them to respond by reference to such factors as *reason*, *revelation* in *scripture* and *tradition*, *experience* (broadly conceived) and *culture*.

I soon had to give it up. I discovered that my innocent request was invariably met by total bewilderment and an embarrassed silence. I came to understand that the problem lay in the artificial grid that I was forcing on to their personal faith. It was not that they were unable or unwilling to talk about origins and influences. When I finally got them to talk, they invariably spoke about people, sermons and services, and significant events and periods in their own and others' lives. (They often did this very eloquently; but I have learned not to equate eloquence of expression with significance or integrity of content.) They acknowledged many learning situations and contexts as occasions of and influences on their faith formation. In particular, they identified significant changes in their beliefs and in the depth of their beliefs through times of suffering or joy. Many of them knew when and where and how they had learned at different levels and in different ways to be Christian, and most of them could identify occasions and learning experiences that had helped them to become more Christian – or, sometimes, less Christian. When they were allowed to name the influences in their own way, putting aside the clean-cut convenient categories of traditional academic theology, the exercise proved to be much more natural and straightforward.

Yet it is never going to be an easy task. Religious faith has deep roots; it is deeply rooted in the tangled morass of the mangrove swamps that constitute our lives. And down below those murky waters, our faith is anchored in even murkier mud. It is only when it grows up into the light and publicly spreads its branches of beliefs and values that we – and others – can get a good view of what it looks like. But clarity is not everything; and a *superficial*, easy clarity can sometimes obscure a deeper truth. By my fruits I may be known, certainly; but the learning *roots* of my faith are also part of my faith flourishing, and if you want fully to know about my faith you should take account of them as well. Each of us knows something about our own roots, usually more than others do, anyway; but some of my roots may be hidden from me almost as much as they are from you. It will take us both some hard work to trace them properly.

One might ask whether it is worth it. I think so. If I have learned one thing about religion and about people over the years, it is that our judgements about both are as a rule quite superficial. If I have learned two things, the second is that the depths are worth the plumbing. We should not despise our earthly origins and early anchors. To affirm them is part and parcel of the Pauline claim that 'we have these treasures in earthen vessels' (2 Corinthians 4: 7). If I need a theological justification for this study, therefore, it is that it embraces a perspective that accepts the doctrine of creation fully, acknowledging that this is how and where and why we are what we are, humanly-speaking and Christianly-speaking. As creatures, we can only learn and know and be, and therefore we can only learn and know and be *religiously*, in this human, messy and muddy way.

And, behold, it is very good.

Chapter 2

Learning Religion

With a very few special exceptions a person comes to believe under the influence of others.
(Ritschl, 1984: 49)

The word 'God' does not come to us from nowhere. It comes to us from the history of its uses.
(Lash, 1986: 263)

I also hold that religion is something that we have largely learned and now learn. This is not to deny that there are some aspects of it that are 'innate', in so far as some attitudes and dispositions that make up the general orientation on which religion builds are natural to us (cf. Clack, 1999: 116–24). By God's intention, human nature is such that 'our hearts find no peace until they rest in you' (Augustine, 1961: 21). But the greater part of the edifice of our religious beliefs is learned, as are the associated religious attitudes, religious values and dispositions to act and experience in religious ways. Our instinctive reactions have developed into religious beliefs, affects and practices under the tutelage of a religious culture. Religion is learned from others, and ultimately from a tradition or history; in one way and at one level it is a *fides ex auditu*. If and when it becomes 'our religion', it is learned in another way and at a different level, through personal reflection and experience and (yes, in this sense) our personal 'discovery' or even 'invention'.

And if learning is the right word for 'a permanent or lasting change in knowledge, skills or attitude which is the result of experience rather than maturation' (Gordon and Lawton, 1984: 105; cf. Gagné, 1972), then religion is something that is still being learned, as we continue to change. As indicated in the previous chapter, this learning is not always facilitated by teaching and even when it is it often occurs outside formal educational institutions of any kind, 'as a process incidental to everyday living' (Lovell, 1984: 30). Learning, it is often said, is like breathing: 'something everyone does all the time – a fundamental human process' (Tight, 1996: 21). On this wide definition of learning, no distinction can be made between what I am calling learning and the 'acquisition' of a culture 'within the family at a very early age' (cf. Davie, 1994: 29), or indeed elsewhere and much later. This too is true of religious learning.

Our religion, then, is a *learned* and a *learning* thing.

The Centrality of the Learner

Religious learning is too often ignored. Admittedly, some will give it a certain sort of pre-eminence just because it arrives chronologically early in the religious life. But even after all the guests are assembled at this particular feast, it deserves to take a higher place than we usually allocate to it. Learning is central to religion. Put more boldly, this may be expressed in the educational aphorism: *the learner must come first.*

Learners First

I admit that, like many good aphorisms, this one has sometimes been run to death and seriously abused. I too have sat through adult education and in-service training experiences in which we were earnestly encouraged to 'share our situation and our perceptions', when what we really wanted – and really needed – was to *learn something*. It frequently felt as though the only thing that was being shared under these circumstances was our ignorance, confusion and sense of frustration. Such situations illustrate a reduction to the absurd of 'learner-centred education'. 'Child-centred education', the equivalent of this approach in the school situation, can similarly be taken to extremes, in this case leading to the nonsense of an 'open education' where the child's interests alone determine what is taught. We must ever beware the dubious morality of an extreme consumerism, even where it is advocated by educationalists. Education is not to be understood 'as one giant department store in which facilitators are providers of whatever learners (consumers) believe will make them happy'. Stephen Brookfield adds an admirably balanced judgement:

> For a facilitator completely to ignore learner needs and expressions of preference is arrogant and unrealistic. But it is just as misguided for a facilitator to completely repress his or her own ideas concerning worthwhile curricula or effective methods and to allow learners complete control over these.
>
> (Brookfield, 1986: 97)

At its best, however, putting the learner at the centre is much less contentious, and much more profound, than these scenarios suggest. It means that in reflecting on and engaging in any educational process, the main focus of attention should be the learner rather than the subject content or the teacher (cf. Knowles, 1975: 18–21). This is an approach that involves treating the learner as a whole person, one who possesses a heart as well as a brain, and also has a life beyond this particular learning situation. In addition, learner-centred education recognizes that 'significant learning' takes place best, or even only, when the subject matter is perceived by the student as relevant for his or her own needs and purposes (cf. Rogers and Freiberg, 1994: 35–7). Most importantly, it acknowledges that 'all learning takes place according to the mode of the learner' (Lee, 1982: 137): that is, as controlled by the motivations, interests and pre-understandings of the learner, and (particularly) according to the processes of human learning and development. Learning does not take place 'according to' the logical structure or originating source of the subject matter content, whether this be physics, a foreign language or a religious tradition. And unquestionably, the nature of the learner's learning does not bypass the processes of her own cognitive, affective and lifestyle learning, and therefore cannot be solely, simply and straightforwardly determined by the influence of the pious or intellectual characteristics of any teacher, nor even of his pedagogical techniques. This emphasis on keeping the learner at the centre is one that is most sympathetic to the so-called 'humanist' theories of learning (cf. Elias, 1982: ch. VI; Rogers, 1986: ch. 3). However, it is both possible and necessary to ensure a focus on the learner in more teacher-centred 'behaviourist' theories and more subject-centred 'cognitive' learning theories as well (cf. Elias and Merriam, 1980; Cross, 1981: ch. 9; Saddington, 1992).

Some of these claims may be disputed, but few would deny that the learner comes first at least in the sense that learning is something that only the learner can 'do'; it is something that can only 'happen to' the learner. However good the teaching, however carefully and intelligently prepared the environment and the experiences that facilitate her learning, learning only takes place when the learner changes. And the way that change takes place is in large part a function of the learner himself or herself. 'What the learner learns' is in the end dependent on, and very much determined by, the processes of – and therefore of the person doing – that learning (cf. Gagné, 1977: 22–4).

To say that the learner and her learning comes first is also to say that where there is no learning there has been no *effective* teaching. Learning is usually taken to be an 'achievement' (thus, 'I tried to learn the dive, but it was quite beyond me'), whereas teaching is normally understood as a 'task' ('I've repeatedly taught him how to do the calculation, but he hasn't grasped it'). But however these words are construed, 'the success of the teacher depends on the success of the learner' (Langford, 1985: 126). When teaching is understood as a task, 'what the teacher teaches' may be thought of as a function of the teacher and the subject matter being taught. The learner's learning, however, is never simply identical with the object or the form of the teacher's striving.

Putting the learner at the centre has implications about how we view the content of education, what is and has been learned. If religion is largely learned, then our religious faith content is a *learned faith* and we are faith learners. Once upon a time we did not have it; even now it is changing, and the word 'learning' is a fitting label for much of that change. Many of these changes originate from outside ourselves, appropriated through our sense organs as a result of our reading, listening and looking. They are, fairly unambiguously, 'the result of experience'. But changes in our religious beliefs may also originate on the inside, as do other changes, through processes of remembering and reflection, of deliberation or arguing with ourselves, and of agonizing with our hearts and our minds. 'Inner' mental and affective processes, although they appear to be more active than does our reception of sensory data, are still things that we experience, interpreting experience in its widest sense. On this broad view, to 'experience' is simply to 'live through' something: to 'encounter or undergo' an event or occurrence 'which leaves an impression on one' (COD, 1999: 501). Our own occurrent thought processes, memories, imaginings and feelings certainly do that. Some would even say that learning may be the proper word for changes in our mental processes, attitudes and behaviour that result from *unconscious* experience. At all events, we may agree that 'there can be no learning that does not begin with experience' (Jarvis, 1995: 66).[1]

---

[1]   We should note that some definitions of learning avoid any mention of the word 'experience', defining it simply as 'a change in human disposition or capability, which persists over a period of time, and which is not simply ascribable to processes of growth' (Gagné, 1977: 3).

It is a truism that life changes us. Here is another: 'Experiential learning in everyday life is almost synonymous with conscious living' (Jarvis, Holford and Griffin, 1998: 56). William Heard Kilpatrick writes:

> Learning is the tendency of any part or phase of what one has lived so to remain with the learner as to come back pertinently into further experience. . . . We learn what we live, we learn each item we live as we accept it, and we learn it in the degree we accept it.
>
> (Kilpatrick, 1963: 239, 244)

Life is all experience, of course, and it is a major part of making us what we are. 'To adults', the adult educationalist Malcolm Knowles has remarked, 'their experience is *who they are*' (Knowles, 1990: 60). An adult *is* what she or he has *done*. Life and learning makes us what we are, through change. 'Learning is *the* major process of human adaptation' (Kolb, 1984: 32).

But there is no life in general, only *our* individual lives. As the learners at the centre, what is changing is *us*. In terms of Christian learning, it is still *our* faith; and it is only our faith because we have learned and still learn it. Christianity is for us, necessarily, a learned faith: our Christ is a learned Christ, our God is a learned God. This is as true of the learning that comes from our own contemporary experience of God or the risen Christ as it is of the understanding of God and Christ that we have learned from other people, with which I am mainly concerned. All religious realities are learned and experienced by me, from and in my human context. They are never known by my 'jumping out of my skin' to embrace a God, a faith or an understanding that is not mine. All my embracing is done from within this 'skin', and it is through my skin that I make what is alien my own. Even if I convert to your beliefs or values, or to those of St Paul, St Francis or St Jürgen Moltmann, that is only because *I* have changed, and my believing and valuing has changed. On the account I want to develop here, then, I *can only* have my own faith; I cannot own anyone else's.

Nevertheless, I have also argued that any faith normally arises – that is, it is learned, moulded and transformed (and sometimes broken) – in a conversational dance with others, in and through my contextualized practice. So it is never just *my* faith and I am never the sole author of it. We are not isolated individual monads each with our own private religious language corresponding to our private religion and theology. I will make much of the personal and individual nature of our theology in this book, but this should not be thought to be incompatible with the social and communal nature of our existence. I agree that our self-understanding 'will never be purely arbitrary or subjective' because of our continuing dialogue and encounter with others, which involves critical rationality and therefore 'accountability' (Pattison, 1998: 83).

Yet my faith cannot be properly described as mine unless it is rooted in my individual and communal commitments and acts: acts that are expressed and performed daily at my home and work and play, in my life choices and through the hard uphill slog of my flawed discipleship. Christian learning is 'learning the Christian Way' along the (*my*) Christian way. There is no other road.

Changing One's Religion

Learning is change. Religious learning involves quite major changes in our attitudes, beliefs, values and dispositions, and even in our skills and capacities. Much of this learning happens, of course, in our infancy, childhood or adolescence. During those very fluid periods we undergo huge changes as a result of the external influences to which we are subject, as well as from developmental changes that are more internally driven. These are, indeed, our most 'formative' years.

But adults also change. Their learning, like all learning, is change; it therefore always involves a transformation. Some educationalists have drawn our attention to a particularly potent example of this and labelled it 'transformative learning'. Usually associated with critical self-reflection, it may be defined in terms of its outcome – a change of perspective or habit of mind. I am very conscious of the extent to which my own adult life experiences have changed the quality and connections of my faith, and most people will have registered something similar going on in their own case. These changes are a result of a great variety of situations. In particular, 'transformative learning is stimulated by encountering viewpoints that are discrepant with our own' (Cranton, 2001: 103). In religion we are sometimes encouraged to ignore such changes and to hold instead to our earlier understandings. But those who think that a set of beliefs and attitudes formed in childhood, or at the time of an adolescent conversion experience, is all we need for our adult religious life are badly mistaken. Life is *about* change: 'to live is to change', as Newman insisted, and we cannot really stop ourselves changing. We need to acknowledge how much we change and have changed as adults, in our beliefs, attitudes and values; and how often these changes can be traced to particular experiences and particular practices in our lives. This is one of the great truths of religion that most adults know; it constitutes another reason why 'we must stop keeping the experience of adulthood a secret' (Simmons, n.d.: 18).

Such claims scarcely require documenting for the history of theology confirms them at every turn. We hardly need reminding of all those conversions, all those 'changes of mind', which include changes in a person's 'past ideas, attitudes, values or behaviour, more generally all four of these accompanied by intense feeling' (Clark, 1971: 531). These changes have also been described as 'transformations of a person's loyalties, pattern of life, and focus of energy' (Rambo, 1980: 22). Such conversions arise in and from particular, and often changing, contexts: Paul, Augustine and Francis; Martin Luther, Ignatius Loyola and John Wesley; Leo Tolstoy and Albert Schweitzer; Simone Weil, Karl Barth and Thomas Merton (cf. Krailsheimer, 1980).[2]

---

[2] Barth complains how slow to learn human beings are, and puzzles over the fact that he did not learn 'much sooner' that true Christian doctrine 'has to be exclusively and conclusively the doctrine of Jesus Christ . . . as the living Word of God' (Barth, 1969: 43). Learning takes time because of a range of internal, developmental and external, experiential factors (including our experience of historical change, which was surely crucial to Barth's own change of mind). Without these, learning would be a different phenomenon altogether and less of a human one. (But perhaps it is the recognition of this that lies behind Barth's complaint!)

These are examples of extreme transformations, of course. But religious change of mind and heart is not limited to such classic cases. More recently, if less famously, the philosophical theologian David Pailin wrote that he was forced to 'revise my views on the saving reality of God and on the relationship between God and human beings' by becoming friends with Alex, a seriously handicapped baby who died at the age of 13 months. He confessed that 'Alex has been for me a source of revelation': 'What he has done is to make me think hard about what the Christian gospel means for all human beings. What is the liberation of the children of God that is true for him as for all finite persons?' (Pailin, 1992: 1, 11, 184)

There are many other examples in theology. And from philosophy too, which is perhaps more puzzling, as philosophy would appear to be more of a 'purely' cognitive activity that one might expect to be less open to the influence of new experiences. Yet although Bertrand Russell's repeated changes of metaphysical mind may have been driven solely by the force of the arguments, Wittgenstein's 'conversion' over the nature of language seems to have been partly precipitated by particular experiences and events.

Elsewhere in philosophy the problem of relativism provides some interesting examples of change. Many theologians and philosophers scathingly dismiss both moral and cognitive relativism because of their (perhaps terminally disabling) paradoxes. But powerful experiences have often generated these positions; and those experiences, at least, should be taken more seriously. Here is the philosopher Paul Feyerabend admitting to an educational context for his own conversion to relativism, which was a conversion that expressed his rejection of the 'superficiality and presumptions of a philosophy that wanted to interfere with a well formed practice'.

> In the years 1964ff Mexicans, Blacks, Indians entered the university as a result of new educational policies. There they sat, partly curious, partly disdainful, partly simply confused, hoping to get an 'education'. What an opportunity for a prophet in search of a following! . . . I felt very differently. For it dawned on me that the intricate arguments and the wonderful stories I had so far told to my more or less sophisticated audience might be just dreams, reflections of the conceit of a small group who had succeeded in enslaving everyone else with their ideas. Who was I to tell these people what and how to think?
>
> (Feyerabend, 1987: 317–18)

This snippet of autobiography may also serve to illuminate Alasdair MacIntyre's more cautious insistence that the issue of relativism arises at the boundaries of a culture, where the bilingual speaker must communicate *both* with his own family or village *and* with a new, and very different, 'outside world'. For MacIntyre, the experience that arises in this practical context 'explains' the origin of the theoretical claim that truth is relative to the different communities of language user. Furthermore, it is in reflecting on how in practice such a situation may arise that MacIntyre develops his insight into how relativism, which cannot be 'refuted', may yet be 'transcended' (MacIntyre, 1994).

These examples, both of one-off experiences and also of widespread, common situations, provide evidence for a clear influence of the originating context in the reflections to which it gives rise. John Hick supplies us with another example illustrative of the theme of relativism, this time with a theological emphasis. Hick believed that he had said all that he had to say in theology and the philosophy of religion when his first book, *Faith and Knowledge*, was published in 1957. His later, more distinctive and more influential, work was provoked by a move to the English city of Birmingham in the late 1960s, and his involvement there in issues of race and the problems of multicultural communities. This experience induced him to think through a theological position that he believed was *implied* by the new attitudes and practices that he, and many other Christians, found themselves adopting towards people of other faiths: 'their frank recognition that there is a plurality of divine revelations and contexts of salvation' (Hick, 1985: 11). Such a pluralistic theology seemed to Hick to follow from the position many Christians adopted over such issues as the proper form of religious education in community ('county', 'state' or 'common') schools, and over debates within the churches about whether redundant church buildings should be made available for non-Christian worship (cf. Hick, 1980: ch. 3). This is the experiential and practical background to Hick's frequently repeated remark that if he had been born in India he would have become a Hindu, rather than a Christian, as would very many others (Hick, 1983c: 78–9). It would appear that similar and equally potent reflections have produced the pluralist theology of religions that is now held by many believers (see p. 158 below).[3]

John Hick was involved in the process of creating a new and more plural agreed syllabus for religious education. Educational contexts of a more 'chalkface' variety are also highly effective in provoking the sort of reflections that lead to theological change, in teachers as well as students. Stewart Sutherland has argued that educational practice 'thrusts upon theologians questions which otherwise and mistakenly they might "leave till the end"'. He adds that certain theological questions and issues, which raise 'matters of fundamental substance about the very nature of theology itself', are 'set in sharp relief by the problems faced in the practice of education' (Sutherland, 1986b: 37).

I recall such a change in a particular group of conservative evangelical students who were preparing to teach religious education in English schools. Their church's official theological position, which they claimed to endorse, was that 'false religions' were demonic; even to study them objectively was to put oneself at risk of spiritual damage. Yet, after a while, these students seemed quite happy to teach about Hinduism, Sikhism, Buddhism and Islam in an educational context. During discussion several of them admitted (or, perhaps, discovered) that their deeper knowledge and experience of other faiths and, in particular, their own experience (practice) of teaching about them, had contributed to a change in their theological position.

Sutherland recognizes that educational contexts are not the only situations apt for posing theological problems. He contends that the centrality of such issues as the challenges of science and the problem of suffering to the lives of ordinary people and the pastoral practice of the church gives them an insistence and priority that

---

[3] Michel de Montaigne made a similar claim in the sixteenth century: 'another region, other witnesses . . . might imprint upon us in the same way a contrary belief' (*Essays* 2: 12).

academic theology rarely matches. But the churches' own official theology is often similarly negligent. In a recent British survey (Hay and Hunt, 2000: 27–8), the largest single group (41percent of the sample) chose as an explanation of why some people do not believe that there is a God, the response that 'there is too much suffering, poverty and injustice in the world for God to exist.'[4] The authors comment, 'The problem of suffering is probably the single most difficult issue for believers in a good God, yet it often seems to be avoided by the representatives of the institution, or covered up by sentimentality' (36).

The experience of life helps to form and change our theology because it is *our* experience that we connect with the Christian story. Much has been written of the way that pain and suffering can change people's spiritual stance and religious beliefs, for good or for ill. 'Suffering is the greatest teacher', von Hügel writes. 'Suffering can expand, suffering can contract' (quoted in Ford, 1997: 137). There are biblical precedents: for example, in the Old Testament narratives and prophecies of Hosea, Jeremiah, Deutero-Isaiah, Job and Jonah (cf. Eichrodt, 1967: 349–71); and the theme is explicit in many of the Psalms (cf. Weiser, 1962: 66–83). The stories about Jesus in the New Testament traditions are open to the interpretation that Jesus' own theology was radically changed through his anticipation and experience of spiritual and physical suffering. Perhaps the Last Supper and Gethsemane marked turning points from a theology of options and possibilities to a recognition of the divine necessity and the forced choices that imposes. Certainly, it was Jesus who was first compelled to develop a theology of the cross (cf. Green, 2001).

One might easily multiply these illustrations of theological change. While academic theology researches the historically and intellectually significant examples, it is likely to ignore more domestic and everyday ones. Empirical studies also tend to concentrate on 'events that were of fundamental importance' in people's lives, although a person's theology – like 'the history of a person's life' – is 'perhaps determined for the greater part by the most trivial and ordinary of experiences' (Zuidberg, 2001: 37). Many adults would claim, for example, that their experience of becoming and of being a parent dramatically changed their values and life perspective. It can change their theology as well. Concepts such as 'creation', 'preservation', 'providential care' and even 'kenosis' can mean something different to someone who becomes a parent. In such a circumstance, some of these concepts may come to mean something for the very first time. One might better understand what it is to be God when one functions to a child as her creator and provider, the one who nurtures her growing independence, and the one who must eventually let her go. It would be interesting to test this claim empirically, along with the hypothesis that human parents are also more 'understanding' of (in the sense of forgiving of) the Divine Parent than are childless women and men.

So positive situations can also help to forge our theologies. Experiences of beauty and of human kindness, and moments of joy and delight in nature and other people,

---

[4]   This was almost twice as many as the number who chose the option that 'science has explained the mysteries of life'.

have served to reinforce or change the beliefs of many people about ultimate reality. Others bear witness that they only came to recognize the theological concept of grace when they experienced in their own lives a positive empowering that seemed to come from outside themselves, particularly in moments of darkness and despair. In these ways life plays a part in facilitating our theological learning.

The Modes of Religious Learning

According to Ludwig Wittgenstein, there are two movements, modes or moments in a typical case of religious learning (Wittgenstein, 1980: 64; cf. Phillips, 1988: 89). I shall entitle them 'learning about religion' and 'embracing the faith'.

Learning about Religion

First, there is a form or stage of religious learning that we could label 'second-hand'; we might also call it 'third-person' religious learning. This is the learning about religion which comes either by means of socialization or enculturation, or through intentional instruction. These processes give us an understanding of the great concepts of faith, by teaching us how to use these notions. They teach us, many would say, the logic or *grammar of faith*. Wittgenstein famously wrote, in the *Philosophical Investigations*, 'Grammar tells what kind of object anything is. (Theology as grammar.)' (Wittgenstein, 1968: § 373). His point is that learning a concept means mastering 'the appropriate ways to refer, to judge, and to describe' (Holmer, 1978: 141) and therefore that, in the theological case, theology gives us the rules for religious discourse that determine 'what it makes sense to say to God and about God' (Phillips, 1970b: 6). According to Rush Rhees, then, learning how the word 'God' is used is truly to learn a theology; we are learning theology when we learn that God is the 'Lord God of Israel' and 'Creator of Heaven and Earth'. Rhees anticipates a cavil: 'This may seem to be making theology superficial. Just learning the sorts of things it is correct to say – is that theology? Well, I do not see how theology can be anything else' (Rhees, 1969: 126; cf. Holmer, 1978: 202–3; Clack, 1999: 78–9).

Apparently the metaphor of theology as grammar comes originally from Luther. It clearly has both descriptive and normative aspects, for a language's grammar tells us how that language *is* used, in the sense of how it is *properly* used. Fergus Kerr comments:

> The kind of object that a thing is comes out in the kind of things that it is appropriate to say about it. . . . To explain what the word 'God' means we have to listen to what it is permissible to say about the subject. . . . Theology, in practice, has always included a great deal of critical reflection on what people are inclined to say about the divine. It is very much a question of learning to trace what may rightly be said, and what has to be excluded as inappropriate or obsolete. . . . Theology as grammar is, then, the patient and painstaking description of how, when we have to, we speak of God.
>
> (Kerr, 1986: 146–7)

In this first mode of learning, therefore, we learn how God is to be spoken of. This is a relatively 'objective' form of religious learning and may be quite impersonal and 'academic', in the sense of dispassionate and uncommitted. Thus Wittgenstein gives the example of sharing the grammar of the word 'God' by 'denying that one could talk about arms of God' (quoted in Kerr, 1986: 146). The method is primarily that of presenting significant instances of the use of the concept, so that the learner learns 'the conditions which evoke it or which it addresses, and the ways it is to be used under those conditions' (Wood, 1993: 76). This need not imply a religious commitment, in which the learner actually speaks of and to the God in whom he believes. It can all be done in a 'subjunctive mood' or 'as if' mode (Kelsey, 1992: 199, 238). Although it mainly involves cognitive learning, an empathetic understanding of religious concepts will also need *some sort* of appreciation of the affective dimension or accompaniments of religious concepts, through an 'imaginative rehearsal' or 'bracketed make-believe' that is dependent on one's previous experience of related emotions (Dhavamony, 1973: 18–20; Smart, 1973a: 32–3; 1973b: 37, Kelsey, 1992: 173; Astley, 1994a: 108–13).

This first mode is a form of socially contextualized religious learning. Either the broader culture enculturates in us the language of faith or the church itself teaches it to us. It is not a learning project that the lone individual can ever pursue, for even books and other media of communication link the individual with others. Neither faith nor theology could be solipsistic. It is in social contexts that we first learn to speak of God.

We may do this at different levels. Let us first distinguish an element in the non-confessional approach to religious education, variously described as 'descriptive', 'objective' or 'phenomenological', which (together with the promotion of the pupils' own search for meaning and value) now constitutes the main thrust of religious education in non-church schooling in Britain and other states (cf. Smart, 1968; Schools Council, 1971; Hull, 1984; Hobson and Edwards, 1999: ch. 7; Schreiner, 2000; Caldwell, 2001). When this process of 'learning about religion' turns to the study of Christianity, most authorities agree that it should be concerned solely with understanding and not at all with religious assent.

> The beliefs-that which the religious education teacher aims to develop are beliefs about Christianity, rather than beliefs about God, Jesus, the church etc. They are therefore beliefs about Christian beliefs, as well as beliefs about Christian attitudes, emotions, experiences, evaluations and actions.
>
> (Astley, 1994a: 107)

Even at this level of religious learning, the understanding that educators aim at comes in degrees. This is not just a cognitive matter; students will understand Christianity better the more they can empathize with the affective states that normally accompany beliefs about God, Jesus and the church in the lives of the Christian believer.

As we have already noted, for many of these learners the reality of such central concepts as God, the risen Christ and the Holy Spirit will be entertained only as possibilities, in a hypothetical mode. But there are some students who will not only understand these concepts empathetically, but also accept that they have real instances. Such a person believes that God exists or that Jesus was a historical figure. Believers will affirm these claims to different degrees, on a spectrum stretching from extreme tentativeness to complete certainty, and they too will have different depths of understanding of the concept in question.

All these different religious learners are learning *about* the faith; they are all examples of the first mode of religious learning. There is one question that seems particularly appropriate at this stage of 'conceptual training' (Wood, 1993: 35). Whenever we are confronted by a believer or a non-believer who has some unusual understanding or belief about religion, it is natural for us to ask, 'Where did you get that from?' People often know the answer, if this is the way they 'got' their religion. They say, 'I was taught it' by certain individuals or through a particular community. Austin Farrer writes, 'How did religion get into our heads? It was taught to us, was it not? . . . Being taught us, it does, or does not, continue to hold us' (Farrer, 1967: 3, 6). 'Who taught you that?', we sometimes ask incredulously of a particular piece of religious believing, and often find that the answer is some Christian minister or another. (Despite what clergy say, it is my experience that the more bizarre forms of theology come as often as not from the church's ministers, than from someone's Auntie or from people working things out for themselves.) In this first mode of religious learning we are inevitably much influenced by what other people take the grammar of religion to be. This opens us to the possibility of being misled, which is an ever-present danger in matters of religion and one that becomes even more serious when it is carried over to the next stage.

Embracing the Faith

For there can be another act to the drama of religious learning. In Farrer's words, the religion that we are taught may – or may not – 'hold us'. For some learners the third-person form of belief becomes something that is much more authentically their own, in what we may call a 'first-person' mode of religious learning. When this happens, there is a deeper, fuller religious understanding that is 'not just a matter of words alone' but involves redirecting one's passions (Martin, 1994: 188). As we saw in Chapter 1, attitudes and emotions such as love, fear, joy, hope, trust, kindness and humility are part of the meaning of the concepts of religion, along with other capacities for response (Kelsey, 1992: 168–9). We do not *fully* understand religious concepts unless we feel these accompanying emotions and are disposed to behave in a manner appropriate to the beliefs and affects that we have learned. 'To understand a religious expression supposes that a passion will also follow the learning. Or better, the language of faith makes words themselves part of the religious passion and life' (Holmer, 1978: 66). This, therefore, is how we learn God:

> The concept and the affections emerge together. The pupil, in short, does not know the true God or know God truly by a simple use of the word 'God'. God is genuinely known only when God's identity is established in a manner that includes one's passions.
>
> (Martin, 1994: 190)

And then? Then we are changed at a different level, and through a different form of learning, as we embrace the faith for ourselves. Martin writes:

> If the concepts enable the learners to speak, they must also be capacitated by them to fear and love God, hate that which is evil, be joyous in tribulation, take little thought about tomorrow, and be hopeful, forgiving, kind and humble. . . . Indeed, the demands imposed upon the learners by the language of faith are so arduous and deep that it is no wonder at all that the language must become genuinely their own, in the first-person mode of expression rather than the third-person, if one is to be changed in the requisite ways. If, instead, the words of faith belong to the pupils only by way of enculturation, by virtue of others and through exposure, this is not enough. The learners, in a more deliberate and self-conscious mode, must embrace the faith and reduplicate it in their own lives.
>
> (Martin, 1994: 188; cf. Holmer, 1978: 154–8)

Martin is here interpreting a short, but highly concentrated, text from G. H. von Wright's edited selection of Wittgenstein's manuscripts, published in English as *Culture and Value*. In 1947, adopting a Kierkegaardian tone, Wittgenstein wrote:

> A religious belief could only be something like a passionate commitment to a system of reference . . . . It's passionately seizing hold of *this* interpretation. Instruction in a religious faith, therefore, would have to take the form of a portrayal, a description, of that system of reference, while at the same time being an appeal to conscience. And this combination would have the result in the pupil himself, of his own accord, passionately taking hold of the system of reference.
>
> (Wittgenstein, 1980: 64)

Of her own accord, Wittgenstein argues, the learner runs to religious belief and grasps it for herself. In the Christian case, she 'seizes' on the message of the Gospels 'believingly (i.e. lovingly)' and 'that is the certainty characterizing this particular acceptance-as-true'. Wittgenstein calls this sort of certainty 'faith': 'faith is faith in what is needed by my *heart*, my *soul*, not my speculative intelligence' (faith, after all, 'is a passion'). What combats doubt here is *redemption* (32–3, 56). This is the second learning. Culture cannot enculturate this, nor any teacher teach it. Rather, 'life can educate one to a belief in God. And *experiences* too are what bring this about. . . . e.g., sufferings of various sorts. . . . Experiences, thoughts, – life can force this concept on us' (86).

Fergus Kerr comments that Wittgenstein's account 'seems a pretty good description of a religious education'. He notes that it is not a description of any process of indoctrinatory persuasion, in which the learner's autonomy is disabled, because in and after the embrace the beginner finally proceeds independently as he does when engaged in secular learning such as learning to count (cf. Wittgenstein, 1968: §§ 143, 145). But in the religious case the context and content are not neutral or passionless, but *self-involving*. 'Religious education does not take place in a vacuum. On the contrary, it comes as a challenge to the values and practices that the learner already has, whatever they may be.' It is often, then, a *confrontational* learning (Kerr, 1998: 77–8).

One might argue that the shift that is portrayed in this account of a second mode of learning includes a transition between different species of belief: a move from a *belief-that* to a *belief-in* God or Jesus or the sacraments. As we noted above, the first stage might only produce beliefs about what religious people believe. Instead of coming to believe that God exists, even in some notional or nominal fashion, one may only come to believe that Christians believe that God exists. A Christian belief-that about God, however, involves an element of assent to or adoption of the belief, in addition to an understanding of it. This already represents a major shift from understanding the concept of God to believing that it is instantiated, that there is a reality corresponding to it. But this believing might remain at the level of intellectual assent or mere 'propositional belief'. It would then arise and be held dispassionately, as just one more belief. While this would be a step forward from simply understanding what the concept of God entails, it is not yet the situation of which Wittgenstein speaks. It is no more than a detached, 'notional' assent to a proposition, to use Newman's language; it is not yet the 'imaginative or real assent' that goes with devotion (Newman, 1913: 119).

In the passionate embrace, however, this belief-that is built on and transcended, as we move to a *belief-in*. To coin a phrase, belief-in is belief-that *with attitude*. Thus belief in God embraces both beliefs-that about God's nature and existence, and affective states such as trust in God and other pro-attitudes towards God (Price, 1969: 447–54). It is partly this dimension of religious beliefs-in that led Jonathan Edwards to claim that 'true religion lies much in the affections', since the things of religion take hold of human souls 'no further than they affect them' and 'he that has doctrinal knowledge and speculation only, without affection, never is engaged in the business of religion' (Edwards, 1961: 27, 30).

Mere knowledge *about* God must be distinguished, then, from knowledge *of* God (Holmer, 1978: 25, 189, 203; Wood, 1993: 32), which is the first-person religious knowledge that 'engages the affections and is embodied in the religious person's life, the affections not so much responding to the knowledge as in their engagement representing one idea of the knowledge itself' (Kellenberger, 1985: 179). Prior to this point, all that education has realized is an understanding of Christian concepts. This is never enough for true faith. Mere understanding of Christianity is something; but it is no more than, say, understanding the idea of love. One may, indeed, 'learn the language of love and never be in love. [One] might recognize it in others, . . . or . . . use it in feigning love' (Rhees, 1969: 124). But this is very different from truly learning what love is *by being in love*. The transition from learning about faith to being in faith marks a similar sea change. The language of faith asks that we 'have the pathos and the passion, and that we let the categories of religion gain their dominance in our daily life' (Holmer, 1978: 71).

Some philosophers of religion are unhappy even with the distinction between belief-that and belief-in in the case of God. Thus Norman Malcolm has complained that a belief-that God exists that is 'entirely devoid of any inclination to religious action or consequence' seems indistinguishable from a belief-that God does *not* exist. He writes, 'I do not comprehend this notion of belief in *the existence* of God which is thought to be distinct from belief *in* God. It seems to me to be an artificial construction of philosophy' (Malcolm, 1977: 155–6). As D. Z. Phillips puts it (using the phrase 'belief in God' for believing solely 'in' God's existence):

> What would it mean to say that one believed in God without this involving any affective state in one's life? Even if sense could be made of these 'beliefs' divorced from active responses, what would be particularly religious about them?
>
> (Phillips, 1993: 112, cf. 118–19)

Such philosophers find fault with some accounts of the distinction between learning the language of Christianity – that is, *knowing about God* – and the embraced learning that is more properly a matter of *knowing God*. In the context of the church, the two modes of religious learning are conflated. Thinking in terms of participating in the linguistic usage of a worshipping community, Phillips argues that 'to know how to use this language is to know God', for 'to *use* this language is to worship, to believe in God' (Phillips, 1965: 50; 1970b: 69). Nevertheless, Phillips and others can and do recognize a distinction between a religious understanding that comes through *participation* and *advocacy* (by using religious language for oneself), and an understanding of religion that a non-believer may come to possess through *elucidation* (as he or she learns how other religious language users employ the language). The difference between 'participant-understanding' and 'observer-understanding' can therefore still be affirmed (cf. Phillips, 1970b: 166–7; 1986: 11–12; Marples, 1978; Kellenberger, 1985: 36–44; Astley, 1994b: 177–80).[5]

However we interpret the distinction between belief-in and belief-that in the religious case, we can still argue that our first mode of religious learning is learning *about the Faith*, whereas this second mode of learning is the transformation of the first learning in the mouth, mind and heart of the believer into the language *of faith*. Thus theology starts for us in an 'about' mood, as 'a sum of truths', 'grammar-like and something like an account that we can get from others who have been there long before us'. But it 'must always move towards a present-tense, first-person mood'; for 'theology, to the extent that it becomes knowledge of God, has to have the form of personal appropriation built in' (Holmer, 1978: 24–5). Here 'faith' is more properly spoken of than 'The Faith', at least on a Lutheran rather than a Thomist model of faith (cf. Swinburne, 1981: 105–15; Astley, 1994b: 189–91). Its belief statements now represent 'the linguistic component of a particular mode of living' (Clack, 1999: 71).

The images that we should have in mind for this second mode, style or stage of religious learning are those of affective embraces, of taking sides, of trusting and acting on trust, and of people speaking for themselves at first-hand. This is a world away from the tentative, dispassionate ratiocination of an intellectual account of religious beliefs, and shares many of the qualities of a moral commitment. It is clearly a more personal kind of change and of learning, and is thus a more individual and particular thing. For that reason, different people will engage in this second learning differently; they will embrace different aspects of the Faith and embrace

---

[5]   For a more nuanced response to the question, 'Is it possible to understand without believing?', particularly with reference to the role of the will, see Kellenberger, 1985: 154–62.

them in different ways. The nature of this second learning will depend much more on the nature of the person and personality of the learner than does the first learning, in the sense that it will be more affected by our attitudes, emotions, cognitive skills, and so on. Our own psychology is therefore more relevant here. The second mode of learning will be influenced too by our fundamental values: that is, by what we take most seriously and regard as intrinsically valuable – indeed as 'worthy of worship'. This may be understood, in the traditional sense, as 'a supreme objective value . . . whose worthwhile-ness does not depend solely upon some human judgement about it' (Ward, 1994: 30); but the *recognition* of that value is something that we must each do, and will be dependent on what each person takes to be worthwhile. Different people will embrace different things.

Phillips writes that 'coming to God is not a change of opinion, but a change of direction; a reorientation of one's whole life' (Phillips, 1988: 118). I have hinted that such a religious commitment or conversion is closely parallel to falling in love. If this is so, it may explain why there are few objective criteria for it. 'Why do you love her?' someone asks. 'Because I do,' I answer. This is a personal evaluation and response. I should not expect you to see her the same way or to react in the same way. 'A declaration of love is a personal matter . . . because the person who makes it does not thereby commit himself to supposing that anyone who fails to love what he does has somehow gone wrong' (Frankfurt, 1988: 92; cf. Astley, 1994b: 228–30, 235–41, and below, p. 38, 42, 43). In so far as this truth is something we are and do, it is also inevitably subjective, in the sense of being personal. This is the sense in which *no one else can live our (religious) lives*. Authentic living and authentic faith are matters of each to her or his own.

I have used the language of embracing to characterize this second mode of religious learning, and likened it to falling in love. Wittgenstein himself writes of 'passionate seizing'. Being English, I am a little surprised to find these metaphors so appealing. But even the English know the difference between a passionate embrace and a mere 'air kiss', recognizing that true religion – however much it may frighten the horses – needs to embrace belief rather than just politely brushing its cheek against it. But none of this should be taken as implying that reason, cognition and understanding have *no* place in the embrace. This is a point to which I shall return, but it is worth noting here that this second form or stage of religious learning may be seen as hermeneutical through and through. Such a personal embrace is at the same time a personal *interpretation* and *understanding*. It has become routine to argue that we can only embrace or 'appropriate' a tradition by and in an act of interpretation in which the interpreter is engaged in a personal dialogue with that tradition or 'text'. As Hans-Georg Gadamer puts it, the interpreter is involved in the process as one is involved in a 'genuine conversation [in which] something emerges that is contained in neither of the partners by himself'. In this way, the text is 'brought out of its alienness and [becomes] assimilated'.

> The interpreting word is the word of the interpreter, it is not the language and the dictionary of the interpreted text. This means that assimilation is no mere recognition of the text that has been handed down, but is a new creation of understanding. . . . All the meaning of what

is handed down to us finds its concretion, in which it is understood, in its relation to the understanding 'I' – and not in the reconstruction of an 'I' of the original meaning.

(Gadamer, 1982: 419, 429–30, cf. 223)

The appropriate question to ask of the first category of religious learning was, 'Where did you get that from?' There is a different question that is more appropriate for this second learning mode. It is, 'Why does that mean so much to you?' Even if the answer in the end is going to be a frustrating, 'Just because it does', the question is still worth asking. This is especially the case if it forces us back to the first movement, which serves as the road to the responsive embrace. There it can illuminate the context of learning, by lighting up times, people, places and life experiences that are intimately associated with this reorientation of a person's passions. As and when you know that much about my story, you will be better equipped to understand me, my embraces and my faith. Nevertheless, the question, 'Where did you get that from?' has its emphasis on the *from*, and therefore on the source of our belief; whereas the question, 'Why does that mean so much to you?' has its emphasis on the *you*, and therefore on the religious learner – once again restored to the centre of our concerns.

In Terrence Tilley's nuanced account of religious tradition, he argues that traditions are best understood 'as communicative practices, in which the communication of the "how to" is as important as, or more important than, much of the "what" communicated'. He writes, 'How to love God with one's whole mind, whole heart, and whole self is primary; doctrines about God, mind, heart and self are derivative' (Tilley, 2000: 80; cf. Lindbeck, 1984: 35). For Tilley, as for many other contemporary theologians, *practice comes first*. Christian learning is thus 'best understood in a practical way'. 'One learns the meaning of the *tradita* [the content – that is, the doctrines, attitudes, skills, practices and so on that are being passed on] as one is inaugurated into participating in the practices of the tradition' (Tilley, 2000: 79). This is the theme that lies at the heart of what has been called the 'faith community' or 'enculturation' model of Christian education, and which accords with remarks in my last chapter about apprenticeship.

There is no doubt, however, that this (usually implicit) educational process only truly bites when the learner truly practises the tradition, rather than 'practising practising' it. Undoubtedly, religious practices may still 'shape persons and reshape them, their beliefs and their attitudes' (Tilley, 2000: 79), even when the learners engage in such practices at the level of 'going through the motions', like a young child encouraged to kiss his Grandma – or to receive communion. But the understanding truly takes off, including the understanding of religious 'know-how', as and when the participation becomes real rather than notional. This comes with, and after, the embrace; only then, surely, do we 'become what we practice' (Tilley, 2000: 152). One can, to a degree, know about practices and even perhaps how to engage in them, without actually participating. But such an understanding will only be an observer's understanding, not that of a *true* or *full* participant (cf. Phillips, 1970b: 230; Astley, 1994b: 178–80). The observer's 'know-how' will be purely theoretical, another form of knowledge-about at one remove – in this case knowledge about how to do something.

The church's educational ministry, therefore, must be more radical. It must create participants. Only then is a religious belief 'really a way of living, or a way of assessing life' (Wittgenstein, 1980: 64). John Westerhoff writes of the relationship between what he calls 'nurture' and 'conversion' along these lines:

> At some point every Christian must fully internalize the faith of the church and affirm their own faith by being confronted with the choice of whether or not they accept or reject the authority of the gospel and are brought to a personal life transforming commitment to Christ. . . .
>
> Children and youth are Christians and members of the community of Christian faith by their baptisms. They are to be nurtured in this community's understandings and ways. They are also to be evangelized by God's transforming Word until in their maturity (adulthood) they experience a moment or period of 'conversion'. . . .
>
> Conversion is best understood . . . as a radical turning from 'faith given' (through nurture) to 'faith owned' (through conversion). Conversion is radical because it implies ownership and the corresponding transformation of our lives.
>
> (Westerhoff, 1978: 413–14)

Moving On

Let us recap the pattern of learning that Wittgenstein traces. There is, first, some learning about the language of the faith, through enculturation and/or instruction. Then there is the passionate taking hold of religion for oneself. This new stage results from a learning from life and experience that generates, and perhaps partly constitutes, the passionate embrace. We may wonder how much of the first stage is needed in the case of those who move to this second stage. The answer, I believe, is that it varies. It will not involve very much in the case of some people, and could in principle be contemporaneous with it; but for others it might take a lifetime. At some point, however, some of those who have learned the language will want to begin to speak it.[6] This is when we truly 'become learners' and 'learn as we go'; when it is true that 'our walking in faith is . . . an ongoing learning about God' (Holmer, 1978: 24).

Although Wittgenstein leaves his account with the embrace, this cannot be the end of the story. A third mode or stage of religious learning is now possible, with endless opportunities for 'moving on' through more learning of the faith, a learning that is now accompanied by a new intensity and a new motivation (a self-motivation) in the learner.

> This is not the terminal point of the training; it is more like a new beginning. The personal appropriation of the words and beliefs of Christianity is not a task for a single hour; . . . [the pupils] are now to be continually built up, instructed, challenged and chastened *by* Christianity. . . . Now the interest, even the happy compulsion, for deeper and more heartfelt faith stems from the new initiates themselves.
>
> (Martin, 1994: 197; cf. Holmer, 1984: 103)

---

[6]   It is arguable that this process of coming to embrace the faith may also stretch over a long period of time.

I introduced a hermeneutical reference in my exposition of the second stage. In fact, however, all three of the stages of learning may be thought of as having the structure of a hermeneutical dialogue between learner and tradition. The learner is never a blank sheet of paper to be written on by the Faith, not even at first – and certainly not after he has begun to embrace it. There will always be some critical dimension to the learner's conversation with the Christian tradition (cf. Groome, 1980: ch. 9); the learner will always have his own words to say, as he has his own beliefs, practices and experiences to bring to the encounter with the religious tradition. To begin with he will be cautious, possibly exercising an 'ideological critique' or 'hermeneutics of suspicion'. In Paul Ricoeur's phrase, he will show the 'willingness to suspect' as well as the 'willingness to listen' (Ricoeur, 1970: 27). But he must do enough listening to learn what he does not yet know – the grammar of Christianity. After the embrace has begun, however, the conversation between the tradition and the learner will become more intimate. It is now a lot less like an exchange between wary strangers, and more of an intercourse between partners; with the conversation flowing, as it were, from Faith to faith, and from faith to Faith. There will be a continuing critical evaluation of the tradition; but this is now also a conversation between lovers, and one in which the interpreter risks 'being caught up in, even being played by, the questions and answers – the subject-matter – of the [religious] classic' (that is, text: Tracy, 1981: 154). This time, as they say, it is truly *personal*.

Personal Religious Learning

I want now to fill out and defend my claim that this learned religion is a 'personal thing'.

The Personal Incorporate

Religions are, of course, essentially corporate entities; Christianity in particular. In history and our experience it is the social that usually comes first. The first mode of religious learning is a product of social formation, even if the public, communal faith of the church is conveyed through a sole teacher or an individual text. To insist that the personal and the individual must come a strong second, however, is not to slip down the greasy inclined plane of the privatization of religion. It is to affirm the centrality of *response* in religion.

> Doctrine is orientated towards faith, representing a demand for personal involvement, rather than passive assent. . . . Whatever social or communal function Christian doctrine may possess, it includes an appeal to the individual. It is an affirmation of trustworthiness, inviting a response of faith. To use Kierkegaard's famous phrase, truth demands 'an appropriation process of the most passionate inwardness'. Doctrines define the object of faith – God – not in order that God may be comprehended but in order that the believer may relate to God in faith. . . . Truth is not simply something one knows about, but something which one possesses and is possessed by. . . . For Kierkegaard, doctrine is to be viewed, not merely as a description of Christianity, but as an existential imperative, a challenge to *become* a Christian. Doctrines are descriptions which propose to be actualised

in human existence; there is a demand for the interiorization of doctrine. Doctrines do not contain the meaning of the truth as such, but define how an individual is – or comes to be – 'in the truth', by orientating his or her existence towards God and Jesus Christ. Implicit within doctrinal formation is an invitation to adopt a 'discovery perspective' on God.

(McGrath, 1997: 78–9)

The reference to Søren Kierkegaard is to a text from his *Concluding Unscientific Postscript*, located in a chapter entitled 'Truth is Subjectivity'. It provides theology with the most famous account of the existential appropriation or response to religion. Kierkegaard wrote:

> For an objective reflection the truth becomes an object, something objective, and thought must be pointed away from the subject. For a subjective reflection the truth becomes a matter of appropriation, of inwardness, of subjectivity, and thought must probe more and more deeply into the subject and his subjectivity.
>
> (Kierkegaard, 1941a: 171, cf. 178)

Kierkegaard always conceded the importance of a public, objective, accessible account of faith; he therefore recognized the significance of learning *about* Christianity. But he insisted that such 'truth' must be personally appropriated: it must become 'my truth'. Otherwise, Christianity remains *merely* an 'objective faith', 'a sum of doctrinal propositions', rather than inwardness. This objective religious alternative is one that Kierkegaard dismissed with scorn:

> It is as if Christianity also had been promulgated as a little system, if not quite so good as the Hegelian; it is as if Christ – aye, I speak without offense – it is as if Christ were a professor, and as if the Apostles had formed a little scientific society.
>
> (Kierkegaard, 1941a: 193)

What is Kierkegaard concerned about here? Clearly at one level all my beliefs, values, attitudes and actions are mine, not yours or anyone else's. But there is another, deeper level of ownership open to us. The most important religious assertions are not logically neutral, but self-involving; they commit us to action, or imply an evaluative attitude at the very least. Unlike scientific assertions, they are not fully comprehensible impersonally, because they are dependent on a person's having what Donald Evans termed 'depth-experiences' – experiences that are looked on as revelations and expressions of the transcendent (Evans, 1968: 112, 127). Such religious truths are not arrived at in a detached way, as one might come to some 'indifferent fact', but are 'discovered' in and with a profound emotional impact and power that is consonant with their nature. This is a religious learning that may best be thought of in terms of coming to 'see for the first time the significance of familiar facts', in what James Kellenberger calls a 'realisation-discovery'. This sort of discovery is a function of our sensitivity and is therefore wholly unlike the confirmation of a hypothesis (Kellenberger, 1972: 16–20; cf. 1985: chs 2 and 3).

This is what Kierkegaard means when he writes of religious truth as 'an objective uncertainty held fast in an appropriation-process of the most passionate inwardness'

(Kierkegaard, 1941a: 182), which is an infinite passion that 'cannot be confused with anything else' (539). For Kierkegaard, such inwardness means 'self-involvement, assimilation and responsibility' (McPherson, 2001: 167). In this deeper sense, religion – *our* religion – is personal; in this more profound manner, it is intrinsically and definitively *owned*. And clearly it is owned primarily by *individuals* rather than by communities, and it is primarily rejected by individuals. (We all have a view about religions, whether we embrace them or reject them.) Contrary to the usual criticisms, such 'individualism' is not irresponsible or hostile to community. Kierkegaard argues both that 'subjectivity means responsibility and responsibility means individuality', and that the *only* people capable of real community are 'individuated selves' who have come to themselves in self-choice (Pattison, 1997: ch. 6).

How do these claims relate to my insistence that our theology is a learned and a learning thing? In learning about religion, the style is that of impersonal learning. When a piece of 'objective' theology is learned (for example a fact about biblical authorship or what Christians believe), the manner and mode of its learning is largely irrelevant. However, the learning of a theology that is 'spiritual' or 'religious' (and in this sense 'subjective'), in which appropriation and response are key, is in part dependent on and in part determined by its context, medium and manner of reception (see Chapter 1). Here 'theological truth' means something different, because it is received through, and only through, a process that is much more personal and idiosyncratic. And it is this sort of theology that is much the more important for most people. Our embracing of faith compels us to speak here of the truth of theology as an 'encountered truth'; it is the sort of truth that we do not just know, but are 'in'.

Searching Through the Junk

All religious traditions have at their heart a set of very powerful, highly *a*ffective and powerfully *e*ffective rituals, symbols, stories, practices and patterns of life that have the capacity to feed on and feed this personal learning of personal faith. They express and generate spiritual beliefs, values and experiences that are positive in the sense that they 'animate' us, and help us to triumph over suffering and to face both life and death. Few would give religion a second glance if this were not the case. These life-giving, personal features are central to the power of every living religion.

Not all religious learning or religious truth, however, has this personal nature. There is much in religion that does not, and perhaps should not, provoke a personal response. Religiously-speaking and spiritually-speaking, a great deal of it is junk. I warm to John Drury's metaphor of the Christian church as a junk shop where 'there is a good chance that amongst the clutter there will be something useful or beautiful' (Drury, 1972: 41). I agree, except that I am less sanguine, fearing that the chance of finding the good stuff is not itself always particularly 'good'. Many lay people give voice to a similar pessimism when they complain that going to church sometimes has little to do with anything 'personal', indeed that it *often* doesn't. This should not be dismissed as the criticism of 'sermon-tasters' or as some equally trivial form of religious consumer dissatisfaction. It is a serious complaint about a serious shortcoming. Religion needs to understand where its heart and its soul is to be found, and what constitutes its strength and distinctiveness. Frankly, the churches just have too much junk in them.

First-hand Learning

I have used the word 'learning' to specify a *process*. Understood as a process, 'my learning' is never your learning. But often the word is used of a *product* as well, as in 'he wears his learning lightly'. It then labels the difference, the changes (particularly in beliefs and understanding; but also in attitudes, values and dispositions) that experience makes in us. It is this second sense that Michel de Montaigne, the sixteenth-century essayist, employs when he complains of the way we 'look after the opinions and learning of others' but do not make them our own. I cannot resist quoting a less polite comment on this theme from the same essay (1: 25 – Montaigne's reflection on 'Pedantry' or 'Schoolmasters' Learning'). Here is his impudent critique of the academic who makes all learning second-hand:

> Whenever I ask a certain acquaintance of mine to tell me what he knows about anything, he wants to show me a book: he would not venture to tell me that he has scabs on his arse without studying his lexicon to find out the meanings of *scab* and of *arse*.
>
> (de Montaigne, 1991: 155)

This heteronomous learning is absurd, Montaigne insists. It is as if, needing fire, we went to a neighbour's house and sat down in front of his hearth, rather than carrying a lighted brand back to our own. It is as though we took pains to eat meat, but did not bother to digest and transform it, and hence it never nourished us. 'I do not like', he writes, 'this dependent and mendicant ability' (loc. cit., in Donald Frame's 1958 translation). In thus relying on the arms of others, we 'annihilate our own powers'.

Charles Wood discusses the danger of interpreting the goal and criterion of theological education simply as the acquisition of 'a theology'. A great deal of theological education is the product of a desire on someone's part that the learners – whether Christian adults, ordinands or undergraduates – should get themselves some theology. But what does this mean? If that theology is inherited or accepted on authority, or 'collected at random', it is 'acquired at second-hand rather than formed for oneself'. In such a case, we may call it a 'second-hand theology', and recognize with Wood that it 'lacks suppleness and vitality' and serves only the 'ceremonial function' of being available to put on display when solicited. This theology does not burn in our own hearth, but is a mere sanctuary lamp of a theology kept lit in a distant shrine of piety and therefore incapable of shedding light or bringing warmth at home. It is not a theology that churns within our own stomachs, but one that is kept preserved and boxed to impress the neighbours, and consequently cannot feed our hunger. Montaigne's rejection of second-hand learning has an obvious theological relevance.

Where Wood writes of a theological judgement as being 'formed for oneself', I prefer to talk of our learning such things in the first instance at second-hand and *then* adopting and embracing them with passion ('vitality'). But I agree with Wood that 'theology is properly an activity' and that 'learning theology must . . . mean learning to engage in that activity', and therefore 'becoming a competent enquirer': that is, *doing theology* and not just learning about the products of other people's theological reflection (Wood, 1996b: 345). And I agree that the embrace should not exclude some element of self-critical enquiry (with 'suppleness', then, 'through a process of careful, critical reflection'). While Wood places more emphasis on critical reason than I am altogether easy with, he is right to recognize that the theological task must have room for the dimension of thinking *for oneself*, as well as feeling for oneself, about theological matters. The embrace that marks our second stage of learning religion is best performed with our wits about us, as is any falling in love; even though, at the deepest level, it is not motivated by wits at all.

Wood is also right to stress that as we 'move on' in our relationship with Christian faith our responsibility for doing theology increases. Now that we are doing theology for ourselves, at first-hand, it is truly *our* theology. 'It is not the mere possession of "a theology" that is the measure of a theological education', Wood writes, it is rather 'one's ability to form, revise and employ theological judgements that counts' (Wood, 1996b: 345).

Wisdom Learning

Let us return to the writings of Montaigne. He does not only contrast second-hand and unassimilated learning with something more direct and immediate. He also uses the notion of *wisdom* to mark out a state that is more personal and individual. He writes, 'Learned we may be with another man's learning: we can only be wise with wisdom of our own' (de Montaigne, 1991: 155). This wisdom of contemporary life is contrasted with the book-learning of antique texts beloved of the scholars of his day. It is a wisdom which involves 'living well': that is, living 'the good life' in the ethical and spiritual sense. This includes living intelligently, happily and morally, and is a theme that has formed an integral part of a venerable philosophical tradition (see Cottingham, 1998). The good life is the life that is worth living. The concept implies certain claims about what it is to be truly ourselves and truly human, and about what constitutes human well-being or 'human flourishing'.

For Montaigne, wisdom is about 'understanding' and 'conscience' more than it is about 'memory'. It is also about 'sense' and 'judgement'. It is, or includes, the 'knowledge of goodness', 'integrity' and 'resolution'. Admittedly, his notion of wisdom partly reflects his ideal of the amateur, dilettante gentleman who browses 'without order, without method', rather than engaging in formal 'study'. But it is also a concept that captures his preference for what others have called 'practical reason', as opposed to speculative, unreliable theorizing unrelated to the choices of life (cf. Burke, 1981: 3–4, 17–18). This is the dimension of wisdom that finds expression more readily in ordinary people than in academics; and it is his privileging of this element that enabled Montaigne eventually to overcome his upper-class contempt for *le vulgaire*, and to insist – as he does elsewhere (*Essays* 2: 12) – that a ploughman can be wiser than a university rector and 'cleverer than all degrees'.

Wisdom, understood as 'sound and serene judgment regarding the conduct of life' (Blanshard, 1967: 322), has its conceptual home in reflection on the conduct of life. Its focus is on living rather than just thinking; it is a matter of practical sagacity, rather than speculation. This is why it is not just for, or particularly associated with, an intellectual elite. It is also why it is often linked with the virtue of humility. There is a healthy tradition that distinguishes it from, and sometimes opposes it to, mere intelligence, expertise or any other form of cleverness that is restricted to the few (cf. Astley, 1999). It is in the light of this sort of account of wisdom that we may begin to give some content to the notion of the wisdom of true religion, and become more willing to appreciate the more ordinary virtues of faith and of theology.

Spiritual, Faithful and Salvific Learning

At the heart of all religions is what makes religions 'religious': that is to say, *truly* religious. Some call it 'spirituality'. In what I have written above I have sometimes called it 'faith'. Whatever it is called, it is something that is *very* personal. Spirituality, on one definition, comprises those 'beliefs, attitudes and practices that animate people's lives and help them to reach out to super-sensible realities' (Wakefield, 1983: 549). This may appear to many to be far too broad a definition already, but we need an even broader one if it is to cover spiritualities that deny the existence of a supernatural dimension, for non-theistic Buddhists and humanists also have their spiritualities.

James Fowler's understanding of 'faith' is wide enough to encompass most of what I understand by spirituality. In Fowler's writings human faith is not defined by its content, but rather in terms of our way of giving our mind and heart to, and pledging our allegiance to, whatever we take to be ultimate. He argues that all of us, all the time 'believe in' something (Fowler, 1981: 31). Some examples of human faith are religious, many others are not. Human faith is only *religious* faith if its centres of values, images of power and master stories (or 'symbols, narratives, practices and communities') are religious (Fowler, 1981: part I and ch. 23; 2001: 164). Used in this way, faith is a word that labels the way we believe in whatever we believe in, whatever our 'gods' are. The form of 'faithing' that our beliefs take, which constitutes the pattern and direction of our lives, represents *the way* we hold *the what* of our faith. And that will affect the way that we do our theology. On this account, faith represents our life stance, our orientation as we lean into the wind and steer through the tempests of our lives.[7]

In this book I shall attempt to develop an understanding of 'ordinary theology' as a form of theology that is fundamentally religious and spiritual, and therefore closely connected to personal faith. Along the way, I shall have to face certain criticisms. One that I shall broadly accept is that it is proper to apply even to this sort of

---

[7]   Both spirituality and (human) faith are concerned with 'commitments' and 'values'. Frederick Ferré has defined religion as 'an institutionalised way of valuing most comprehensively [for what is valued is relevant to the whole of life] and intensively [it is valued above all things]' (Ferré, 1967: 73). On people's 'deepest commitments' and 'intensive concerns', see also Bailey, 1997: 8–9; 1998: 17–25.

theology a range of normative criteria of what Christian theological belief ought to be, including criteria representing norms of belief derived from scripture, tradition and church order, as well as norms of rationality. But I also need to say something about why such normative theology will appear to many 'ordinary believers' to miss the point. For ordinary theology is a theology to live by, and to die for. It is self-involving, personal, even pragmatic. It sustains people; it heals, restores, challenges and makes them whole. It saves. How *people* think and what *they* believe is not constitutive of normative theology; many argue that it is wholly irrelevant to theology understood along these lines (but we shall see). It *is*, however, constitutive of religion. The reason for this is that the most objective of claims to divine truth, disclosure and salvation must assume a subjective pole if it is ever to make contact with human knowledge and human lives. 'Revelation', after all, is an achievement word, similar in logical form to the word 'learning' (see above, p. 19). It can only be used when something has been revealed, it does not refer solely to God's 'task' of offering the revelation. 'Revelation, to be revelation, has to be in principle, subjectively effective' (Abraham, 1997: 213).

The same goes for salvation, with bells on, for 'to know Christ means to know his benefits' (Melanchthon, 1969: 21). Even if we wish to speak of an objective salvation, we must recognize it as something that must be subjectively appropriated and will therefore depend on what is salvific *for us*. What matters here is what saves us, what heals us, what works for us; and therefore what *we* need to be saved from and for. Although we may not dare to apply the adjective 'salvific' to theology itself, we must at least affirm that the religion, spirituality or faith that it expresses is salvific, and recognize that the focus of all of these will be individual, personal and experiential. When confronted by norms of orthodoxy and rationality, ordinary belief is likely to respond in the way adopted by the man born blind who was healed by Jesus: 'I do not know whether he is a sinner. One thing I do know, that though I was blind, now I see' (John 9: 25). The application of theological standards and rules of evidence or logic do not rank among the most important issues where matters of healing are concerned.

Salvific, Selective Learning

Of course ordinary theology *connects* with the prescribed norms of scripture, creeds, councils, 'what father says' and so on. But it connects as experience always connects with tradition, in the way that conversations connect two people with different perspectives. The norms and the individuals engage in a 'critical conversation' in which the norms may certainly challenge and change the believer, but in which the believer's beliefs will also challenge and may even, eventually and given a sharp enough bit of challenging, change what *counts* as the norm of belief (see Chapters 4 and 5).

At the very least, what we find to be salvific for us will affect what we count as central to the tradition and therefore which Psalms we don't sing, which bits of the creed we reinterpret, which words of father we take seriously. That is how Christianity changes. It is a process built in to the structure of a developing theology, as it is to the structure of a proper critical Christian education (Groome, 1980: 217–18, cf. 229; Browning, 1991: 218–22). It is futile to deny that the tradition, and the norms of belief and practice we take from it, change in this way. If they did not, people would still be singing the whole of Psalm 137. But they do not. Verse 1, 'By the rivers of Babylon – there we sat down and there we wept', often sounds across the nave, but not verse 9 (addressed to the enemies of the exiles): 'Happy shall they be who take your little ones and dash them against the rock.' I have never heard that text sung and rarely heard it read, even by fundamentalists. This selectivity constitutes one very practical way in which people exercise a critical perspective on their tradition, and my point here is that it is usually driven by an appeal to their own experience of what is salvific for them.

Conversion Learning

I have called the second mode of religious learning a form of conversion but that is perhaps unhelpful. It is not a change of mind that involves a change in the descriptive content of what is believed, but a change in the *form* of believing from a belief about these things to believing in them and believing for oneself. It bears some resemblance, therefore, to Fowler's account of a transition from Stage 3 to Stage 4 faithing: from the 'Synthetic-Conventional' style of receiving one's faith at second-hand, to the 'Individuative-Reflective' choosing of faith for oneself (Fowler, 1981: 178–83). However, Fowler does not call such a change in the way we hold our faith a 'conversion' (281–6).

Other psychologists of religion, however, do so label it, and regard it as crucial for the unification and integration of the self, which is such a central feature of identity formation and 'knowing where one fits' (Gillespie, 1979: 126, cf. 192). Walter Conn distinguishes the 'horizontal' conversion of adopting a new faith content from this 'vertical' conversion, which he describes as 'restructuring content (old or new) into a totally new horizon' (Conn, 1986: 27). This may include both a 'critical moral conversion', which is post-conventional in that 'one must discover the final criterion of value in one's own critical judgement', and also a surrender – not of oneself or one's personal autonomy – but of 'one's illusion of absolute autonomy'. This last type (for him, 'stage') of conversion is described by Conn as rare, presumably because he specifies that it is a *total* surrender and a *complete* transformation. But he also describes it in a way that would fit the more common phenomenon that I have represented here as a learning process (rather than purely a developmental process). Conn writes that this change is only possible 'for the person who has totally fallen-in-love with . . . God', and that it 'might be best understood as a conversion from religion to God' (Conn, 1986: 29–31).

Although religious conversion usually involves much more than this second form of religious learning, the second learning is an essential part of it. Some of the other elements detailed in accounts of the phenomenology of conversion may also apply to the second learning. They include the 'intense feeling' and felt state of assurance that William James analysed as incorporating the sense that all is ultimately well, the sense of perceiving truths, the sense of the world appearing new and (most characteristically) an 'ecstasy of happiness' (James, 1960: 247–57). These affective states are most likely to be associated with the full-blown conversion of the 'twice-born' who, on Francis Newman's typology, are the 'sick souls' who recognize their need of rescue from sin and evil. As we have seen, Wittgenstein's account of the second learning has something in common with this rhetoric of affect. It too may involve, in the words of the psychologist of religion Paul Pruyser, people who 'first pluck up the courage to cry for help and then find an answer that will be at least as loud and clear as their crying' (Pruyser, 1974: 135).

In my view, religious conversions are rarely *intellectual* conversions in which a change of beliefs is precipitated by some argument or other. I am not denying that such conversions happen, but I do not think that they occur as often as people claim. Even when they do, I would insist that an essentially cognitive conversion would only be superficially 'religious'. Coming to hold a new cool, neutral belief on religious matters is not the same as having a religious conversion. In the religious case, as in the moral case, conversion is more commonly mainly a shift of attitude and emotion. This is the essential element. I would argue that it arises primarily in response to the presentation of a model; Christianity is, after all, a conversion to *Christ*. In an early study, L. Wyatt Lang argued that the decision of the conversion-process is not one that is analogous to a reasoned judgement. It is rather, he writes, the embracing of an ideal.

> In the case of conversion, the decision is whether to be or not to be a Christian personality. This is a personal or spiritual decision and not at all detached or strictly intellectual. . . . The main religious appeal should be to gain a decision to have a Christian character, . . . a conversion-decision is a choice between personal types or values. Evangelistic appeal should, therefore, be mainly personal.
>
> (Lang, 1931: 188–9)

When we learn the concepts of God and Jesus, we learn the description of a character, the rendering of the identity of God as revealed in Christ. This character is capable of finite reflection in our human characters, in the form of the Christian life. It is what people are converted 'to'; they pledge their allegiance to it (to God, Christ, the Christian life); they 'believe and trust in Him'. They may later use such a concept in arguments and belief systems to *explain* their predicament and their salvation. But to be converted is not the same as finding a convincing explanation of anything.

Apologists and evangelists frequently go in for a deal of parading and defending Christianity as an explanatory scheme. In my view, however, these explanations only 'work' in any real, self-involving sense, as and when we have already fallen in love with and embraced the key terms that are used within the explanation. And that is such a basic shift that we cannot be intellectually argued into it or out of it. Explanations in terms of God (or Christ or the Christian life) will only satisfy us as and when God has become *our* god, when we have come to recognize supreme value and worth in the perceived character of God. It is only then that we shall kneel down in worship.

Subjective Learning

None of this, I would insist, impugns theology's claim to objective truth, even of an 'absolute truth' out there. At the level of salvific spirituality, what we call 'truth' is a particular species of truth. It is inevitably one that can only be specified as a truth-for-me. It is what works-for-me, it is that which 'means something' to me. In the story from the fourth gospel to which I referred above, in which Jesus' enemies quiz the man whom Jesus had cured of his blindness, we read an account of a particular form of 'objective theology' that asks about the sinlessness of Christ. It is answered, however, by a particular form of 'personal theology' or 'subjective theology' that answers in terms of a particular individual's needs and his discovery of how those needs have been met. This is not to say that Jesus did not exist or did not cure blindness, for the debate assumes such objective claims. But although objective realities (loosely 'facts') can bring physical healing, they cannot *save* on their own. If the man born blind had not wanted to see or came to regret having been cured of his blindness, there would have been no salvation and therefore no true healing. For this event to *be* salvific, he has to think of it as salvific, to feel it as salvific, to perceive it as salvific. That is the sense in which religious truth has to be subjective. It has to be, we might say, 'at least subjective'. That which is objective cannot *on its own* save. But that which is objective *can* save, if and when persons (subjects of experience, thoughts, feeling and consciousness) are saved. Salvation belongs to us, and *therefore* it belongs to God.

What I have called 'spiritual truth' is greatly dependent on our evaluations. In the end, it is *founded* on judgements about what we take to be intrinsically valuable, valuable-in-and-of-itself. As I claimed above, this is what makes such judgements ineluctably personal; in this sense, evaluations too are 'subjective'. Like our grounds for falling in love, they are 'ultimate' desires (Edgley, 1969: 159–63). We should allow reason a considerable role in judging most emotions, in so far as they are based on beliefs that may be adjudged reasonable or unreasonable. Reason is also our best guide in tracing and testing the pathways that allow us to judge some things to be *instrumentally* valuable. But reason surely reaches its limit with ultimate desires and intrinsic evaluations, for these are not subject in the same way to objective, rational criteria of justification.

Yet it is these deep valuations that furnish me with my 'reasons' for spiritually embracing *or* for spiritually rejecting many of the norms of belief that are on offer from a religious tradition. Our positive or negative response to the ideal that is presented by a religious or spiritual tradition expresses a personal appraisal that is a function of our particular psychology, and is not based on 'reasons' that would necessarily count for others. Our reasons are, rather, 'private or personal reasons' (cf. Lyons, 1980: 80). Nevertheless, our response is not just about our psychology. 'If I were pressed to say why I love him', wrote Montaigne in his essay 'On Friendship', 'I feel that my only reply could be, "Because it was he, because it was I"' (de Montaigne, 1958: 97). Our embracing of a moral or spiritual ideal may be very similar. In theistic traditions this ideal, *mutatis mutandis*, is acknowledged to be the character of God, who is embraced to the extent that God's nature is seen to be spiritually, morally and religiously 'attractive' (see Hanson, 1973: 1–2). The form and content of our subjective religious learning is not just something about us, then; it is also about the nature of the God we embrace. This is the objective pole of our subjective evaluation.

I once stirred up a little local theological controversy by tentatively remarking in a sermon in a college chapel that the God portrayed in the Book of Judges was a 'bit of a bastard'. I stand by that. We have to accept that *what we value* determines which of the concepts of God on offer we are willing to adopt, which sort of God we will regard as 'worthy of worship'. And the God of the Book of Judges just is not, in my view, up to it. For that God to be my God, I would have to recognize in the narrative a character of supreme worth. Otherwise, he *cannot* be my god. As Luther put it: 'What does it mean to have a god, or what is God? . . . Whatever . . . thy heart clings to . . . and relies upon, that is properly thy God' (quoted in Niebuhr, 1941: 23).

We have no choice in this matter. We do not really *choose* which God to believe in, because we do not really choose the beliefs or the values we hold; at all events not *directly*. We just find ourselves with them, as we find ourselves with emotions that have such cognitions and evaluations as their component parts (cf. Astley, 1994b: ch. 8 and 251–4). It is safest, of course, if we continue to feel and value in this way after we have worked hard to 'open ourselves to argument, persuasion and evidence' (Solomon, 1973: 40); but this still does not mean that we can directly change or choose the basis of our affections or cognitions, or our evaluations.[8] They are *too* personal, too much a part of us, for that.

Is this not the heart of authentic religious learning, and therefore – for most people – the heart of their theology?

---

[8]   This is not the place to attempt to defend in any detail my own views on valuation, which many will find far too subjectivist. My argument in this chapter does not really depend on any particular position on this topic. However, I should perhaps point out that sophisticated subjectivist views (sometimes called *expressivism*) recognize that values are not just preferences and that to acknowledge that something is good is not simply to like it, otherwise condemning racism or torture would be reduced to the same level as a distaste for peanut butter. Unlike taste preferences, moral judgements express the speaker's acceptance of a system of *norms*, and are *prescriptive* (they prescribe what other people ought to do and to feel) and *universalizable*. The attitudes evoked in moral situations are much 'more strident' than taste preferences, causing us to 'wish disfavoured actions discouraged by some kind of social sanction' (Sprigge, 1988: 61). The expressivist (or 'projectivist') Simon Blackburn recognizes 'no interesting split between values and desires'. He agrees, however, that you can always ask of any feeling or desire whether it is morally 'good' or not, just as you can ask of any perception whether it is an illusion or not; but he argues that you can only answer by relying on *other feelings*, in the same way that you can only judge illusions by relying on other perceptions. He contends that 'we judge oughts . . . because of the shape of our prescriptions and attitudes and stances, because of our desires, and because of our emotional natures.' But all that, he insists, is 'something that is true' (Blackburn, 1998: 275, 320). He thus allows for talk of 'moral truths', although they are not like truths in physics, and of 'moral knowledge' ('to indicate that a judgement is beyond revision', 318). For such a sophisticated exponent, morality is not *simply* non-factual ('non-cognitive') and subjective. See also Gibbard, 1990: parts II and III.

Chapter 3

Portraying Ordinary Theology

I am at last ready to begin the real topic of this book. I have defined and defended the notion of a 'learning context' for theology, and argued that it is a context to which we should attend more closely. I have attempted an account of what it is to learn religion and noted a number of significant features of this learning. My belief is that the learning context of theology is displayed most clearly and unselfconsciously, not within those scholarly investigations that utilize the specialized disciplines of academic theology, but in a more homely place – in a type of theology that is more personal and more 'ordinary'. Religious learning, itself a rather everyday and commonplace set of processes, is much closer to the heart of 'ordinary theology'. Keeping the learner in sharp focus should encourage us to take this form of theology more seriously.

Taking Ordinary Theology Seriously

But first we must have the joke. This anecdote is often repeated in the banter of sociologists of religion and invariably evokes an amused response. It originates in a survey in North London (Islington) in the 1960s, where the researcher asked the question, 'Do you believe in a God who can change the course of events on earth?' One respondent responded, 'No, just the ordinary one' (Abercrombie *et al.*, 1970: 106).

The original researchers offer this as an example of someone who has difficulty understanding the question (109), a question that was posed, interestingly, as a way of 'trying to pin down a more genuinely religious belief in God'. Other commentators have been tempted to treat the response as one from a 'less articulate respondent', interpreting it as typical of 'the profoundly inarticulate nature of common religion' (Ahern and Davie, 1987: 39, 54), for which the 'ordinary God' is part of a non-institutional set of beliefs that are often unorthodox and superstitious (cf. Davie, 1994: 79).

I will say rather more about the category of 'common religion' at the end of this chapter. I want to ask here, however, just what is so ordinary about 'the ordinary God or gods' of the theology of common religion (Davie, 1994: 5, cf. 79, 91)? I will argue that the respondent from Islington may indeed have been confused, but her response (as we have been given it) does not justify this inference. Nor was it religiously or theologically inept.

My view appears to be shared by the poet and critic Donald Davie, who in 1988 published a poem entitled 'Ordinary God', which his daughter-in-law Grace Davie reprints in her 1994 book on the sociology of British religion. The poem expresses the view that 'it is not/ stupid to believe in/ a God who mostly abjures' (to determine events). It concludes with these words:

> The ordinary kind
> of undeceived believer
> expects no prompt reward
> from an ultimately faithful
> but meanwhile preoccupied landlord.
>   (Davie, 1988: 49)

Belief in such an 'ordinary' non-intervening (and perhaps non-providential) God, although an unorthodox view theologically, has been defended by a number of religious thinkers who are not without academic sophistication. Many writers of the seventeenth and eighteenth centuries were deeply impressed by the new scientific account of a deterministic, machine-like cosmos, with its implication that the divine clockmaker did not need to revisit his handiwork to make adjustments to it (Baumer, 1960: ch. II; Brooke, 1991: ch. IV). A number of them took the view that God brought the universe into existence but involved himself no further with it, either by a continuous act of preservation or through additional acts of providence, miracle, grace or revelation. Although this position was regarded by the orthodox as a remote, cold and lifeless theology, there was surely nothing stupid about it – indeed it purported to be the only rational option.

Although it would be fruitless to search for such 'deism' among academic theologians today, a less extreme position is certainly represented within their ranks. One step along the spectrum of God's active involvement with creation, but still well away from the God of special providence or miracle, we may locate the God of non-interventionist theism (Langford, 1981: 5–24). Such a God not only brought the universe into existence but also (unlike the God of deism) continues to act in sustaining his creation in being. He does not, however, intervene within it. In recent theological debate, this non-interventionist position has been held by Maurice Wiles, who envisages God's action as one uniform and universal action directed to the entire cosmos. On this view, the universe as a whole is to be understood as 'a single act of God' (Wiles, 1986: 29, cf. 107–8). Wiles holds that we should not therefore think of particular events within the world as different divine actions, the products of new and particular divine initiatives, but as all expressing the same divine activity. John Hick's writings express a similar theology, which envisages the entire process of the universe as God's action of continuous creation/salvation. It is this universal activity, 'and not only a few exceptional incidents within it', that constitutes 'the divine creative action' (Hick, 1983a: 72, 78). Gordon Kaufman is another theologian who has adopted a kindred view of God's activity, acknowledging along the way that such a theology 'is more austere than the pietistic views often found in Christian circles'. 'This is no God who "walks with me and talks with me" in close interpersonal communion, giving his full attention to my complaints, miraculously extracting me from difficulties into which I have gotten myself by invading nature and history with *ad hoc* rescue operations from on high' (Kaufman, 1972: 146).

In the Islington question, nothing hangs on the word 'can'. The description, 'a God who can change the course of events on earth', is presumably to be understood as referring to an 'interventionist' deity in the sense of a God who not only 'can' but 'does' and 'will' perform miracles and particular additional acts of care and revelation.[1] If this is the case, the ordinary person's rejection of this theology is one that is shared by some worthy advocates in the studies and lecture rooms of theology. I suggest, therefore, that such a theology should not be presented as part of the immense 'muddle that passes for religious belief' among the general populace (Davie, 1994: xii). It would, of course, be easy enough to find other examples of ordinary religious thinking that are replete with 'comfortable contradictions', partly because such religious belief is not particularly systematic (Ahern and Davie, 1987: 35 – cf. Chapter 5 below). But, as Donald Davie insists, this piece of Islington theology is 'not stupid'; this believer is 'undeceived'. Instead, it is possible that we have here an example of an ordinary person espousing an intellectually respectable theological position, one that would not be lightly dismissed by academic theologians.

I intend to argue that there is much else in ordinary belief that is worthy of our theological attention. The 'Islington joke' strikes me as significant because it suggests that it is only the academically sophisticated who will be taken seriously when they suggest that God does not (or that God does) intervene in human affairs – *or* that God is (or is not) finite, that God is (or is not) a mere concept, or whatever. These theological positions, and many others, have been held both by academic theologians and by ordinary believers. It is, therefore, rather perverse to ignore, and worse to scorn, such beliefs when they are expressed by people with no theological education. What comes to mind here is a variant of the classic cartoon joke: 'If that remark had been made by an academic theologian, I should regard it as interesting and important.'[2]

Who will speak a word in favour of ordinary theology?

Ordinariness Analysed

The word *ordinary* relates to the noun 'order' and the verb 'to order', both of which derive originally from the Latin *ordo, ordinis*, the word for a 'row', 'order', 'rank' or 'class'. 'Ordinary' translates the Latin *ordinarius*, 'regular', 'orderly', 'usual'. Surveying recent Oxford dictionaries, we may note that the word has come to mean what is 'regular, normal, customary, usual, not exceptional, not above the usual, commonplace' (COD, 1982); 'belonging to or occurring in regular custom or practice'; 'of the usual kind, not singular or exceptional, commonplace, mundane' (NSOED, 1996). The ordinary is 'normal or usual' (COD, 1999).

---

[1] Abercrombie *et al.* described a positive response to the question as expressing a belief in 'an interventionist being', that is, one who intervenes or at least (according to the dictionary) 'favours intervention'. David Brown defines 'an interventionist view of God' as one in which God 'performs' (not only 'can perform') actions over and above his general ordering of the world (Brown, 1985: x).

[2] In the original, for 'academic theologian' read 'man'.

Some of these synonyms merit closer attention. *Usual* is that which is 'habitual', 'commonly or customarily observed or practised', 'current' or 'prevalent'. The noun *commonplace* labels a 'notable passage' (one that is worthy of putting into a 'commonplace-book') as well as an 'ordinary topic; an opinion or statement generally accepted'. The word *common* – 'belonging to the public', 'of ordinary occurrence', 'generally known', 'of the most familiar type' (from the Latin *communis*) – shares an etymology with the word *community*, which indicates 'joint ownership', the 'state of being held in common' or a 'body of people holding something in common' (Latin *communitas*). These are all neutral, even honourable, connotations.

Normal is a significantly ambiguous word, reflecting our dual understanding of the word *norm*. This noun refers either to 'customary behaviour' – what people normally (usually or typically) do, or to some 'standard' that is to be attained (the Latin *norma* denoting a carpenter's square). The first is a *descriptive* or 'statistical norm', the second a *prescriptive*, 'social norm' or ideal. The two senses are related in that, in some areas at all events, an account of *what ought to be* is subtly influenced, or even (as in the case of fashion) largely determined by, *what usually is*: the prescriptive norm deriving from the descriptive norm. Thus, in its legal usage, 'custom' is defined as 'established usage having the force of law'. Similarly, *regular* not only means (neutrally) 'done or happening frequently'. It can also connote 'following or exhibiting a principle'; being 'consistent', 'constant', 'not capricious or casual', 'correct'; 'conforming to a standard', 'properly constituted or qualified'; even (colloquially) 'complete', 'absolute' or 'indubitable'. (The word is cognate with 'rule' and 'regulate'.) The connotation here is of what is *properly orderly*. 'Pattern' is similarly ambiguous.

We shall revisit this distinction in Chapter 5 below; it is sufficient to note here that English uses the words 'normal' and 'regular' both of what ordinarily happens and of what ought to happen. Hence a thesaurus is likely to offer the word 'norm' as a synonym both for words such as 'average', 'mean', 'medium' and 'ordinary', *and* for words such as 'example', 'gauge', 'mark', 'standard' and 'touchstone'.

However, many of these words also display a less prestigious alternative connotation. So *common* also means 'undistinguished by rank or position', 'of inferior quality', 'vulgar'. And, used as an adjective, *commonplace* has the sense of 'trite', 'lacking in originality, novelty or distinction'. Why should this be? By 'indiscriminate use', the dictionary tells us, a phrase may become hackneyed,[3] common, trite; it turns into a cliché and thus becomes uninteresting.

The explanation of this linguistic phenomenon is presumably that something that is frequently seen or observed, because 'there is a lot of it about', soon ceases to hold our interest. It doesn't stand out, it is too 'everyday'. So it becomes acceptable to disparage features that are widely shared, or situations that are frequently encountered, or people who are 'nothing out of the ordinary'. We tend to prefer the unusual, the extraordinary and the 'special'. 'Ordinary people' are only interesting when they become famous.

---

[3] A 'hackney' was not only a horse used for ordinary riding, but also a person hired for servile work – particularly a prostitute.

Ordinary life is something we want to escape from or rise above. We often lust after something 'extra' in our lives and for someone who is 'extraordinary'.

Robert Schreiter comments on a common contrast between 'popular religion' (the religion 'of the people') and religion that is more elite in a variety of senses, depending on whether the elite in question is considered to be superior as a cultural or socio-economic elite, or as a minority of initiates who are thought to have received an esoteric tradition. Schreiter defines the first and third of these categories in ways that illuminate my category of those whose theology is 'out of the ordinary'. He describes them as having a 'more literate, verbal, and conceptually sophisticated approach'. They are people whose level of 'theological sophistication' distinguishes them from the 'more rudimentary level of understanding of the great majority of adherents' (Schreiter, 1985: 125).

Elitism of this kind is natural; in some circumstances it is entirely justified. The danger comes, however, when it blinds us to the value that is also to be found in what is without a special status; so that we do not see the worth of the everyday, the usual, the *ordinary*. Such a myopia is particularly problematic, I shall argue, in the domain of Christian theology. My position on this issue is continuous with my views in other areas of personal and social life. Briefly put, my overall perspective is that we suffer from a tendency to undervalue the ordinary, or at least that this is the case in the society and culture with which I am most familiar.

My concern in this book is with the situation in education and religion. Both education and religion, of course, involve growth, development and enrichment. In each of them we change – we are 'drawn out', we 'move on', we 'progress'. Ignorance and undeveloped talents are not to be preferred to wisdom, understanding, knowledge, skill and excellence; any more than sin, mistrust and doubt are to be preferred to morality, faith, hope and love. I am not suggesting that for a moment. In fact my perspective depends on its denial, for my claim is that the second set of values is often to be found in those who may seem on other grounds – particularly intellectual, academic grounds – to be undeveloped, uneducated and ordinary. In particular, I contend that there is much about 'ordinary believers' that others who are less ordinary should recognize as being valuable.

Theology and the Ordinary

I would go further. 'Ordinary life' itself is the primary locus of our spiritual health. The 'affirmation of ordinary life', understood in terms of the life of production and reproduction, is a feature of Charles Taylor's account both of Christian spirituality and also of our understanding of what it is to be human (Taylor, 1989: 13, 70, 211–30; cf. Kerr, 1997: 144–7). Taylor argues that our dignity – 'our sense of ourselves as commanding (attitudinal) respect' – is something that is very often grounded in our exercise of the everyday roles of ordinary life, perceived as being at the centre of the good life (Taylor, 1989: 15–16, 23–4, cf. 44–5, 57–8). This focus on ordinary life as the locus of the good life is described by Taylor both as a 'massive feature of the modern identity' (cf. de Certeau, 1984) *and* as originating in Judaeo-

Christian spirituality, particularly through the theology of the Reformers and Puritans. It is an emphasis that in principle takes us well beyond the dominance of the concerns of a limited theology, with its associated sense of 'the irrelevance of things secular' (Taylor, 1960: 170, 178–80; 1989: 215–18).

Taylor is not alone in recognizing the significance of the ordinary for a rounded and responsible Christian theology, and I should acknowledge at once that a number of academic theologians have pointed the way in this regard. I offer a small selection here, in homage to all those scholars who, in their different ways, recognize the value of the ordinary religious life.

Dan Hardy has drawn attention to what he claims is the peculiar emphasis of English theology of beginning from 'common practice' and seeking to make evaluative judgements as to its truth. Common practice, understood as 'the way people live, think and pray together as mediating the work of God', is thus to be regarded as some sort of touchstone for all theology (Hardy, 1989: 30–42). Rowan Williams lends his support in claiming that the theologian is 'always beginning in the middle of things', because 'there is a practice of common life and language already there' and 'the meanings of the word "God" are to be discovered by watching what this community does – not only when it is consciously reflecting in conceptual ways, but when it is acting, educating or "inducting", imagining and worshipping' (Williams, 2000b, xii). In the same vein, David Kelsey would have us concentrate theologically and empirically on the 'common life of Christian congregations' as the place where 'the Christian thing' (using Chesterton's phrase) is concretely encountered (Kelsey, 1992: 134, 203–4, 229–31). 'The way to the generally relevant and universally true', Kelsey writes, 'passes through the particular and concrete' (135).

Thomas Groome is representative of a larger group of Christian educationalists who are willing to add their voices in support of non-specialist theology. Groome writes that, despite the essential role played by theological scholars in resourcing the educational task:

> We must refuse to hand the theological enterprise over to the exclusive domain of the specialists. Theology is to arise from Christian praxis as much as it is to inform further Christian praxis. It should arise from the faith of a community reflected on in light of the Story/Vision and not from a group of scholars isolated from the community to reflect on the community's behalf. The latter kind of 'theology' (and we have it in abundance) contributes little to the ongoing faith life of the Christian community.
>
> Thus, while shared praxis needs to be informed by the expertise of the scholars, the scholars need to be informed by the shared praxis of the people.
>
> (Groome, 1980: 229)

The highlighting of 'women's experience' by many feminist theologians presents a further variation on our theme, by incorporating a celebration of such 'ordinary' experiences as friendship, love, sex, embodiment, childbirth and nurture (cf. Moltmann-Wendel, 1994). In doing so, feminist theologians offer a theology that is more inclusive, humane and integrated than much of academic theology. Mary Grey adopts the phrase 'sapiential yearnings' as a metaphor for feminist theological education, so as to distinguish this education for wisdom from more utilitarian and materialist approaches. It is a yearning that enables creativity to triumph even in the midst of the crush of the everyday. The pattern here is 'not of separation from the chaos and messiness of ordinary living, but of *immersion in it*'. Grey adds, 'There is no other way for the embodied wisdom of holistic education and spirituality to develop than through a willingness to make that its starting point' (Grey, 1996: 82). Arguing for a similar position, Janet Martin Soskice wryly notes that in the Christian tradition 'such things as attending to a squalling baby are seen as honourable duties, consonant with God's purposes, rather than in themselves spiritually edifying' (Soskice, 1992: 66).

Few theologians, however, have been as consistently (or as radically) in favour of democratic ordinariness as Don Cupitt, who sees it as 'the place where everything begins and everything ends' and even goes so far as to praise elements of folk religion such as 'luck' and 'the Trickster' (Cupitt, 1998a: 4, 44).[4] This emphasis is consonant with Cupitt's general philosophy of religion. His spirituality of Being is a return to ordinariness that has political as well as theological implications, for he warns us that 'we should not be nostalgic for the mystique of super-natural power and authority once wielded by a pyramid of old men in big hats' (Cupitt, 1998b: 94). 'It is much better', he writes, 'that *everything* should be on the level, freely negotiated and transparent' (1998a: 163).

Finally, I turn to a philosopher who makes quite explicit the particular claims that I wish to develop: that theology can be done by those who are 'ordinary' and that the academic theologian has no real advantage in this task. In his book *The Grammar of Faith*, Paul Holmer writes:

> We learn about God in the way a grammarian of language discovers the rules. He masters the language and assesses carefully what we all have access to already, our common working speech. So the theologian gets no new revelation and has no special organ for knowledge. He is debtor to what we, in one sense, have already – the Scriptures and the lives and thoughts of the faithful. . . . This puts theology within the grasp of conscientious tentmakers, tinkers like Bunyan, lay people like Brother Lawrence, and maybe someone you know down the street who shames you with his or her grasp. . . . Theology is often done by the unlikely. . . . God's ways are still discovered by his friends and not in virtue of techniques and agencies of power.
>
> (Holmer, 1978: 21)

D. Z. Phillips comments that Holmer wants 'to impress on ordinary believers that everything needful already surrounds them, and that they are not dependent on whatever intellectual systems theologians are able to devise' (Phillips, 1988: 235). Although, as we have seen in Chapter 2, Holmer makes much of the importance of learning religious concepts as part of the life of faith, he insists that these concepts do *not* include the abstract, highly specialized ones of academic theology. He draws an analogy with the fact that the motor mechanic does not need the concept of atomic weight.

---

[4]   I shall refer to his recent lexicological studies in Chapter 4.

Using concepts like those for foods, for cars, and for everyday things does not presuppose knowledge of the concepts for vitamins, atomic weights, or other specialist-described ingredients. Likewise, the concepts of theistic metaphysics are not components in most of the concepts of God wrought for us by Scripture, prayers, and liturgy – perhaps, too, by most sermons.

(Holmer, 1978: 174)

Indeed, Holmer insists, the specialized concepts usually 'mean less' and 'have very little work to do', by comparison with the rich, workable and liveable concepts of religious faith that have established roles that are independent of theistic metaphysics.

I believe that my own concern to take seriously a theology that is grounded in the challenges and fulfilments of ordinary life and its ordinary religious concerns, rather than in the controversies of the academy, can accommodate a number of these insights, without necessarily implying or endorsing every aspect of the particular theological positions embraced by their authors. I also welcome the implication that the ultimate object of theology (God), and its proximate object (faith), are not necessarily better known by the experts than by those who do their theology outside academia.[5]

Patently, there are significant theological and religious issues at stake here. Speaking quite generally, however, many would agree that something theological and religious is being missed if 'we characterise religion as discontent with the ordinary; a discontent which sets off a search for the extraordinary' (Phillips, 1993: 150).

Defining Theology

Does this mean that theology is simply identical with Christian believing or, perhaps, with the wider categories of Christian faith, experience or practice? Most accounts of theology demur, preferring to portray it as something distinct from what Christians preach, live and believe. Thus it is said that theology is 'the church reflecting on the basis of its existence and the content of its message', and that theology includes within its list of tasks those of testing, criticizing and revising the church's language about God, and testing it by its norm ('namely, God's self-disclosure to which testimony is given in the Bible') (Thomas, 1983: 1–2).

While distinct from faith, however, theology is closely related to it (cf. Green, 1990: 12). According to Geoffrey Wainwright, 'theology characteristically means the reflective enterprise that both feeds on and intends to serve [the] primary manifestations and deliverances of Christian faith that occur as revelation, narration, proclamation and worship' (Wainwright, 1993: 369). I shall explore this 'reflective' dimension in more detail later. It is sufficient to note here that the introduction of a distinction between faith and theology, a distinction that I immediately concede to be a proper and necessary distinction, allows for a very radical separation indeed in some accounts of theology.

---

[5]   This puts academic theology in a relatively unusual position on the university campus, although similar claims might be made for subjects such as anthropology.

In particular, theology is often characterized as an academic and scholarly *subject*. Thus *A New Dictionary of Christian Theology* defines it as 'the rational account given of Christian faith, as furnished by a series of sub-disciplines', as these are studied in institutions of higher or further education 'such as faculties of theology, seminaries or theological colleges'. On this account, theology is viewed as something 'appropriate to a minority of Christians, usually seen as an intellectual elite'; although the author acknowledges that this account has to face the challenge of Jesus' appeal to those without formal education and of Paul's critique of human wisdom, as well as protests from the champions of spiritual humility, mystical and other forms of religious experience, and sociology (Sykes, 1983).

Those definitions of theology that unashamedly refer to it as a *science* (the science of the Christian faith) do so on the basis of its special content and its 'conscious and methodical explanation and explication' of that subject matter (Rahner, 1975: 1687). The word 'science' is to be understood here in the traditional sense (rather than the modern, purely empirical, sense), as 'a discipline [better, disciplines] dealing with some field of knowledge with an appropriate method' (Braaten, 1984: 17).[6]

But introductions, dictionaries and handbooks of theology also offer broader definitions that suggest that theology is to be understood more generically as 'reflection about God' that makes use both of rational processes and of imagination (cf. Macquarrie, 1975: 82). David Ford allows a 'broad sense' of theology, which he defines in terms of 'thinking about the questions raised by and about the religions', and distinguishes it from academic theology, which deals with particular sorts of questions ('of meaning, truth, beauty, and practice') 'pursued through a range of academic disciplines' (Ford, 1999: 10, 15). So, although theology becomes a 'science of God' at one end of the intellectual spectrum, its definition can also be said to include 'reflection upon personal and group experience' in 'experiential theology' and in forms of theology that are (in a wide sense) 'allegorical' (Hastings, 2000b). Cutting the cake of theology in a rather different way, theology is commonly taken to refer to 'the views of any individual thinker on the nature of God', and thus to 'an individual's "talk about God"', in distinction from *doctrine* ('communally authoritative teachings') and *dogma* ('doctrines defined as essential to Christian faith by universal assent') (McGrath, 1993).

The etymology of the word 'theology' may appear to allow its use both within and outside of an academic context. An apparent ambiguity resides in the Greek noun *logos*, which in combination with *theos* (God) provides our topic. Logos ('word', 'reason') gives us the English noun ending -logy that usually denotes 'a subject of study or interest' (for example 'zoology'), but it can also label 'discourse' or 'a characteristic of speech or language' (as in 'trilogy', 'tautology' and 'eulogy'). However, even when dictionaries offer a number of variants for the meaning of the

---

6   In its original sense *scientia* was simply knowledge. Aristotle considered theology the noblest of the speculative sciences, as the (deductive) study of eternal and immutable being (cf. Aristotle, *Metaphysics* 1026a, 1064b).

word 'theology', they usually all favour the academy as the context for theology or at least assume scholarly, rational, analytic or systematic thinking as its defining characteristic. Thus the ninth edition of *The Concise Oxford Dictionary* defines theology as 'the study of theistic (esp. Christian) religion', 'a system of theistic (esp. Christian) religion' or 'the rational analysis of a religious faith' (COD, 1995). Mere thinking about God ('reflection'), or giving an account of God or religion by talking about them ('discourse'), would not seem to qualify as theology under these constraints.

Theologia and *Habitus*

Edward Farley has written with insight and passion about the changing understanding of theology or *theologia* (his preferred term), drawing attention to an older understanding that we have now mainly lost. For most of Christian history, Farley argues, theology had a broader meaning than that of a scholarly discipline or inquiry, a 'science'. Until the eighteenth century, 'theology was not just for the scholar or teacher but was the wisdom proper to the life of the believer'. This form of theology was not abstracted from its concrete setting, but understood as personal knowledge of God – 'direct cognitive vision'. It was a theology concerned with and developing within 'the believer's ways of existing in the world before God'. Farley claims that this enduring orientation, the 'sapiential and personal knowledge' that attends salvation, is in truth a fundamental dimension of every Christian's piety and vocation, 'a part of Christian existence as such'. This is 'theology in its original and most authentic sense' (Farley, 1983: xi, 31, 35–7, 47, 156; 1988: 81, 88).

On this interpretation, theology may be taken simply as a name for one's understanding of God and the meditative reflections that lead to that understanding (cf. Kelsey, 1992: 86), here construed as a 'cognitive disposition and orientation of the soul' (Farley, 1983: 35). It is in this context that Farley employs the word *habitus*. This is a wider conception than our modern 'habit', and includes elements of capacity and settled disposition, and of ability and inclination to act in characteristic ways. Synonyms for it might include 'aptitude' or 'character-trait' (Wood, 1996b: 349–50).

According to Farley, this sense of the word theology is one that badly needs to be recovered, as something prior to theology construed as a scholarly discipline of investigation and specialist reflection. It is hard to disagree with the broad thrust of this case. I would argue that it is in this sense that 'theology is a task laid on every Christian' (Moltmann, 1997: ix), as a part of every Christian's vocation. Here is a type of theology that is ordinary and everyday in a way that the academic or scholarly enterprise of theology, to which it quite properly gives rise, is not. It is this latter task that takes us 'out of the ordinary', to develop theology as a science. By contrast with theology as a *habitus* of the soul, academic theology articulates abstract impersonal knowledge that is distanced from human Christian living and being; in particular, it develops the 'dialectical' aspect of *theologia* in a way that is more rigorously self-aware and self-critical (cf. Kelsey, 1993: 127). The wisdom of faith, however, in which *both* these aspects of theology are rooted, is practical rather than theoretical knowledge, having to do with making sense of one's life and living one's life before God. But faith always involves a kind of knowing; even when it is a function of the heart as much as the mind, faith is pre-reflectively 'insightful', 'cognitive' and 'interpretative'. 'Inasmuch as faith is wisdom in an unreflective mode, *theologia* must be that same wisdom in a reflective mode – a *habitus*' (Kelsey, 1993: 126). *Habitus* may be understood, then, as 'the cognitive component of piety, . . . the insightfulness and knowledge that runs out of and shapes the attitudes and dispositions of the self in its apprehension of God and the world in relation to God' (Osmer, 1990a: 145).

The habitus of theology is no mere cleverness or lust for information, therefore, but embraces an orientation towards God that involves, and is an expression of, learning how to live before God – and, in this sense, *to live theologically*. It is the form in which faith (with its pre-reflective insights) becomes reflective, and comes to understanding as 'the reflective wisdom of the believer' (Farley, 1983: 156–7; 1988: 88, 96). 'Farley uses the term *theologia* rather than *theology* in order to underline that it is a kind of wisdom and not, as *theology* tends to suggest, a body of information and theory about God' (Kelsey, 1993: 102).

Andrew Louth confirms that for the Greek Fathers *theologia* was a matter primarily of contemplation. He cites Evagrius: 'If you are a theologian, you pray truly, and if you pray truly, you are a theologian' (Louth, 1983: 4). *Theologia* here is an apprehension of God that is not to be separated as something intellectual from its affective or 'spiritual' dimension. Philip Sheldrake also agrees that '*theologia* is a much broader concept than theology as an academic subject'. Like 'spirituality', it is self-implicating: a matter of personal commitment and action, of having one's perception transformed, of 'being a theological person not merely using theological tools' (Sheldrake, 1998: 22–3). The person who does theology is involved *as a person*; her personal faith is central to her doing theology and is therefore transformative. For this view of theology, ortho*doxy* is grounded in ortho*praxis*: right (reflective) belief in right (reflective) practice. David Tracy writes: 'Theological truth is ultimately grounded in the authentic and transformative praxis of an intellectually, morally and religiously transformed human subject. . . . Personal transformation ("doing the truth") is the key to theological truth as speaking the truth' (Tracy, 1981: 71, 73).

Farley and those who share his concerns provide me with my jumping-off point for my own account of theology. I am not claiming that my position wholly coheres with his, nor even that it is a natural development from it. I simply take from this discussion a concern to distinguish disciplined theological study from a form of theology that is more universal, more personal, more spiritual – and more fundamental. This is the distinction I have in mind when I contrast academic theology with *ordinary theology*.

Defining Ordinary Theology

People tend to think of a person's theology in terms of the subject matter and pattern of her or his religious talking and thinking. But, as the discussion above shows, theology is process as well as content, and therefore includes the set of processes and practices of holding, developing, patterning and critiquing these beliefs, thoughts and discourse. Theology is thus both beliefs and believing, both thoughts and thinking, both the content of what people say about God and that talking itself (and also their talking about their God-talk), both something we 'have' and something we 'do'. In short, it is both theology and theologizing.

Adopting this shorthand, I offer a definition of 'ordinary theology'.[7] Ordinary Christian theology is my phrase for *the theology and theologizing of Christians who have received little or no theological education of a scholarly, academic or systematic kind.* 'Ordinary', in this context, implies *non-scholarly* and *non-academic*; it fits the dictionary definition that refers to an 'ordinary person' as one who is 'without exceptional experience or expert knowledge' (NSOED, 1996).

At base, as we have seen, theology is 'God-talk': 'a form of discourse professing to speak about God' (Macquarrie, 1967: 11; cf. Hodgson, 1994: 3). This sounds an admirably open and democratic definition. Although the overwhelming majority of contemporary 'God-talkers' have not studied theology formally at all, they are inevitably engaged in doing their own theology if and when they speak and think about God, or at all events when they do so with any seriousness. This is an acceptable claim if theology is essentially the attempt *to speak reflectively of the divine*, or more generically of what we worship. 'Ordinary theology' would then be an appropriate term for *the content, pattern and processes of ordinary people's articulation of their religious understanding.* In the case of adults – and I am mainly concerned with adults in this book – ordinary theology might be called *the theology of the non-theological adult.* This is a deliberately paradoxical phrase, as it equivocates between my wider concept of theology and the more usual narrow sense – 'non-theological' being understood in this context as a label for those without an academic theological education.

Ordinary theology is itself often grounded in a less articulate and more inchoate complex of human and religious attitudes, values, commitments, experiences and practices. Some of these elements have been variously classified as a part of 'folk', 'common' or 'implicit religion' – as well as of official or 'conventional' religion; or simply as 'spirituality' or 'human faith'. A proper study of religious believing must also include an examination of these less manifest and less cognitive faith foundations (see pp. 39–44 and pp. 88–95 below).

As we have also seen, however, theology is usually understood much more narrowly than this. In fact John Macquarrie's definition of theology, which was quoted above, is immediately followed by a qualification that narrows its scope considerably. He writes, 'Not all God-talk would qualify as theology, for we reserve this name for the most sophisticated and reflective ways of talking about God' (Macquarrie, 1967: 11; cf. 79 and Macquarrie, 1975: 82). Evidently, the attempt to make room for something called *ordinary* theology may necessitate elbowing aside

---

[7]   Some might wish to describe the activity of *studying* ordinary theology as 'ordinary theology' as well, but I do not myself use the phrase for this second-order exercise (see Chapter 4).

those academic theologians who wish to reserve the noun for a particularly 'articulated' and 'sophisticated', 'critical' and 'highly reflective' form of God-talk. *That* form of theology is not just 'reflective', but 'disciplined' and 'systematic' thought or talk about God.

But Farley's scholarly diachronic defence of the original, *unscholarly* connotation of theology is something to which we can appeal. Thus broadened, there is room for a generic concept of reflective God-talk or -thought that may be said to exist among ordinary believers who have received no formal academic theological education, as well as in the lairs of academic theologians. And it is to an account of this form of theology that I now turn.

Characterizing Ordinary Theology

In this next section I shall attempt to give an account of the more significant aspects of ordinary theology. Readers deserve to know where this account comes from. I admit that it is not as grounded in empirical research as I would wish, although some empirical studies will be cited and others have informed much of the rest of my discussion. Most of these are interview studies with adult churchgoers in England.

I have also drawn on more anecdotal evidence from my experience as an adult Christian educator and Christian minister working in a variety of contexts with individuals, groups and congregations for over thirty years. Nevertheless, I am conscious (as I confessed in the Preface) that this part of the book in particular should be regarded as an essay, an 'attempt' rather than a definitive statement. I trust that it is an attempt worth making.

My definition of ordinary theology is couched in terms of those who have received little or no academic theological education. This is its defining characteristic. While not wishing to be too specific as to what would fall under the heading of 'theological education', I am thinking in particular of university education and its near neighbours, and therefore of the study of Christian theology as an academic field, discipline or set of disciplines. Most church education programmes with children and adolescents would not qualify, even those that are directed towards confirmation or church membership. Then again, I have met a few examples of this sort of Christian education that border on the 'academic', thus blurring the boundary. But what if an adult reads a book of academic theology or attends a course on some aspect of the Christian Faith, does that mean that he or she has received some 'academic theological education'? Well, it might; it would depend on the content of the book or the course, and on what was actually learned through it. We would have to see. I do not think that I need to specify in more detail and a priori what would or would not count as an academic theological education.

Readers may wonder whether I intend to be equally vague about the other characteristics that mark out ordinary theology. In fact, my categories both of ordinary theology and of academic theology are essentially *ideal types* in the (Weberian) jargon of the social sciences. That is to say, they are mental constructs derived from observable reality but not conforming to it in detail. I acknowledge that, as ideal types, they incorporate some deliberate simplification and exaggeration, and that I have selected and accentuated certain elements in an attempt to order more clearly the phenomena I am studying. In particular, I have concentrated on polar phenomena to make my point.

I believe, however, that we can all think of individuals who match the portraits that I paint, at least in many of the features displayed and to a large degree. Of course, with most continua it is much easier to distinguish the extreme examples at the ends than it is to wield a dichotomous classification in the grey area of the middle ground. And in many such cases, a difference essentially of degree ('more or less' something) can become a marked difference in kind at the extremes; just as organisms which gradually evolve as they disperse into different habitats, while continuing to interbreed with their close neighbours, may eventually become so different in genotype from the individuals 'left at home' that they have to be recognized as a separate species.

A similar point may be made with respect to many of the categories I will include in this section so as to characterize ordinary theology. They often represent, at least in some form, continuous variables that may be plotted on a spectrum of differences in degree. Ordinary theology may then be said to be more or less 'tentative', 'religious', and so on. Further, these qualities are only *characteristic* of ordinary theology, they are by no means *unique* to it. They are not, therefore, invariably absent from academic theology.

I should sound one final cautionary note. I shall argue later that, as the academic theologian always began life as an ordinary theologian, the usual rules will apply, and therefore that his academic theology may be seen as a *modification* of a more basic, earlier model, many parts of which will still be operating. To switch metaphors once more, we may say that inside the academic the ordinary theologian slumbers.[8] One cannot, therefore, easily separate the two.

Bearing in mind all these provisos, I will proceed to attempt to characterize my understanding of the nature of ordinary theology.

Learned and Learning Theology

While arguing for a properly empirical study of how people learn religion and therefore of how they are, in a vast variety of ways, taught it, the Christian educationalist James Michael Lee identifies the contribution that theology has received from an educational perspective.[9] 'The priceless gift which religious instruction bestows on theology is none other than its placing theology in the human context of social and psychological reality where life is lived' (Lee, 1971: 238). This

---

[8]   To appeal to a different biological analogy, ordinary theology could be said to constitute the inner core or 'heartwood' marked by the early annual rings of the wider, and more complex, academic theological 'tree'. See pp. 86–8 below for yet another analogy of the relation between these two types of theology.

[9]   For technical reasons, Lee calls the teaching element of Christian education 'religious instruction'.

may serve us too, appropriately reworded, as a maxim for the significance that a focus on religious learning should have for our understanding of ordinary theology.

In the first two chapters I discussed the learning context of theology and analysed the nature of religious learning. In my experience, 'ordinary theology' is the type of theology for which this account is most relevant, for ordinary theology both reveals and recognizes its learning context and nature much better than does scholarly, 'theologically educated' theology. I am not pretending, here or elsewhere, that ordinary theology is never in want of educational improvement. To the contrary, it will often benefit in particular from further reflection, probing and self-criticism, processes that will lead to significant new learning. But these tasks are not best done by plucking ordinary theology out of its personal learning context, and subjecting it to an analysis, critique and development that purports to be somehow context-free. We must beware of academic 'help' of this nature from the theologically erudite. They are likely to advocate such procedures with enthusiasm, seeking to emulate in others their own earlier ascents out of darkness. But sometimes they are far too determined to rise above their own context and beyond its personal grounding in religious learning. Some exponents of academic theology appear to believe that their work has succeeded in escaping from all contexts. Many others become forgetful of their theology's more humble beginnings, at its mother's knee or in other unassuming postures and surroundings. This forgetting is often welcomed as a relief and as something of an achievement. Nevertheless, 'We all have to start somewhere, and we all have to accept that we will never entirely banish the circumstances of our beginnings from the further development of our thought' (Pattison, 1998: 62).[10]

Most religious believers are not helped by contextless critiques, nor will they always welcome them. Ordinary believers are far more willing to recognize that their theological beliefs are personal and often idiosyncratic. Many of them will express pride in the fact that they bear upon their furrowed brows the marks of the formation of their ordinary theology. 'That's what *I* think, anyway', they often say. 'I came to see it that way when . . .', 'As a parent [or a woman or a convert], I suppose I'm bound to think that . . .', 'You see, I came from this sort of background [social, cultural, intellectual], so naturally I believe that . . .'

'Where did you get that from?' was one of the questions that I argued was appropriate to the processes of religious learning. It is a question that should be posed more often to the 'extraordinary', academic theologian. But when academic theologians are willing to answer it they often provide an answer that is not sufficiently 'radical', in the sense of 'of the roots'. Perhaps they are unwilling to go too far back, intellectually, biographically, psychologically or culturally. Academic theology, after all, would have us direct our attention to its prize blooms and away from its more humble (seedy?) origins, and the rank, dark, moist environment in which it originally took root (see Chapter 1). Although various influences will be

---

[10]   However, as Pattison insists, this is no recipe for historical determinism – as 'the man is not simply a larger version of the child' (Pattison, 1998: 62).

acknowledged, or even paraded, they will be influences that have made their intellectual impact well up the growth of the stem; and among them impersonal texts will usually rank above more personal influences. Ordinary theology does not answer like that. It is much more ready to speak of its roots and its nurturing influences, partly because it is reluctant to claim that it has 'flowered' or 'fruited' at all. This reticence marks it out as a more humble theology than some others, and we may note that this adjective appropriately originates from the Latin *humus*, the word for ground.

Ordinary theology is an overtly contextual theology; it is an explicitly learned theology. It is also a learn*ing* theology. It is not just its origins that it bears upon its sleeve. Those who are innocent of theological training are also more likely to show the 'theological workings' of their current theologizing than to display the 'completed calculations'. In this way, ordinary theologians can reveal in a fascinating way a great deal about theology as a process. They show us a theology-in-construction, a belief system that is 'on the way'. It displays features of its present direction, motivation and underlying logic that more sophisticated thinkers would perhaps think twice about mentioning, even if they recognized them as relevant. In this context, it is interesting that Montaigne's endorsement of a plain style over against the jargon of pedantic scholarship led to his creation of a new literary genre, the essay, a form that serves my own needs here. Montaigne's *essais* were 'attempts', 'trials', 'thought-experiments' or 'exercises'. The distinctiveness of this original form has been said to lie in 'the author's attempt to catch himself in the act of thinking, to present the process of thought, . . . rather than the conclusions' (Burke, 1981: 62). Ordinary theology is expressed best in this more tentative, personal and *developing* form.

Of course, academic theology is a learned theology as well, and particularly prides itself on being a learn*ing* theology. But the academic is most likely to be one who 'composes his thoughts in private. The students are permitted to see the product of his thinking, but the process of gestation is hidden from view' (Belenky *et al.*, 1986: 215). Furthermore, because of its different style – impersonal, universal, objectifying – academic theology all too often teaches one 'to be cool and to remain at one remove from your subject, dealing with it in a manner that ensures it is never going to make the slightest difference either to your life or to anyone else's' (Cupitt, 2000b: 47). This is a different sort of learning. Indeed, as the same author insists, academic theology may be said to 'systematically [train] the student to objectify religion and to miss the point of it' (22). In any event, and less controversially, the primary objective of much academic theology, certainly in a British context, is to create students of religion, not religious thinkers, feelers and doers. 'You don't learn to be a performer; you learn only how to be a good critic of other people's performances' (47).

Doing theology for oneself has been largely replaced in the academy by critically studying other people's theology, which leaves much of it deliberately stuck at the 'about' mode or stage of religious learning. One might argue that this is both inevitable and perfectly proper in a secular educational institution. But I also think that it should give us pause before we summarily dismiss theology as it is practised outside the academy. Ordinary theology *is* part of people's religious performance, and it does engage in a personal form of theological reflection aimed at thinking through the meaning of God. The theology that takes place within the academy, however, is mainly reflection *on* theology, and is devoted to thinking through the meaning of the theological conceptualizations of *other* theologians. It is learning about theology. Sadly, it is quite possible to study, and indeed to teach, academic theology without *doing* theology in any real sense at all. (I know, I've been there.)

Tentative Theology

I have said that ordinary theology is most often expressed tentatively. When pressed to state their views, ordinary believers speak hesitantly about what they believe. This reluctance is partly explained by their sense that theology is a subject for experts (either clerical or academic) and therefore is not for them. They have little confidence in their own beliefs or believing because they sense (rightly) that most professional theologians would quickly dismiss them. But this reticence is not on all fours logically with their attitude to their own views about other subjects in which they lack academic expertise: for example, history, economics or the natural sciences. Hence a tentative theology may often be accompanied by a rather confident, but equally 'non-expert', expression of opinion about medical science or political history. To some extent, then, theology is being treated as a special case.

But then theology should be a special case if it is an account of the mystery of God and an attempt to put into words that which will not go into words. This should be true, however, even for the professionals. If theology is, in part at least, an attempt to be articulate about a mystery that it can never embody, it can only ever be a partial understanding. This is both a logical and a theological point. God's mystery is an inevitable consequence of God's transcendence, God's radical difference from all other realities over against which he stands as their creator and Lord. 'Theological humility' is therefore a virtue that is essential to every form of theology. 'Ideally, indeed, God is best communicated in silence. . . . Faith will always be cautious of its assertions – and the more detailed, the more cautious.' 'We can be sure about God; but we must be tentative in theology' (Ramsey, 1965b: 61; cf. 1963: 89–90). Even those who claim some direct religious experience or revelation must acknowledge that their language can only be a provisional, exploratory and uncertain mirroring or expression in a different medium of that experience or event. This, of course, is axiomatic even of our accounts of sense experience (cf. Hospers, 1967: 542), although there it is more a matter of the 'technical tentativeness' of corrigibility, and should not prevent us from using the everyday language of indubitability or 'practical certainty' (Ayer, 1956: 52–7, 68; Malcolm, 1967: 79, 81; Quinton, 1973: 146–8). At the very different religious level, we may speak in a similar way of a proper 'practical confidence' in matters of faith, which is essentially a religious, spiritual or psychological confidence, and may be distinguished from an (equally proper) tentative and provisional theology (Ward, 1994: 29–30). Confidence in religious commitments does not, and should not, be simply translated into theological or epistemological claims. 'The certitude of faith has much more to do with confidence, or freedom from fear, which is partly an emotional state, than it has to do with judgments of certainty or great probability in any evidential sense' (Adams, 1987: 18; cf. Runzo, 1986: 155, 220–25 and ch. 5).

This excursus into epistemological matters is included solely to highlight the distinction that needs to be made between claims concerning religious experience and the spirituality and psychology of faith, on the one hand, and *theology* (God-talk, particularly in the form of representative language about God and God's actions) on the other. Between the two some sort of gap has to be acknowledged, and the recognition of this should lead all God-talkers to a theological humility which finds expression in what has been variously called their 'significant stuttering' and 'theological stammering' (Ramsey, 1962: 542; 1965a: 61; 1967: 263), or their 'thinking *towards* God' (Pattison, 1998: 114). It would appear that the content and form of ordinary theology express this element particularly well.

Lay Theology

Ordinary theology is also, in many senses, a lay theology. The second half of the twentieth century saw a significant, if patchy, development of lay institutions within the churches, coupled with increasing pressure for serious reflection on the theology of the whole 'people of God', and of the place of the laity in Christian mission and ministry both within and outside the churches (cf. Kraemer, 1958; Gibbs and Morton, 1964; 1971; Küng, 1971: 363–87; Green, 1990: 123–6). Much current writing on ecclesiology and ministry is critical of any 'clerical spirituality and sense of oneness with God' that is presented 'as inherently superior'. Instead, 'the new way of being church requires an ecclesial community that is being created *of* people, rather than provided *for* people' (Greenwood, 1994: 144, cf. 32, 146, 170–71).

We have already noted Charles Taylor's recognition of the significant shift in theology that is implicit in the focus on secular, ordinary life. One might say that this takes us beyond *the clerical paradigm*, to employ the current jargon. Edward Farley initially used that phrase to refer to 'the prevailing (post-Schleiermacher) Protestant way of understanding the unity of theological education'. He argued that, according to this paradigm, 'the disparate fields and courses are connected by their capacity to prepare the student for future clergy responsibilities' (Farley, 1983: 98). Under these circumstances, theology was defined not by its subject matter but by a particular (and limited) goal, namely, the training of the clergy. In its functionalist form, the clerical paradigm elevated the tasks of the ordained ministry as the (often sole) rationale of theological studies (Farley, 1983: 115). Theology then becomes restricted in its scope to knowledge needed by the professional leadership of the Christian community. Farley writes:

> This 'clericalization' of theology is so much the air we breathe that it is very difficult to imagine a time when it was any other way. . . . Theology at one time meant a disposition and knowledge which resembled wisdom, and as such had no clerical restriction. It was simply the sapiential knowledge which attended Christian life. This is not to say that a lengthy and rigorous clergy education was lacking. It does mean that that education as the

'study of theology' was thought of as an education in something which attended Christian life as such, something shared in by non-clergy. Clergy then are 'masters of divine knowledge which they are to teach others'. In the clerical paradigm, 'theology' is not something attendant on Christian existence but something clergy need in order to function as leaders of the church community. In the functionalist form of that paradigm, the leadership itself is defined by an assortment of discrete tasks, and theology is a theory or a theory of practice about those tasks.

(Farley, 1983: 130)

Farley argues that this has led to a separation between formal theological education and 'church education' or catechesis, with the apparent consequence of compounding differences in status, power and influence between lay people and professional theologians (Farley, 1983: 131; cf. Orr, 2000). It also leaves the clergy ill-equipped to reflect theologically on their own practice and that of their congregations (Kelsey, 1992: 163). It is for these reasons that 'the clerical paradigm' is a phrase that is most often used in criticism of an approach to theological education in institutions, such as seminaries, theological colleges, theological courses or divinity schools, that teach theology with both eyes on the ministry of the church and its professional formation (cf. Kelsey, 1992: 162–3; 1993: 107–9, 121). With respect to this approach, Francis Schüssler Fiorenza writes:

Then theological education becomes sharply removed from other forms of theological education, for example, university education, religious studies, education for interested adults. In addition, the concrete parochial expectations of ministers and the *de facto* wishes of church leadership become normative rather than those criteria demanded by good theology or by the purposes of the church.

(Fiorenza, 1996: 337)[11]

There is an important ongoing debate over the influence of the clerical paradigm in theological education. This is relevant not only to the concerns of those who are involved in lay Christian education and 'ministerial training', but also to the work of secular institutions of higher education engaged in teaching academic theology. My interest in this book, however, lies not so much with formal education as with the informal processes that lead to Christian concern and commitment, processes that are relatively independent of formal teaching and study (see Chapter 1). How does this debate impact on my concept of ordinary theology? I have, of course, defined ordinary theology in terms that largely preclude its application to those who have received an academic theological education under the auspices of university, seminary or church. As most clergy and ministers are authorized only after

---

[11]   Fiorenza recognizes three possible approaches to theological education. They are theological education as an education in theological enquiry concerned with the nature of theology, theological education focused on the nature and activity of the church, and this third approach which arises from the perspective of specific conceptions of ministry. He argues that the three approaches are interrelated and complementary, and each suffers from limitations, particular in specific contexts (Fiorenza, 1996: 334–8).

undergoing some formal education of this kind, their 'clerical theology' (using that adjective quite neutrally and certainly not pejoratively) is no longer an ordinary theology. Or, rather, it is not simply an ordinary theology; for, as I have already hinted, while theological education may overlay, modify and develop people's ordinary theology, it never wholly expunges it from their mind and heart.

The adjective 'lay' originally meant 'non-clerical, not ordained', but it has also come to mean 'not professionally qualified' and 'not expert'. This second meaning is close to the meaning I intend to convey by the adjective 'ordinary'. However, if we take 'lay' to refer to the 'laity' – that is, to the non-ordained members of the church – we conspire with the worst implications of the clerical paradigm by subtly defining one part of the church (by far the largest) in terms of the other, and by defining it negatively and in a manner suggestive of a lower status. We shall also be adding insult to injury by using an adjective originating in the Greek word *laikos*, which itself derives from the noun *laos* that denotes the whole people of God, laity and clergy together.[12]

This is certainly a linguistic minefield, but I am content to note three points with regard to ordinary theology. First, ordinary theology is lay by definition, in the sense of not expert and not professionally qualified. Secondly, it is also most often lay in the further sense of having a perspective that is very different from that of the clergy, as well as being very different from that of the academic student of theology. Thirdly, and perhaps most significantly, taking ordinary theology seriously can only help in overcoming that 'great gulf fixed' between clergy and laity in most of our churches. In my experience, lay people feel this gulf most with regard to their own beliefs. As one put it to me, 'Religion is really for the clergy; they just let us have a lend of it.' And in the words of another, 'You sit in the pew wondering if everyone else has "got it", and you are the odd one out.' A study of ordinary theology should help the clergy to hear more clearly these cries from the heart. But more about that later (see Chapter 5).

None of this, of course, precludes the possibility, reality and importance of recognizing and developing lay theology in two different senses: (i) creating an academic theology of (about) the laity, and (ii) promoting a theological education of lay people that will produce expert academic (lay) theologians. The number of lay people who fall into this group has rapidly increased over recent years in Britain, at the same time as the proportion of students of theology in higher education who intend to be ordained decreases. The frustration of these academically trained lay theologians is being voiced more and more vociferously within the churches, as they rightly demand that they should also be listened to by the clergy. Patently, however, they do not provide examples of ordinary theology in my terms.

Significant Theology

There is a pertinent but rarely asked question that we may pose of any academic theological study of the work of another, whether that other is a contemporary

---

[12]   Partly because of the ambiguity of this language, many prefer to use other all-embracing terms such as 'the baptized', 'the covenanted people of God', 'the priesthood of all believers' or 'the ministry of the whole church'.

theologian or a biblical author. The question is, 'Why should I study this (or him or her)?' The answer will most often be couched in terms of the *significance* of the author, text or topic. We shall be told that it is 'worthy of attention' or 'important'. But to whom is it significant and in what ways?[13]

The adjective 'important' has been defined in terms of 'carrying with it great consequence (to person concerned or purpose etc.)' (COD 1982: 501). Later editions of this dictionary drop the parenthesis, although its qualification must always be implied. Bernard Williams has written that it is not at all clear what is meant by the notion of something being 'simply, important' or 'important *period*':

> It does not mean that it is important to the universe: in that sense, nothing is important. Nor does it mean that it is as a matter of fact something that most human beings find important; nor that it is something people ought to find important. I doubt that there can be an incontestable account of this idea; the explanations people give of it are necessarily affected by what they find important.
>
> (Williams, 1985: 182)

Furthermore, 'caring about something *makes* that thing important to the person who cares about it' (Frankfurt, 1988: 92).

Perhaps there is no perspective-innocent, and in that sense non-relative and 'objective', way of calculating the importance of something. As is the case in other disciplines, academic theologians must rely on some sort of consensus among themselves about the theology and theologies that are deemed to be significant. Other contenders will be brusquely shown the door or quietly ignored. In fact, a great deal of theological debate involves arguing for the significance of certain ways of thinking and certain (often 'sadly neglected' or 'inexplicably ignored') authors. But the communal and public (that is, intersubjective) nature of this exercise can hide from those engaged in it the personal perspective that undoubtedly lies behind all appeals to significance. Even when we are just reporting on the theology of others, we are most likely to engage with the theology that seems significant to *us*, in some way and at some level. And its importance is, to some degree, a function of our agreeing with it. It shares the significance that we inevitably give to our own theology. How could it be otherwise?

One of my concerns in this essay is that we should take more seriously than we do the ordinary beliefs of ordinary believers, and indeed the ordinary non-beliefs of ordinary non-believers. But why should we? We may not find them significant; they may not have much importance for us. In these circumstances nothing is more natural than our ignoring or dismissing them. But note this: even though we may be unwilling to take their believing seriously, these believers will.

Yet this may not always appear to be true. I have claimed that the non-academic,

---

[13] Another response might be that the author or her work has had 'a considerable influence' or has 'led to important results'. But this just pushes the question one stage further back. If these effects are being claimed to be significant, important and worthy of attention, we may still ask 'to whom?'.

'untrained' theologian is often reluctant to express her beliefs or her thinking about God. However, her intellectual modesty and religious reticence should not be misunderstood. They do not mean that she does not believe that her theology is of much importance *to her*. At a deep level, ordinary beliefs are usually taken very seriously by the people who have them. They own their belief because it is significant to them and it is significant to them because they own it. Ordinary theology is, almost by definition, a significant theology – to the ordinary believers who profess it. Our own theology is always that sort of thing; that is how belief works. It is implied by calling a person's belief a 'belief-in' something, or by describing a person's attitudes as their 'values'. These things are truly ours; they matter to us. Hence your theology is also always more significant *to you* than mine could ever be to you, or the theology of 'the church' could, or that of Paul, Augustine or whoever. However 'ordinary' (non-academic) a person's theology is, it is necessarily more significant to that person than any other.

Nevertheless, in conversation with these other theologies, my own theology may change. I may come to adopt something of their view, as their theology becomes significant for me, as and when it becomes *mine*. This is essentially the same process as the second, 'learning of' mode of religious learning discussed in the last chapter. In both cases, the sort of person I am will partly define what I will embrace, what can become significant for me, because the claim that 'this is important to me (or for me)' is an expression of my very identity. In religion, what is of consequence and import to us is what meets our deepest needs. *Significance is salvific.* It serves to make us whole.

I have implied that this dynamic is often at the heart of academic theology also. But that is not always the case, and personal significance is not essential to theology as an academic discipline for the same reasons that being a believer is not essential to it. An interest in academic theology can quite easily be fired by the same sort of impersonal passion (to adopt a somewhat paradoxical phrase) that people can have for any discipline or field of study. But ordinary theology is never like that, I suggest; for such theology only begins for most people (as it does, of course, for many academics) when they face such questions as, 'What do *you* think?' and 'Who do you say that I am?'.

There are, however, some problems with placing the religious believer so much at the centre, as my account of ordinary theology does. As I have argued elsewhere:

> Other people's religious beliefs are of most interest to us when we feel that we have to take account of them in constructing our own theology, or atheology. We are inveterate 'meaning-making' animals, and each and every religious belief serves as grist to our mills. We try to make sense of it: to fit it into our (albeit undeveloped) belief-system, or to reject it if it does not fit and we are unwilling to change our own beliefs to accommodate it. Basically, we are interested in testing and critiquing others' beliefs because we have related beliefs of our own.
>
> (Astley, 1996: 69)

This may appear to imply an unsophisticated total relativism, for which truth (or, at any rate, religious truth) is only what-is-true-for-me. As it happens, I am more sympathetic to relativism than most, but only to a *qualified* form of relativism that can still accommodate our everyday senses of the 'objective', 'universal' and 'non-arbitrary' nature of truth and values, and will still allow us to criticize other people's beliefs. These elements are central to the distinctive grammar of our language about, and the phenomenology of our experience of, reality, truth, and morality.[14] I remain adamant, however, that in these matters, where it does matter, our judgement counts. Indeed, of course, it is in the end the only judgement that can count *for us*. For even if I convert to your views it is because I have changed my mind or, to put it more accurately, because you have changed my mind. And it is here that I may seem most vulnerable to the charge of slipping into a total relativism, one for which 'only my views count' and each person is somehow 'the measure of all things'. I need to defend myself against such a serious indictment.

Immanuel Kant notoriously argued that 'even the Holy One of the gospel must first be compared with our ideal of moral perfection before we can recognise him to be such' (Patton, 1948: 73). Basil Mitchell has rightly described this remark as 'preposterous', adding:

> It is absurd to suppose that the fisherman of Galilee – when he made the confession: 'Thou art Christ, the Son of the Living God' – had compared Jesus with his ideal of moral perfection (just as it was before any encounter took place) and had satisfied himself that he had, so to speak, achieved the required standard. He had, of course, judged for himself, and in judging he exercised moral insight, but he could not himself have preached the Sermon on the Mount.

Mitchell goes on to appeal to a famous claim by T. S. Eliot, drawing out its implications for any position that insists that we possess 'autonomy' ('self-government', 'standing on our own feet') in our judgements and decisions.

> As Eliot maintains, a great artist creates the standards by which he is to be judged. Autonomy requires that the standards used shall be, in some sense, the judge's own standards; not, however, in the sense that he must have invented them; only in the sense that he must have rationally accepted them.
>
> (Mitchell, 1980: 152–3)

My view is quite consistent with this claim. We can only 'judge for ourselves'. This may quite properly be described as a rational process, in the sense of a *reasonable* (well grounded, justified) one, although it is not based on ratiocination alone and the 'reasons' we have for it may not serve as reasons for those who do not share our evaluation/acceptance. No one can come to believe in different things, whether they be truths, facts, values or gods, without those different objects of belief entering into his or her own viewpoint. But this does not mean that our beliefs or values, in their *current* form, stand in judgement imperiously 'above', 'over' and 'separate from' all

---

[14] I believe that a sophisticated account of relativism can find a place for these concerns (cf. Arrington, 1989: ch. 6; Runzo, 1986: *passim*; Astley, 1994b: ch. 10).

other theologies and moral systems. The measuring-rule by which we assess the height of these other structures is ever-changing, as it incorporates material from those structures themselves in a psychological process that is more complex than even this convoluted analogy suggests. To move to a different image, we might argue that we view other people's theologies from a platform that is partly built out of other people's theologies, and which we are continually reconstructing by incorporating more of their materials (cf. Sykes, 1984: 241–2).

Friedrich Schleiermacher, one of the founding fathers of hermeneutics, held to the conviction that what is to be understood must in some sense already be known. He argued that this is true even of the child learning the meaning of a word: on the one hand, she must relate it to what she already knows; on the other, she has to assimilate something alien. Anthony Thiselton comments, 'Schleiermacher adds that since understanding new subject-matter still depends on a positive relation to the interpreter's own horizons, "lack of understanding is never wholly removed"' (Thiselton, 1980: 104), and hence that a hermeneutical *spiral* is needed that allows for a *progressive* understanding. The essence of the experience of learning to understand is well-captured in this analysis. It is something that formal educators have to take very seriously in their own practice, recognizing that no text is ever understood 'unless there were at least some minimum of common ground between ourselves and the text'. If it 'did not link up at any point with our experience, we could make nothing of it' (Macquarrie, 1960: 45).

I presume that this element is what partly explains the capacity we all have to respond to the thinking of another person *as if it were our own*, even though we may never before have consciously formulated these thoughts for ourselves (cf. Stiver, 1996: 153). This is a very important feature of religious belief and insight. In religion, it is not unusual to hear something for the first time yet to recognize it as a truth 'one has always known'. (Ordinary believers often comment on this phenomenon.) Poetry can produce this effect very powerfully; our response to a poem is often an enthusiastic and affirmative, 'Yes!', although we may never have previously encountered, nor ourselves engendered, such an insight. The influence of great prose writers also often depends on this factor, not least when their insights are most directed to everyday human life. Both Pascal and Emerson apparently said of the writings of Montaigne, 'I seem to have written this myself.' There is perhaps no higher praise that we can give to another person's thoughts, even in theology.

All of which encourages me to claim that an emphasis on ordinary theology as a significant theology does not preclude the ordinary theologian finding significance in sources outside herself, nor does it push my account into any extreme form of relativism.

Meaningful Theology

Ordinary theology has a significance for people in so far as it is 'meaningful' to them. The notion of meaning being employed here is not to be understood in a semantic or linguistic sense, as a conceptual skill relating to the meaning of language; but with reference to the meaning of events, experiences and situations, and of life itself. This wider understanding designates the perceived value, purpose and significance of elements within our life, and of our life taken as a whole. This is the context in which we talk of a universal human 'meaning-making' or (as some would insist) 'meaning-finding', activity. Fowler's understanding of human faith (see Chapter 2) is essentially about meaning. He construes faith as a disposition, 'a stance', 'a way of moving into and giving form and coherence to life' (Fowler, 1978: 24). Faith is defined as:

> the composing or interpreting of an ultimate environment *and* as a way-of-being-in-relation to it. [It] must be seen as a central aspect of a person's life orientation. . . . It plays a central role in shaping the responses a person will make in and against the force-field of his or her life. Faith, then, is a core element in one's character or personality.
>
> (Fowler, 1978: 25)

The expression and articulation of this sort of faith-spirituality in language comprises much of ordinary theology, where the 'ultimate environment' is interpreted in terms of God, and a person's life is seen in that religious context and therefore as *ultimately* meaningful. Other accounts of spirituality may be less explicit about this element or may understand it very differently. Nevertheless, the dimension of perceived and embraced meaning lies at the heart of all spiritualities, secular as well as religious. This is what enables people to cope with suffering and to face death. It is what gives their lives some sense of point and purpose. Psychologists rate this element very highly, and many relate it to the mythic, narrative and symbolic structures of religion. Jung writes:

> That gives peace, when people feel that they are living the symbolic life, that they are acts in the divine drama. That gives the only meaning to human life; everything else is banal and you can dismiss it. A career, producing of children, are all *maya* [illusion] compared with that one thing, that your life is meaningful.
>
> (Jung, 1977: 275)

One cannot overestimate the importance of this understanding of meaning to human life. When it fails, they sense, all is lost. Where it is present, almost any ordeal or anguish can be borne. In surveys of both adults and adolescents in Britain and Western Europe, a majority agree that life has 'meaning' or 'purpose' (cf. Abrams *et al.*, 1985: 60; Harding *et al.*, 1986: 199–205; Osmond, 1993: ch. 1; Robbins and Francis, 2000; Francis, 2001: 26–7); even that there is 'a patterning of events' that has on occasions convinced them that 'they were meant to happen' (Hay and Hunt, 2000: 13, 44). There is a human resilience expressed in these data that is at first sight surprising, but it is confirmed in many interview studies and pastoral conversations with a wide range of people. Ordinary believers, in particular, witness to this sense that life is meaningful.

Donald Evans writes of assurance as the most fundamental constituent of trust, which is itself the most fundamental of what he calls our attitude-virtues: pervasive stances for living that undergird our religious as well as our moral beliefs and practices. Evans argues that assurance has two components: reality-assurance and satisfaction-assurance. *Satisfaction-assurance* is the assurance that our needs will be satisfied: that we shall receive our bread for tomorrow; that we shall eat, drink and be clothed. The concerns and strengths of *reality-assurance* lie rather deeper in the soul. Evans defines reality-assurance as 'the assurance that life is worth living because it has already received the meaning and reality which are necessary for human fulfillment' (Evans, 1979: 23). In this context he quotes a spiritual insight reported by Sam Keen from the time of his father's death:

> In the face of the uncertainty of life and the certainty of death no human act or project could render existence meaningful or secure. Nothing I could *do* would result in my being saved, ontologically grounded against tragedy and death. Either dignity and meaningfulness come with the territory or they must forever be absent. Sanctity is given with being. It is not earned.

(Keen, 1971: 17)

I would argue that what 'comes with the territory' for the spiritually mature woman or man is an assurance of worth, and an assurance that 'life is worth living' and 'is meaningful', that are so fundamental that they are not dependent on any further facts, not even facts about our flourishing – or our survival. We just recognize the value of our existence, unique and irreplaceable. This is an assurance that is not extinguished even by the diminishing of our flourishing, by the fading of the assurance of the satisfaction of our needs. It is of the essence of a religious perspective on life.

Ordinary theologians will not often use language that is so poetic or profound as that of Keen, but I maintain that their ordinary theology is forged in circumstances of exactly this kind. We note again that they are personal situations of learning-change, not academic contexts. Facing the death of others and facing our own death (which is always a part of our experience in facing the death of others) fires the crucible of ordinary theologizing. The resulting theology can powerfully express spirituality's concern with meaning. It would be foolish, however, to assert that it always does. Ordinary theology, like academic theology, may be either profound or superficial, either positive or despairing, reflecting the people who are engaged in it. What I *can* say, and with some confidence, is that ordinary theology is more directly concerned with the perceived meaningfulness of the speaker's own life than is much of the theology of the academy.

Subterranean Theology

My concept of ordinary theology has some affinities with what the sociologist David Martin has called 'subterranean theologies' (Martin, 1967: 74–5). For Martin, these are part of that unofficial and implicit 'luxuriant theological undergrowth which provides the working core of belief more often than is realized', even among regular churchgoers. Martin unpacks his arresting phrase along these lines: 'By subterranean theologies I mean series of interlocking attitudes about fairness, about the sources of contemporary social difficulties, the choice of superhuman culture heroes, the selection of significant metaphor, and notions about how and why people act' (Martin, 1969: 108–9).

This is a wide-ranging and rather chaotic list. The category is presumably also intended to include components that are rather more cognitive, particularly patterns of religious thought that persist and are transmitted below the level of literary culture (Martin uses the phrase 'sub-cultural'). Martin sometimes appears to distinguish subterranean theologies from 'superstitions', but not in any systematic or convincing way.

Robert Towler has interpreted subterranean theology to mean 'patterns of thinking about supernatural matters'. This is narrower and more focused than Martin's own usage, and therefore suits my interests better. Towler declares that such theology is 'underground' in two different ways. It is 'below the level of universally available, publicly articulated, religious ideas such as are adumbrated in books and sermons'. It is, therefore, 'hidden' to those who seek for theology in libraries or by listening to clergy, but is 'readily available to the observer who simply listens to the talk in pubs, in bingo-halls, or in bus queues'. But subterranean theology is also underground in the sense that it lies 'closer to the immediate experience and consciousness of ordinary people' than are the official theological formulations that are taught and defended in the university or the church (Towler, n.d.: 5). Towler adds that, in his view, the term subterranean theology is useful:

> because it draws attention to the fact that theologies exist apart from those which conventionally bear the name of theology, and by employing the same word we restore to these beliefs the dignity of which they are robbed when they are designated superstitions, for example, and distinguished from respectable ideas of the highly educated for which the word theology is reserved.
>
> (Towler, n.d.: 5)

It should be clear by now that I share these concerns; I have adopted my own terminology partly for these same reasons. However, I prefer the term ordinary theology both because it speaks of what is normal, usual and commonplace (and, therefore, widespread), in distinction from the out-of-the-ordinary nature of academic theology, and because 'subterranean' may itself be interpreted in a pejorative fashion – as something that is *deliberately* hidden, secret or even subversive, or as something that is unconventional and experimental (as in the phrase 'the underground press').

I also need to consider the extent to which theology may be said to include the range of phenomena that Martin seems to include: that is, values and attitudes, sociological or psychological explanations, the adoption of 'heroes', and the use of significant metaphors.[15] I would make two points here. First, that we should not artificially isolate beliefs and believing from their affective (especially attitudinal) companions (indeed, beliefs-in comprise beliefs-that wedded to pro-attitudes). Secondly, that a person's understanding of deity and salvation may well be better

---

[15] Presumably this is something akin to Pepper's 'root-metaphors': cf. Pepper, 1935.

expressed in his 'secular' rather than his 'religious' beliefs. Nevertheless, my own understanding of ordinary theology is of something that is more explicitly and more recognizably *theological*: that is, the reflective God-talk which expresses and articulates beliefs about God, Jesus, sin, salvation and so on. I do not use the word 'theology' in an analogical or metaphorical sense, nor as synonymous with the (wider) term 'religion' (see the next section, as well as pp. 88–95 below). *My* focus is on explicitly religious beliefs and believing.

Although our religious practices, attitudes, values, emotions and experiences can never be wholly separated from our religious beliefs, 'it is the beliefs that are peculiarly open to reflection and debate: to argument, criticism and development' (Astley, 1996: 61). Our beliefs can be dissected, both because (logically) as beliefs they are more directly and appropriately subjected to critical evaluation, and because (psychologically) they are less intimately and closely embraced than our affective stances, existential commitments and overt lifestyle. I should acknowledge in this context that academic theology is often effective precisely by being cool, ritualized and impersonal. That is, very often, very useful. It can be particularly helpful for those who *need* to distance themselves a little from their own first-hand theology, to lay it down in front of them (and others) for dissection and analysis as if it were not a part of themselves. I do not deny that academic theology has its uses!

Religious Theology

'Subterranean theology' is one of many phrases that have been employed by sociologists, phenomenologists and historians of religion to speak of a common or popular religiosity that is not controlled either by the church or (in its more theological expression) by the academy. I shall examine a range of such terms at the end of this chapter. All of them employ the noun 'religion' rather than 'theology', and thus appear to have a wider concern than is apparent from my term 'ordinary theology'. Religions, after all, include much more than theology. They comprise attitudes and values, religious practices and more general forms of behaviour, feelings and experiences of various sorts, communal and social expressions, moral beliefs and principles, artefacts and artistic expressions, and many other dimensions. Ordinary theology is an expression of and a reflection on such religious experience, attitudes and practices, but is itself – as I have indicated above – a much more specific thing. Theological language is a form of religious talk that articulates religious beliefs and thinking, particularly about God. Ordinary theology is therefore a *part of* 'ordinary religion', particularly as that part is made known in speech.

But if ordinary theology is the theology of ordinary religion does that make it a *religious* theology? John Macquarrie, along with most theologians, distinguishes *theological* language from *religious* language, arguing that the former arises out of the latter 'when a religious faith becomes reflective and tries to give an account of itself in verbal statements'. While recognizing that theology should not stray too far away from its religious source, lest 'it degenerates into empty and arid disputes' or comes 'to appear senseless', Macquarrie seems to assume a considerable distance between a theological belief and any 'immediate and unreflective utterance of faith' that may form its basis (Macquarrie, 1967: 19). Does this allow *any* form of theology to be qualified by the adjective 'religious'?

Ordinary theology is the test case, and the next section will explore the nature of this religious dimension in more detail. In describing ordinary theology as a 'religious theology', I am treating it as a form of theology that keeps close to the religious impulses and especially to the spirituality that drives people and heals them. Of course, some scholarly theology also succeeds in keeping close to its religious origins and effectively draws on spiritual attitudes, values and experiences. Despite the secular environment in which the majority of them now work, in Britain at all events, many of the academic theologians who embrace Christian beliefs and engage in Christian practices would argue that their academic theology should also qualify as a religious theology in my terms. But not all academic theology is like that and much of it is not.

The scholarly disciplines that theology rightly utilizes in its work, particularly in the context of and for the audience of the secular university, tend to separate theology from its religious context, at the same time as they sever it from its learning context. This is particularly true where academic theology understands its 'scientific' status in a manner that is too closely modelled on other studies, particularly the empirical sciences. Many oppose such a conflation, arguing that religious believing has little to do with hypothetical speculation or evidence gathering, but everything to do with its beliefs being beliefs that we can live by – whether we can 'digest them, whether they constitute food for us' (Phillips, 1970a: 71; cf. 1976: ch. 2 and 1970b: ch. III).

Yet some might claim that academic theology is to be *preferred* to ordinary theology as a means of relating to ordinary spirituality and religious experience, on the grounds that the primary task of academic theology is to explore, critique and remodel theoretical truth. When it has achieved that goal it may confidently provide, by deductive reasoning, the religious and practical implications of that truth. Academic theology will then tell us how it 'should work' in our ordinary religious lives. But this pattern is too prescriptive for our needs, and places too much emphasis on the critical, reconstructive nature of theology and too little on grounding theology from the outset in the religious life. We need, rather, *to begin with the working*: to look and see what works in practice, and then to reflect theologically on that.

Where academic theology does try to keep close to religion, it sometimes does so in ways that limit the relevance and the value of these links to those who share an academic theological education. For example, not unnaturally, academic theology often draws on the spiritual and religious resources of a theologically articulated Christian tradition, or of the scholarly author himself or herself. This produces a very different sort of religious theology from that generated by an ordinary theology that arises from the ordinary spirituality of those who have not been taught to structure their religious orientation in dialogue with the theology of the academy, and who are more likely to appeal to its learning context in their own religious lives. A similar point may be made of the salvific dimension of theology (cf. above, pp. 39–41). Ordinary theology is itself salvific, sharing in the salvific nature of the religious and spiritual life from which it springs. Academic theology may also be salvific, but usually only for those academic theologians whose spiritual and religious lives resonate with its concepts and modes of reasoning. Most religious believers are not in this situation. For them, academic theology frequently appears to be too distanced from their religious lives and too 'second-hand'; academic theology requires too much 'bracketing out' of the personal, or too much critical testing of beliefs, for it to serve them as a medium for their healing.

Kneeling, Celebratory Theology

In many academic contexts, much of what is called 'theology' is not truly theology at all but rather 'religious studies' in the form of Christian studies, the study of Christianity. This labour of historical criticism, textual analysis or sociological reflection constitutes valuable, worthwhile and appropriately academic study. Its disciplined work can certainly illuminate the Christian religion and Christian spirituality. But it does so by generating perspectives *on* religion and applying tools to it 'from outside'. I have argued before that only some of what goes on in university departments in England involves *doing* Christian theology, in the sense of the critical and reflective articulation, development and defence of Christian beliefs. And the extent to which *that* activity is a truly religious theology that keeps closely in contact with the heart of Christian spirituality is an open question.

None of this is meant as a criticism of what goes on in academic institutions under the title of theology. Quite the reverse, in fact, for secular universities *should* do their theology in a different way from religious believers and their churches. I make these points solely to show how different an animal ordinary theology can be. In particular, I wish to stress that ordinary theology is not so much a perspective on theology, but a perspective *in* or *of* theology.

Rowan Williams has distinguished three styles of doing Christian theology (Williams, 2000b: xiii–xvi). As a *celebratory* phenomenon, as in hymnody, preaching and certain kinds of scriptural communication, 'connections of thought and image' are displayed so as 'to exhibit the fullest possible range of significance' in the language used. It is in this way that images and patterns are cross-referenced and 'an ever-more complex texture to the language of belief' displayed. This is theology for a believing public. In its *communicative* style, theology behaves rather differently. It seeks to persuade the unbeliever and commend the faith to her, by experimenting with the 'strange idioms and structures of thought' of the rhetoric of her uncommitted environment. The third style of theology, *critical* theology, tests the language of both celebration and communication, by asking whether their emerging thought forms are still identical to, or at least continuous with, the 'fundamental categories' of theology, and by asking probing questions about what those categories really mean. This third style of theology embraces both the ancient negative theology and the philosophical theology of western modernity.

Williams stresses the interaction between these different styles of doing theology, which parallels the overlap that others have noted between the different 'publics' that theology addresses (cf. Tracy, 1981: ch. 1). While ordinary theology is well placed to engage with the wider non-Christian or non-church public in its communicative mode, and while it is not without its own critical element (as I shall argue in Chapter 5), I suggest that much of ordinary theology is a great deal closer to the celebratory style than to the other two categories that Williams has rehearsed.

To adopt a distinction originally proposed by Hans Urs von Balthasar, ordinary theology is more of a 'kneeling theology' or 'theology at prayer' than it is a 'sitting theology' or 'theology at the desk' (von Balthasar, 1960: 224; 1989: 208). Karl Ernst Nipkow comments on the distinction:

> The theologian takes a step aside, as it were, now standing beside him or herself, giving up the former identity, at least to a certain degree. Today, theology as an academic discipline participates in this separation by systematically reflecting and critically checking the forms of 'faith-theology-identity', and thereby more or less dissolving the identity.
>
> (Nipkow, 1985: 31)

Ordinary theology incorporates 'the more or less immediate cognitive articulation of living piety' that is characteristic of kneeling theology. This rests on 'the inner identity of theology and faith', whereas engaging in academic theology involves a 'critical dissociation' between the two.

What is meant by *articulation* here? 'Articulate' is an adjective that may be used of anything that is jointed. 'Articulate speech', therefore, like an articulated lorry, has separate and distinguishable parts that are flexibly connected together. Interestingly, the phrase is used first of the distinct pronunciation of words and then (presumably by extension) of speech that is both fluent *and coherent*. As with many of the accounts already offered of the distinction between ordinary and academic theology, the differences noted here are differences only of degree rather than rigid and dichotomous distinctions of kind. Being 'inarticulate', we should note, also admits of degrees. At one extreme the inarticulate person is wholly speechless or 'dumb'.[16] But speech that is indistinctly pronounced and/or lacks clarity may also be labelled 'inarticulate', and this covers quite a range of inarticulateness until we arrive at the category of those who are said to 'speak clearly' without qualification, either in their vocalization or in the clarity of the meaning they seek to convey (which is 'unambiguous, accurate, without confusion').

Academic theology majors in the distancing process of critical reflection *on* theological positions. It has therefore been defined as 'the deliberate, critical and systematic reflection upon the fundamental assumptions and . . . activities' of the Christian religion (Mason, 1989: 10). While ordinary theology also has its critical dimension, there is a marked difference in degree between the two – and also a difference of 'position'. To return to von Balthasar's metaphors, academic theology may occasionally come down to its knees, but it mainly reflects in the sitting position; whereas ordinary theology is mostly to be found – and is most at home – in a kneeling posture. The essential questions here are questions of degree. Just *how*

---

[16] The word 'dumb' is also used with a range of connotations, from a complete inability to speak, through the temporary silence of those 'struck dumb' and the relative silence of the taciturn or reticent, to the merely colloquial dumbness of the ignorant or stupid.

much is 'enough' in the claim that the theological critic must create 'enough distance from the text'? And *at what stage* do problems arise for the non-critical reader who both 'looks into the text from outside' and 'accepts its invitation to enter in wherever it leads' (Thiselton, 1992: 316)?

Stewart Sutherland has extended von Balthasar's typology by introducing the further category of 'holding at arm's length' theology.

> Much of what goes on in theology and in education involves holding at arm's length what is most naturally and appropriately held in embrace. The beliefs and values which we hold out for scrutiny lest they be the products of blindness or prejudice are, again most naturally, matters of deep-seated conviction which involve emotion as well as intellect, soul as well as mind.
>
> Critical openness, central as it is to our Western culture, both liberates and causes problems. We have all experienced the fruits of liberation in the quality of our lives, but the problems also belong there, and they arise because critical openness requires the mastery of a very difficult technique – that of distancing oneself from what is nearest to one and in that sense primary. This distancing requires one to objectify that which most fully belongs to one's subjectivity. One has to hold at arm's length both what is personal or individual and partly experienced in that sense, and also what is experiential in the different sense of belonging to the communal and 'institutional' world of ritual.
>
> (Sutherland, 1985: 140)

Sutherland notes that the dangers of this procedure include the over-objectification of human life and values (142). This is all very well put, and presents us with an arresting image of the 'posture' of academic theology and (to capitalize further on the metaphor) of the distance between its own stance and that of ordinary theology.

Academic theology is able to move from its sitting posture easily enough into this more extreme position, and is never far away from doing just that. Ordinary theology, however, in this metaphor starts from a very 'different position'. Although ordinary theology can from time to time adopt the sitting position, or something close to it, I suggest that its work is hardly ever done 'at arm's length'. This may be regarded as a limitation (see above p. 72) but its kneeling posture is also a plus, for it allows a self-involving expression of a person's deepest spirituality. The articulation of ordinary theology partakes to some extent of the power of the things it expresses: things that heal, restore and give life – that is, the believer's faith, wisdom and knowledge of God. Ordinary theology is the *natural* way of doing theology for people on their knees, as they lean into the eternal mystery that is both inside and beyond us all. For ordinary theologians, their kneeling God-talk also incorporates the deepest value convictions on which they rest their lives and their deaths. To attempt to pluck all that from their hearts, and to hold it as far away as possible, would be well beyond where most ordinary theologians wish to go in their critical reflection on their faith. So ordinary theology, lying close to its religious origination, keeps to the styles and linguistic forms of religion: confessional, expressive, poetic, affective, exhortatory and communal. Its nature both expresses and encourages this particular way of engaging with religion.

Irregular Dogmatics

Karl Barth's category of 'irregular dogmatics', which he distinguishes from 'regular or academic dogmatics', shares many similarities with this category of ordinary theology (Barth, 1975: 277–8). Like ordinary theology it operates outside the theological school and does not attempt to 'cover the whole ground with the same consistency'. It is a form of theology that is often not easily distinguishable from proclamation and relies more on aphorisms than on explicit argument. It seeks nothing beyond a fragmentary account of faith, leaving the goal of a systematic enquiry to its academic cousin. Like ordinary theology, irregular dogmatics tends to be 'strongly influenced by the person and biography of their authors'. Barth argues that this 'free dogmatics' existed first but that it continues *alongside* the more academic mode of theology, which 'has always had its origin in irregular dogmatics and could never have existed without its stimulus and co-operation'. All told, we are presented here with quite a positive picture, painted by a major theologian who was nothing if not scholarly but who also saw the academic task of theology as a confessional task of *church* dogmatics.

For Barth, however, dogmatics is always a science, in the broad sense of *Wissenschaft* (an academic discipline), and therefore a 'human effort after truth'. This emphasis takes dogmatics beyond any simple testimony of faith and life to the critical revision of the church's talk about God. For Barth, of course, this revision is no distancing, neutral evaluation. It is to be undertaken instead in the light of the content of the distinctive utterance of the church, which must be considered as its very 'being as the church' – that is, Jesus Christ (Barth, 1975: 3–5). If this revisionary role is part and parcel of *all* dogmatics, then irregular dogmatics will surely not be spared it. This alerts us again to the need for ordinary theology to have some self-critical dimension, although to what degree is still open to debate.[17]

Mother-tongue Theology

Some might argue that the contrast between ordinary and academic theology is even more extreme than I have so far allowed, and that its effects are much wider than the religious case, on the grounds that it is located deeper within the diverse forms of human language.

Ursula Le Guin, in a powerful essay, distinguishes two types of 'tongue' (Le Guin, 1989: 147–51). She argues that there is, first, the 'mother tongue' of the home, the intercourse of conversation, which is constituted by language that expects an answer. This tongue is the language of communication and of relationship. It markedly differs from the 'father tongue', to which the mother tongue appears to be 'inaccurate, unclear, coarse, limited, banal . . . repetitive . . . earthbound,

---

[17] I should acknowledge that Barth himself insists that a universal, true insight from irregular dogmatics can only be accepted as such when it has survived the rigours of the academic theological 'school' (Barth, 1975: 279).

housebound'. The father tongue is the language of 'disinterested' analysis, of 'thought that seeks objectivity': a language that distances the speaker from the subject and forces a gap between human beings and their world. According to Le Guin, the father tongue is also the language of social power, the language that makes somebody do something and that gratifies the ego. It is the language of *succeeding*. Like a traditional lecture, the father tongue is one-way communication rather than a conversation and to that extent it does not expect any answer. This form of language is not 'native' to us in the way that the mother tongue is. Most significantly, the father tongue is a tongue that we have to go to college to learn fully.[18]

In a commentary on Le Guin's distinction, Rowan Williams accepts her underlying point and applies it to a church context. His comments are worth quoting at length.

> There is (broadly) purposive talk, designed to change situations in particular ways, and which therefore opens up contexts about the sorts of change looked for and who is to execute them; and there is the talk that is *designed* for nothing, that simply articulates a situation, identifies it, we could say, as a *human* situation, one that can be brought to speech. We could put it another way and say that such talk is not dominated by 'interest', by considerations of power and advantage. What matters is not victory but keeping the exchange going. This, I suppose, is the sense in which Le Guin can say that the mother tongue expects an answer: it is about maintenance, the unobtrusive and hard-to-formalise ways in which people attend to the background regularities of a shared world, and so it values bare continuation, participation in the exchange, in a way that can be baffling or infuriating for someone conditioned to the idea of verbal exchange as an exchange of information or of signals about who's in charge. Death, for example, is surrounded by clichés; many a priest engaged in a bereavement visit will have discovered the extraordinary importance of saying or allowing to be said a whole range of what might look 'objectively' like empty bromides. Some things require saying, and originality is not what's looked for.
>
> (Williams, 2000a: 74–5)

There is an obvious connection here with the world of ordinary theology. Is ordinary theology, we may wonder, the theology of the mother tongue? Williams' example of the pastoral visit illustrates its context. I would suggest that situations of this kind are frequently rich in ordinary theology. They are also occasions where academically trained, theologically educated ministers often find themselves at a theological disadvantage, while the more ordinary theologian knows quite naturally what 'requires saying'.

---

[18] Le Guin does not say that the father tongue is the language of *rational thought*, for she recognizes that there is more to reasoning than distancing. Le Guin's dichotomy is in some respects similar to Basil Bernstein's distinction between two different forms of social interaction and ethos that underlie language styles: a 'restricted code' that reinforces social solidarity and an 'elaborated code' whose language communicates abstract concepts (cf. Bernstein, 1971: ch. 5).

But the differences of which Ursula Le Guin speaks may be of another kind; Le Guin herself understands them as a gender distinction. Williams is reluctant to map the mother/father tongue distinction directly onto human sex or gender, since both modes of speech may be used by both men and women. I share his reluctance for the same reasons. The historical, philosophical and sociological truth of the matter, however, is that more women than men continue to speak the 'mother tongue' naturally, especially in situations where relationships are to the fore, or appear so to be to the women concerned (cf. Tannen, 1990; 1995; and Belenky *et al.*, 1986: ch. 6 – on 'separate' and 'connected' knowing). Le Guin herself says of the mother tongue that it is 'the language spoken by all children and most women', and explains that she calls it a 'mother tongue' because 'we learn it from our mothers and speak it to our kids'. Many men, she writes, 'learn not to speak it at all' (Le Guin, 1989: 150–51).

However, Le Guin also writes of a third language, 'my native tongue', in which mother and father tongues wed and weld, fruitfully creating the 'baby talk' of *art*. It is important to understand that this includes, or is best expressed in and most readily flows from, the art of living well – 'living with skill, grace, energy', and of 'making order where people live'. These are, she adds, 'the low arts, the ones men don't want' (Le Guin, 1989: 151–5). Equally significantly, they are the *ordinary* arts of *ordinary* living. They are not, in principle, gender-specific. Nevertheless, the gendered dimension of this analysis of tongues should not be underrated.

If men and women do often speak and think differently, then it is likely that their ordinary God-talk will also be different. Those who have undertaken empirical studies using unstructured or semi-structured interviews sometimes report a difference in the way that the two sexes speak about their faith. Generalizing from my own experience in a way that I hope is not too irresponsible, it seems to me that on the whole the style of theologizing that comes naturally to women does tend to reflect a conversational form of God-talk. We may dignify it as *disinterested* talk, but in a fashion that is wholly different from the disinterestedness of academic-speak. Women's talk in general is not a distancing discourse, apt for competitive disagreements; rather it is disinterested in the sense that is without a purpose ulterior to the expression and maintenance of a relationship. I wonder if this is why women's talk *about* God often sounds so close, in the content and manner of their speech, to talking *to* God; whereas on the whole men tend to distinguish these two modes of religious language. Religious self-expression, particularly in prayer and worship, does seem to be very much a matter of mother-tongue work. It is concerned with just 'keeping the exchange going' (even though, at one level, this might appear to be a rather one-sided 'exchange') and with 'articulating a situation', in the sense of expressing how one feels about it – without (usually) striving to get things done or to secure some advantage. Talk directed to God is about maintenance, rather than information-exchange, clarification or making any 'progress'. As is the case with the discourse of lovers and parents, some things will 'require saying' in religion and originality will not be 'what's looked for'.

Such discourse is truly 'without interest', in that it is not directed to serving an end beyond the relationship and the speaker does not engage in it with the thought of that reward. What is often described in the academy as 'disinterested theological analysis', on the other hand, is only truly disinterested if it is done for its own sake, and not as part of a desire to win *my* argument or prove *my* point. A great deal of academic theology, unfortunately, by the very nature of the educational and academic context in which it has its home, is constrained to recognize winners and losers (of arguments), and to identify and assess end results, conclusions and originality. This is an additional reason why it may appear so alien – and sometimes rather distasteful – to those believers whose theology is more continuous with their religious life and devotion. And it may be that this is particularly the case for many women.

In interviews with men, on the other hand, the father tongue is often rather more evident, even when they *haven't* been to college to learn it fully. Men tend to be more distanced in their God-talk: more analytic, speculative, 'cool' and detached. They are therefore more naturally inclined to engage in what *sounds like* academic theological discourse. Their ordinary theology shows more readiness to debate, to argue, and to clarify and defend a position. Many of them seem to find conceptual analysis and sparring over intellectual positions more in keeping with their natural way of speaking, and perhaps of living. In research interviews they are more likely to use phrases such as, 'I don't think I can accept that', 'You may disagree, but *I* believe . . .', 'Yes, keep me to the agenda', 'I have often wondered whether . . .'.

I have come to expect differences between the sexes in my own pastoral conversations, interviews and reading of interview scripts. But the evidence, such as it is, may be misleading. The putative gender difference that seems to be implied by these differences in language and reasoning styles may be better characterized as a difference between 'masculine' and 'feminine' outlooks, attitudes, orientations or viewpoints, rather than a difference between the sexes (cf. Bem, 1975; 1981; Belenky *et al.*, 1986: 102–3; Francis, 1997; Francis and Wilcox, 1998). Not surprisingly, males are more likely to show (stereotypical) 'masculine' ways of thinking and of being religious, and women are more likely to show the more 'feminine' styles, but the difference is not in fact a difference of sex or gender, but of psychological type.

Perhaps I may illustrate the paradigmatic male or masculine perspective with an anecdote about the first theological student I ever taught. He was an adult churchgoer setting out on a rather formal Anglican lay education scheme. Following the syllabus requirements, he wrote an essay on a topic in Old Testament history (the conquest of the promised land). He read the appropriate passages in the appropriate books, but interpreted his task as that of coming up with his *own* theory of the relationships of the tribes of Israel to the land, and his own speculative reconstruction of the history of the thirteenth century BCE. Looking back, it seems to me that this neophyte student was engaged in a peculiarly masculine style of theologizing, in which he embraced speculation for its own sake (and to that extent was 'disinterested') but in a manner that had not yet been regulated and routinized by a scholarly method, nor properly informed by the findings of other scholars in the tradition. That he was not yet engaged in academic theology was most clearly signalled by the fact that he had not yet learned the importance of describing and discussing other people's theology (or, in this case, history). He still thought for himself; he had not started to think other scholars' thoughts after them. But like many men I have taught on adult Christian education courses over the years, and unlike the vast majority of the women, he had a certain delight in speculation that took him a very long way from his own personal and religious life.

Admittedly, in this case the process mainly went wrong because the area of 'theology' chosen for his task was not really theology at all but a (particularly recondite) historical topic, in the face of which the unscholarly should have been more explicitly warned to give up their amateur pretensions and listen to the experts instead. In most areas of ordinary theology, by contrast, such as our understanding of God's character, our interpretation of human suffering or our reflections on God's vocation for us, the ordinary theologian is frankly not much hindered by ignorance of 'the literature'. With regard to these truly theological topics, theological 'expertise' is more widely disseminated, although speculation needs some controls there too, from logic as well as from experience.

Nicola Slee's research on women's faith development takes us well beyond such anecdotal evidence, being based on a careful analysis of in-depth interviews. Her interviewees were all graduates, and a substantial proportion were theologically highly educated (including ministers and lay religious), so the study is not included here as an illustration of ordinary theology but to indicate some themes that *may* be particularly characteristic of women. Slee describes a number of general features that characterized her respondents' 'faithing strategies':

> First, there is a dominance of concrete, visual, narrative and embodied forms of thinking over propositional, abstract or analytical thought. Whilst conceptual thought was not absent from the interviews, there was a marked preference amongst the majority of the women for a more concrete language of metaphor, story or exemplar as the vehicle for the expression of their faith experience. Second, there is a dominance of personalised and relational forms of appropriating faith over abstract and impersonal means: faith was worked out in relation to the other, and this is demonstrated in the preference for metaphors emerging from personal life and relationship, the use of exemplars drawn from personal life and narratives centred around issues of inclusion and exclusion from communities of belonging, as well as in the conversational nature of the interview itself, in which faith was articulated in dialogue with the presence of the other. Third, each of the faithing strategies is rooted in a dynamic context of meaning-making in which the *process* of the interaction between interviewer and interviewee is as significant as the content. It was not only *what* was said, but the *way* in which it was said, and the para-linguistic features that surrounded and supported the narrative, which indicated the nature and style of the women's faith.
>
> (Slee, 1999: 126–7; cf. Slee, 2001)

Can such studies tell us anything about ordinary theology? Both men and women have an ordinary theology, for this is just my label for the theology of those who are innocent of theological education. It may be, however, that the nature of this theology will differ between men and women, or between 'masculine' and 'feminine' approaches. The ordinary theology of men might appear rather 'cooler' and 'dispassionate' than that of women. These are, perhaps, better adjectives than either 'disinterested' or 'objective'. In any case, they are qualities that academic theological study encourages, but they may sometimes be displayed by what is still an *ordinary* theology. It may be that women's ordinary theology employs more concrete, narrative and personal ways of thinking. Their theology could thus be said to be more of a 'mother-tongue theology'. Perhaps that roots it more strongly in the primary religious discourse of Bible and prayer than in the distancing father tongue of men and of the academy. The relevance of all this for the (often sticky) relationship between ordinary and academic theology will need much more careful exploration, both empirical and conceptual. But it does seem probable that the difference between ordinary and academic theological styles may be either amplified or toned down by the effect of gender and/or psychological type.

Onlook Theology

According to some accounts, all theology arises in some form of religious experience or discernment, in which God reveals himself and we struggle to respond with our inadequate theological descriptions. This interpretation provides us with an experiential theology with a vengeance. In this section, however, I have in mind a less extreme version of the appeal to experience, which seems to me to fit ordinary theology better.

   Much of the discourse of religion, and sometimes of theology as well, uses the language of sight and vision in more general ways. Religious discernment and revelation is thus expressed in terms of seeing new things or of seeing the same things differently (cf. Job 42: 5; Matthew 11: 4; 13: 11–17). This, too, is something that we learn. In the biblical narratives, '"seeing" is used as a metaphor for a learning that is experiential, rather than vicarious. In these texts, "seeing" and "sight" connote not only a visual experience but the ability to *perceive* more than what is actually visible' (Melchert, 1998: 282). In religion and philosophy, 'seeing' is a familiar metaphor for learning (Melchert, 1998: 106) and, significantly, the word 'wisdom' is etymologically related to the concept of vision (Hodgson, 1999: 88–9). The related language of 'discernment' and 'disclosure', and of situations in which 'pennies dropped' and 'lights dawned' was popularized by Ian Ramsey. Ramsey argued for a wide range of revelatory situations that he described as 'disclosure-situations'. They included the experience of discerning a universal such as yellow while surveying a range of yellow objects, and discerning other minds as they disclosed themselves through their bodies and behaviours. But the genus also included a category that we might call 'recognition disclosures' (Astley, 1978: 103–10), in which we recognize, for example, a bird as a goldfinch, a plane as a Tornado jet or the physiognomy of a friend.

   We have to *learn* how to recognize these things. So the histologist learns how to 'see' (that is, how to recognize, acknowledge and therefore react appropriately to) the particular morphologies of cell structure that denote a malignant growth. Michael Polanyi has detailed the ubiquity of such 'tacit knowledge'. He contends that much of our knowledge involves a focal awareness of something that can only come through a subsidiary awareness of something else, attending *from* the implicit, proximal clues *to* the distal object. 'We know the first term only by relying on our awareness of it for attending to the second' (Polanyi, 1967: 10). This is an important skill in everyday life; and it is significant that 'we know more than we can tell' in such areas, since a shift in focus to what immediately presents itself to us undermines our focal awareness. Hence an 'unbridled lucidity', according to Polanyi, 'can destroy our understanding of complex matters. . . . We can make ourselves lose sight of a pattern or physiognomy by examining its parts under sufficient magnification' (Polanyi, 1967: 18).

Is this relevant to religious seeing? Polanyi writes of religious worship as a 'heuristic vision' and of 'skilful religious knowing' that is based on a 'tacit act of comprehension which originates faith from [a framework of] clues' constituted by words and gestures (Polanyi, 1962: 280–82). All such tacit knowing 'implies a movement of consciousness beyond experiential data to the underlying meaningful order', a conceptualization that is wholly sympathetic to a theistic framework of meaning (Martin, 1998: 182). Again, this may be something that cannot be had regardless of the way it is acquired (see Chapter 1); in this case independently of some sort of training in religious recognition. And, for Polanyi, all such knowledge is ineluctably *personal* and never simply objective.

This account of things also lies close to John Hick's claim that much of our experience takes the form of 'experiencing-as', a theme that he developed from a passage in Wittgenstein (1968: IIxi). Hick argues that, just as we can see an ambiguous picture *as* a duck or a rabbit, so we hear a sound *as* a telephone or a car. He writes, 'to recognize or identify is to experience-as in terms of a concept' (Hick, 1969: 25). Hick's account of *religious* experience envisages an indirect or mediated experience of God.[19] He boldly describes religious faith itself in terms of the interpretative element within religious experience. To experience religiously is a matter not just of experience but of 'experiencing-as' (Hick, 1973: ch. 3). Faith is our 'recognition of God's activity in human history' and consists of 'seeing, apperceiving, or interpreting events in a special way' (Hick, 1983b: 69). In this way the prophet experiences the armies attacking Jerusalem *as* the hammer of Yahweh's wrath.

In *The Logic of Self-Involvement*, Donald Evans has written in a somewhat similar way of *onlooks*. An onlook is more than an intellectual 'opinion', 'conception' or 'view', and implies more commitment than an 'outlook' or 'perspective' (Evans, 1963: 125). Onlooks take the form, 'I look on *x* as *y*' (sometimes 'I see x as y': 129). Thus, 'I look on death as the mockery of human hopes', 'I look on my work as a vocation' (or as 'a necessary evil'), 'I look on this mentally handicapped adult as a person'. Onlooks express our feelings and our attitudes for and against something, as well as our personal involvement with it and our behavioural intentions towards it. 'One undertakes to do certain things, viewing them or interpreting them in a certain way', Evans writes (128). Onlooks are sometimes self-verifying, as may happen when we see life as a struggle, or view our suffering as a time of moral growth (139).

Religion contains many such onlooks which bestow a particular status. We look on ourselves as pilgrims, warriors, subjects, children (Holmer, 1978: 28, cf. 157). Nature is considered as a gift, and other people as our sisters and brothers. The poor widow is seen as one who has given more than all the donors to the Temple. Major

---

[19]   There may be other forms: cf. Swinburne, 1979: 249–52; Davis, 1989: chs 1 and 2; Alston, 1991: ch. 1.

Christian doctrines may also be interpreted using this category, for Christians look on the cold and empty tomb as filled with the afterglow of the incandescence of resurrection, the fractured bread of the Eucharist as the broken-healing body of Christ, and the cross of defeat as his triumphal arch and the foundation of his throne. And at the heart of education into Christianity, and of our ordinary *Christology*, is our learning to see Jesus 'as Lord'. According to Vincent Brümmer, onlooks ascribe meaning to things: we know the meaning of something 'when we know what attitude we ought to have towards it' (Brümmer, 1981: 121, 127–9). In religion this often works by relating it to God (260). In my view, onlooks form a very significant component of ordinary theology.

I also believe that this dimension of our interpretative experience is one of the best ways of capturing the difference between those who are truly religious or spiritual and those who are not. 'Being schooled in certain modes of thought and living (and indeed being schooled in religious concepts and the religious life) enables one to see a different world, to detect possibilities and patterns of meaning which would otherwise be closed to us' (Clack, 1999: 73, cf. 86–7).[20] This different seeing flows partly from our character and nature. As William Blake put it, 'as a man is, so he sees'; significantly adding, 'as the eye is formed, such are its powers' (Keynes, 1961: 835). But vision also flows back into character, as it leads to change and learning in us. The spiritual person is the one who is able to recognize this, that and the other as God's rule, hand and intention. This is what it is to have the eyes of faith, and to have the eyes of faith is a major aspect of being a person of faith. In New Testament theology, to be able to see the kingdom is already to be a part of it.

All this is crucial to the learning context, for learning to have a certain attitude or emotion towards something is closely related to learning to see things in certain ways (Hamlyn, 1978: 124). Many others have argued for a fundamental educational dimension in forming, developing or permitting the requisite moral or spiritual vision, perspective, perception or discernment (see Holmer, 1978: 29–30; Dykstra, 1981: *passim*; McGhee, 1992: 244–5; 2000: 112–15; Brueggemann, 1996; Spohn, 1999: ch. 7). A great deal of Christian education is best portrayed under metaphors such as 'directing people's attention', 'widening their horizons', and 'opening their eyes' (cf. Astley, 1994b: 250, 255–6). Christian learning may thus be interpreted, in large part, as 'learning to see various things, in the world and in one's life and experience, as manifestations of God' (Alston, 1981: 143). The learner is encouraged to notice things she would normally not notice, and to see the things that she does see differently or, as we might say, 'properly'. Learning to see the true meaning of the widow's mite or Caesar's coinage was part of the burden of the teaching ministry of Jesus. It was also the educational point of his life, and of his death. 'Truly this man was the son of God',

---

[20]   For one detailed account of such a 'discovery perspective', which demands that a person overcome his blindness and 'see the significance of facts already familiar to him', in a way that is very different from the confirmation of a hypothesis, see Kellenberger, 1985: 104–11. For Kellenberger's account of 'realisation-rationality' and 'blindness-rationality', and of the cognitive failure that is blindness to religious realizations, see also chs 2 and 3 *passim*, especially 180–81.

the centurion says, when he *sees* how Jesus dies (Mark 15: 39). This insight was not an inference from unambiguous facts but a shift of perspective – an *envisioning*.

Ordinary theology is replete with expressions of 'onlooks' and 'experiencings-as' of this kind, directed to events, individuals and situations that are viewed as freighted with religious meaning. It is natural to regard them as separate, additional interpretations, involving a step of discursive reason. The pattern would then be: first you experience your mother die, then you interpret it theologically; first you look at your relationships, then you think them through theologically. But the suggestion here is that the experience, the looking, is already an interpreting; it is an onlook, an experiencing-as. There is no separate act of cognitive reflection.

Yet the vision remains dependent on concepts and understanding. One of Wittgenstein's examples of seeing-as refers to that well-known example from the psychologist's menagerie, Jastrow's duck-rabbit (Wittgenstein, 1968: 194–5). To see this ambiguous picture either as a duck or as a rabbit, one needs to have the appropriate concept already. Similarly (to adopt another of Wittgenstein's examples), to recognize the oddly shaped piece of metal to the left of my plate as a fork, I must already have the concept of a fork. This 'flashing of an aspect on us seems half visual experience, half thought', Wittgenstein writes. Better, it is seeing something 'according to an *interpretation*'; better still, it is a perception of 'an internal relation between it and other objects. . . . "The echo of a thought in sight"' (1968: 197, 200, 212). But in these cases 'seeing-as' contrasts with and presupposes 'just seeing' (a rabbit), a distinction that does not apply in the religious case (Barrett, 1991: 135, 142–4). In religion, therefore, we do not normally speak of 'seeing an aspect', as we do when we perceive in a picture a likeness to a rabbit. We do, however, often speak of seeing the world as God's world, events in the world as providential, or seeing other people as God's children. And this *is* to experience them in a certain way, in terms of – or 'under' – a certain description or concept. It is also something that we *learn* to do, as we also do in the more secular cases, by learning the concept under which we recognize something as that thing. We then *see* it *as* the other, and continue to look on *this* as *that*. Ordinary Christian education permits and provokes this form of ordinary religious experience that is intrinsic to much ordinary theology.

A further dimension of the interdependence of belief and experience is well brought out in Basil Mitchell's instructive analogy of the ship's lookout who, in peering through the mist, claims to see land. Mitchell shows that such a perceptual claim, especially in conditions of doubt and obscurity, cannot stand alone; the direct experience needs the support of indirect reasoning in order to be justified as a claim to *knowledge* by observation. So the navigating officer's maps and calculations, which contribute to an 'overall appraisal of the situation', need to be brought alongside the lookout's putative observation and other perceptual claims (Mitchell, 1973: 113). This discursive, critical evaluation serves in the world of the story for academic theology's 'overall appraisal' and testing out of the claims of an ordinary theological insight (cf. Barth's comments, above p. 77). (But note that the navigator may be wrong and the lookout right: both the ordinary experience and the academic framework must be open to criticism.)

Some framework of religious beliefs must be in place so that religious experiences can be fitted into it, before a person can know what it is that he sees. It is this learned conceptual scheme of religion that results in the religious experience being designated a religious (and a Christian) experience in the first place, and it is the same conceptual scheme that will be appealed to in any debate about, or concern over, the nature and value of the experience. Yet the academic theologian does not *create* this scheme, he only contributes to it and amends it. The scheme is already there – not in a form that is as well systematized or connected together, perhaps, as the scholar would like, but there nonetheless – as the 'ordinary-theology-sailor' squints into the mist. The lookout does not mumble, 'I see a something-I-know-not-what.' He yells, 'I see land' (or, possibly, 'I think I see land'). At both the ordinary and the academic level, then, vision and theology must go together.

To repeat: a great deal of ordinary theology may be regarded as onlook theology; it is a theology that expresses such ways of seeing. The concepts and the understanding that lie behind the vision are not present in ordinary theology as objects ripe for analysis, or concepts ready to be slotted into specialized forms of theological argument. They are not framed in the conceptualizations of the academy, as the navigating officer's understanding of 'land' is framed by mensuration and calculation. But they are still *interpretative* schemata or background *concepts*, in terms of which we see the world. They are ordinary concepts, if you will, not technical ones. They are there so that they can be *used*.[21] Nor does ordinary theology examine them directly, on this account; it expresses what it experiences in terms of them. This is a much less explicit way of doing theology than we find in academic theology.

From the Ordinary to the Academic

In attempting to characterize ordinary theology under these different headings, the temptation to make too hard and fast a distinction between ordinary theology and the more 'extraordinary' (academic, scientific, scholarly) type has been hard to resist. But in the end it must be resisted, because the difference between these two types of theology, like the difference between many of the pairs of concepts referred to explicitly or implicitly in this chapter, is a difference of (sometimes marked) degree rather than a difference of kind. It is not true to say that all ordinary theology is thoroughly spiritual or experiential; nor that every example of academic theology is irredeemably impersonal or theoretical. We should continue to think instead of our continuous spectrum, the extremes of which are more easy to distinguish than are the intermediate (or 'mixed') forms.

A spectrum is a rather static visual analogy, however, where a more dynamic one might be more helpful. I sometimes think of the relationship between the two forms of theology as analogous to the pattern of a stone thrown into the middle of a large pond. The ripples go out from the disturbance at the centre so that, given the right conditions, they eventually change the entire surface, interacting with the pond's own contours as they spread from the point where the stone hit the water. In this analogy

---

21   Note that 'even the "simple faith" that prefers to accept things without explanation is a form of theory' (Heitink, 1999: 151–2).

(or allegory), the pond represents ourselves with our thoughts and feelings, its surface is our language. Whatever we take the stone to be, the splash represents some sort of religious experience, religious change or religious learning. The ripples that lie close to the point of the stone's impact are large disturbances, which form regular circles around it. These ripples then move out across the pond, changing as they move: their amplitude declines somewhat and they accommodate themselves more to the structure of the pond, metamorphosing from perfect circles to more irregular and sometimes interacting patterns (as they 'bounce off' rocks and other features).

Ordinary theology is like the early ripples coming out from a religious change. These represent the devotional language that arises as a direct reaction to religious experience or conversion, together with the language of personal confession, testimony and commitment that is engendered in any effective religious learning situation. They are more intense, more 'moving' and more 'disturbing' than the later changes in our hearts and minds that flow from them. At the very edges of the pond the water still rises and falls in response to the experiential and learning changes at the centre, but other influences are now involved, so that the causal connection is less obvious than it was at the centre – and the observer who has missed seeing the stone hit the water, and now sees only the ripples, may not be able to track their originating source at all. These smoother, more mature, more distant and less violent perturbations at the edge will be more affected by the pond's environment and the rocks, shoals and vegetation that determine its three-dimensional shape. These ripples are the changes that represent academic theology: movements of thought and language that are more distant from the source of the original disturbance, more influenced by other factors, less particular and local, and more wide-ranging.

I do not wish to hang too much on this picture, but one thing that might be said in its favour is that it captures the sense that ordinary theology can lead smoothly into academic theology, the first theological agitation triggering the second, given a pond of sufficient width (and perhaps of depth). The point at which an 'ordinary theological wave' becomes an 'academic theological wave' is a matter of judgement, for the variables concerned are continuous ones. At the two extreme ends of the wave's path – (i) the immediate zone around the splash, and (ii) the edges of the pond – the differences will be very marked and it will be easy to allocate our two different labels. But at a number of points in-between one may not be sure whether to call this theological ripple 'ordinary' or 'academic'. It will depend on its particular features, and that will depend on the extent to which the pond has been changed.

The ripples essentially represent a person's language as it expresses the form of the pond. The pond's morphology stands for both his mind and its belief system, thought processes and intellectual skills; and his heart and its attitudes, values and stances for living. A pond such as this can be restructured, enlarged and landscaped by an academic theological education. The 'theologically educated pond' has been *changed*, and that change will affect the way the water moves across it. At its margins, therefore, the ripple effect may seem very different from that observed at the edges of a pond that has not been restructured in this way.

Another advantage of this analogy is the suggestion that the rippling of academic theology can ultimately be tracked back to more ordinary disturbances, and therefore that we may speak of some ordinary theological element, contribution or dimension even of the most academic theologian's theology. This suggests another way in which the academic theologian may be, in part, an ordinary theologian.

Folk, Common and Implicit Religion

I shall conclude this chapter by saying something further about a range of other terms that exist in the literature that may be thought to bear some relation to my understanding of ordinary theology.

I referred earlier to David Martin's *subterranean theology*. Some students of religion welcome his introduction of this term, despite the vagueness of his account of it, if only because it avoids the more pejorative expression *folk religion*. In Britain at all events, this latter phrase 'seems to suggest a mixture of individualistic magic, moral obduracy, theological infantilism and social impropriety' (Bailey, 1990: 506; cf. 1997: 41; 1998: 32–3). Bruce Reed's account of folk religion is particularly negative. He uses the term to mark a species of 'dysfunctional religion' in which the individual remains 'in a half-world between fantasy and reality' which is 'filled with grotesque and seductive images', and flees from 'the harsh realities of the world of intra-dependence' where his confirmation and sustenance would be understood as resting in his own hands (Reed, 1978: 76, 92, cf. 32). According to Reed, folk religion uses symbols in 'a credulous, superstitious or unreflective manner' and 'its devotees do not concern themselves with truth and logic, or reflect upon the validity of their belief. . . . Belief is "above their heads."' The behaviour associated with folk religion is also slighted as 'bizarre and sometimes repellent' (103, 105–6, 108).

I have already noted that one obvious difference between ordinary theology and such terms as folk religion lies in the nouns employed. Folk religion, whatever else it is, is some sort of *religion*. Thus definitions of folk religion include references to 'a spirit' and 'a way of life' (Bailey, 1989: 155), as well as to 'general religious behaviour' and attitudes of respect for religious referents such as God and Jesus (Carr, 1984: 29). The related concept of 'popular religion' (see below) includes social activities and celebrations, private devotional activities, attitudes to the world and membership of associations, along with beliefs. It has also been characterized as a form of spirituality (Schreiter, 1985: 128–31, 141).

David Clark understands folk religion, which he describes as 'the underlife of religion', as comprising 'non-institutional religious beliefs and practices as well as variants or reformulations of official religion' (Clark, 1982: viii, 5). The belief component of folk religion may be quite significant. It is usually taken to include theological-type elements such as explanations of the existence of evil in the world, or 'implicit theodicies' (see Berger, 1973: ch. 3; cf. van der Ven, 1993: 172). These might include a belief in luck, fate or chance; or various superstitions, beliefs (and practices) to ward off evil.[22] It also often incorporates other convictions, particularly

---

[22]   Compare the customs, beliefs, rituals and charms described in Williams, 1999: ch. 3.

convictions surrounding birth and death, occupations and the cycle of the year (cf. Clark, 1982: *passim* and Bruce, 1995: 54–5, 103–10).

Whereas ordinary theology primarily focuses on (the linguistic expression of) religious belief and religious believing, folk religion and its cognates cover a much wider canvas. I accept that the study of theology, and therefore of ordinary theology, should include reflections on its related practices, experiences and attitudes; indeed, I have argued that theology cannot be understood except in the context of these broader concerns. But theology is not itself religious practice, experience or attitude. The practice of thinking and talking about God or religion is not the same thing as 'doing religion' or being religious (performing religious activities or adopting religious attitudes), although it connects intimately with both.

The location as well as the meaning and extent of folk religion distinguishes it from ordinary theology. The majority of commentators on folk religion describe its beliefs and practices as lying 'outside the church' (Clark, 1982: viii); its 'adherents' are characterized as 'ordinary folk who would not usually describe themselves as church-going Christians yet feel themselves to have some sort of Christian allegiance' (Habgood, 1983: 78). It is recognized, however, that part of the religious behaviour they exhibit – 'but not necessarily all' – 'looks to the available rituals of the church' (Carr, 1984: 29). Ordinary theology, by contrast, is a category that embraces the majority of regular (even orthodox) churchgoers, as well as extending right across the range of irregular churchgoers and the wholly unchurched.

In fact, it is routine to assert that the pigments of folk religion are also to be found splashed over the church pews. Many of the attitudes, values, beliefs and practices that are labelled by the term 'folk religion' are also held and practised by those who attend churches, particularly those who attend only occasionally. While they may not 'find a warrant in the formal teachings' of the church, such 'unofficial aspects of doctrine, theology, organisation and worship' are frequently at home within it (Clark, 1982: viii). Indeed, Richard Toon takes 'conventional religion' (see later) as including, regulating and endorsing elements of folk religion within certain of its rites of passage, as well as in such folk celebrations as Mothering Sunday and Remembrance Day, and on civic and state occasions (Toon, n.d.: 5).

I turn now to a consideration of a variety of other terms. The first of these types of religion, or 'dimensions of the definition of' religion (Toon, n.d.: 8; see below, p. 91), is *common religion*, a phrase that is sometimes used synonymously with *popular religion* (see Towler, 1984: 4; Schreiter, 1985: 124–5; cf. Bailey, 1997: 41).[23] Robert Towler offers this as his formal definition: 'those beliefs and practices of an

---

[23] In his study of rural communities, James Obelkevich defines *popular religion* as 'the non-institutional religious beliefs and practices, including unorthodox conceptions of Christian doctrine and ritual prevalent in the lower ranks of rural society' (Obelkevich, 1976: 305; cf. Hempton, 1988). Bailey takes the term popular religion as referring more widely to 'local versions of global traditions' of a mainly non-specialist (lay) nature (cf. Bailey, 1998: 32). For S. C. Williams, popular religion includes 'both folk beliefs as well as formal and officially sanctioned practices and ideas' (1999: 11, cf. 88, 166–8). 'Folk' and 'popular' both mean 'of the people'.

overtly religious nature which are not under the domination of a prevailing religious institution.' Common religion, he writes, is 'the underground religion of the common people' (Towler, 1974: 147–8). In Britain it includes surviving elements of pre-Christian, local folk religions. In a later text, Towler comments:

> The alternative expression, folk religion, is probably a more satisfactory one, except that people tend to think that it comprises a relatively coherent tradition, whereas common religion deliberately refers to a miscellany of themes, of different degrees of antiquity, and drawn from diverse sources. Common religion is employed to refer to the whole range of 'religious' beliefs and practices, from the use of the Church's rites of passage by those who are otherwise unattached to a church, to the consulting of astrologers and palmists, to belief in the power of fate, to belief in ghosts and paranormal phenomena. The expression, folk religion, does not immediately suggest this motley collection, and yet it is with just such a heterogeneous medley of beliefs, practices, and experiences that we must be concerned in examining popular religion.
>
> (Towler, n.d.: 6; cf. also Krarup, n.d.)

Towler explicates common religion by means of a contrast with *official* or *conventional religion*, which is in turn defined as 'beliefs and practices which are prescribed, regulated and socialized by specialized religious institutions' (Towler, 1974: 148–9). The assumption is sometimes made in the literature that common religion's independence of the church is associated with its being transmitted, mainly through childhood peer groups, quite independently of the church's influence. Away from any effective control, in 'non-institutional' isolation from the church community, these elements may take the form of a *privatized religion* (cf. Cox, 1965: 16; Martin and Pluck, 1976: 49, 55; Lash, 1996: 16). The belief component in these cases is often identified as 'less orthodox' than conventional, church-oriented religious belief, although Davie recognizes a continuum between the two (Ahern and Davie, 1987: 35–6, 57, 59; Davie, 1994: 75–6). Where religious believers do not engage in active membership of a church their beliefs are frequently in danger of slipping into *superstition* (Abercrombie *et al.*, 1970: 124; cf. Davie, 1994: 122).

They do not always slide this far, however, and Michael Hornsby-Smith has proposed the phrase *customary religion* for a category of religious belief that has avoided this danger. His term covers those beliefs and practices that originally arose through church-related processes of religious socialization, but which have now become unstructured and heterodox because they are no longer under the church's control. According to Hornsby-Smith, common religion is a term that should be restricted to the more extreme phenomenon of 'non-institutionally contexted religious beliefs and practices particularly of a magical or supernatural nature' (Hornsby-Smith, Lee and Reilly, 1985: 247; cf. 250 and Hornsby-Smith, 1991: ch. 5).

It is certainly the case that Towler's work on common religion treats it as distinctively different from the beliefs and practices of organized religion. This is particularly clear in some of the examples that he and others present, such as fortune-telling, belief in fate and ghosts, New Age beliefs and 'Forteana' (see Toon, n.d.: 6; cf. Abercrombie *et al.*, 1970). It is acknowledged by other writers in the field, however, that such beliefs may also exist alongside, and interact with, the orthodox theology of conventional religion (cf. Clark, 1982: 3; Williams, 1999: 166–8). This may be true of many other elements designated as folk religion.

The category that Thomas Luckmann contrasts with official religion is *natural* or *invisible religion*. Unlike common religion and conventional religion, this social form of religion makes no reference to the supernatural, but fulfils the same symbolic meaning-making and meaning-affirming functions that are to be found within official religion. These functions are said to be intrinsic to the human condition. Invisible religion is thus a 'subjective system of "ultimate" significance' and is described in terms of a complex of attitudes and values such as individual autonomy and self-expression, mobility and family-centredness. This rather incoherent 'assortment of religious themes' is said to represent 'the modern sacred cosmos' (Luckmann, 1967: 76, 103, 113).

The religious dimension of invisible religion is implicit rather than overt. Within this category, Richard Toon places invisible religion on the 'unorganized' end of a scale that has *surrogate religion* at the organized pole. Both are 'religions' in the sense that 'they are functionally equivalent to religion or display qualities which are analogous with the qualities of religion.' Invisible religion's themes of central concern and meaning (for example self-realization and sexuality) are clearly not 'organized' in any particular way, but form part of an individual's private life. Surrogate religion, on the other hand, denotes organized equivalents to religion, and is exemplified by such activities as Sunday pastimes, psychoanalysis and political ideologies, together with organized Humanism, hobbies, sport, art and music (Toon, n.d.: 7). The level of organization displayed by these examples ranges from loose to tight. Roland Robertson describes 'surrogate religiosity' as part of a 'functional-equivalent thesis' that holds that Communism (for example) 'has social consequences . . . similar to those of conventionally and intuitively understood religion' (Robertson, 1970: 39).

Toon helpfully maps these 'dimensions of the definition of religion' on the chart reproduced as figure 3.1.

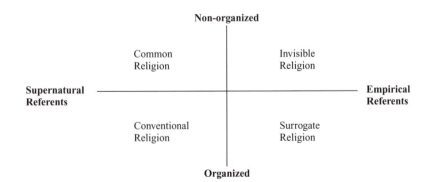

Figure 3.1 Dimensions of the definition of religion
Source: Toon, n.d.:8

Both 'invisible religion' and 'surrogate religion' would appear to be covered by Edward Bailey's term *implicit religion*. Bailey's category is very broad and ambitious, comprising many attitudes, beliefs and behaviours that he sees as examples of unarticulated or unrecognized religiosity (cf. Hamilton, 2001). In a variety of publications, Bailey notes that this concept shares some similarities with a range of other terms: 'invisible religion', 'unconscious religion', 'civil religion',[24] 'everyday religion', 'secular religion', 'folk religion', 'popular religion', 'common religion' and Paul Tillich's 'ultimate concern'. One of Bailey's briefer characterizations of implicit religion is as 'intensive concerns with extensive effects'. This specifies local *human commitments* – 'human depths' that reveal what people really stand for – that are manifested in a far-reaching way through people's beliefs, actions and solidarities (Bailey, 1997: 8–9; 1998: 17–25). This very broad conception of the religious implications of everyday life lies closest to Luckmann's invisible religion and Bailey acknowledges that 'the two terms are almost twins' (1997: 39; cf. 1990). But some of his examples portray *organized* activities that function in a way that is analogous to explicit religion, with their own rituals, sacred times and places, and so on. As applied to these cases, the concept appears to be closer to the category of surrogate religion. This is especially evident in Bailey's fascinating study of 'the implicit religion of a public house' (Bailey, 1997: ch. 4).

However, when the perspective of implicit religion is applied to the commitments of a particular English residential community ('parish') it seems to function more like Luckmann's term, generating an account of a society's 'wilful divinities' (children), 'revelatory ethic' (friendliness), 'profoundest solidarity' (individualism) and 'sacramental language' (buildings such as people's homes, and the local church and churchyard). But the implicit religion of the English also includes the notion of church as an ideal community as its major symbol, and 'Christianity' as its professed faith. 'Christianity' is here understood rather non-specifically as true religion, a commitment to believing as an end in itself, and a strong endorsement of the virtues of kindness and caring (see Bailey, 1989: 153–5; 1997: ch. 5; 1998: 65–7; cf. also Richard Hoggart's 'primary religion' – Hoggart, 1958: 112–19). Not only is this sort of analysis more reminiscent of the concept of invisible religion, it is in this context that implicit religion is also most readily identifiable with folk religion (Bailey, 1989; 1998: 33), at least in so far as that term is not *restricted* to a religiosity that is in interaction with conventional, ecclesiastical contacts.

We should note that Bailey accepts that explicit religion might well be a vehicle for implicit religion (Bailey, 1997: 7). On occasions, indeed, instead of arguing that implicit religion is simply analogous to explicit religion, he goes so far as to claim that 'explicit religion will only actually be religious . . . when it is also in fact implicitly-religious' (Bailey, 1998: 72). Implicit religion, interpreted as human commitments, is

---

[24] The category of *civil religion* is often included as an element within folk religion. This expression, which is ultimately derived from Rousseau, is used to cover such examples as self-propagating festivals and cults, heroes, prophets and martyrs, and family religiosity. Civil religion includes and expresses a set of values, together with beliefs about God, the afterlife and judgement, that are institutionalized in a society (see Bellah, 1970: 168–89).

thus perceived as lying at the heart of all true religion. In a broad sense, this overlaps with conceptions of a person's spirituality or 'human faith' (see Chapter 2).

Ordinary Theology among its Relations

I hope that I have said enough in this chapter to prevent ordinary theology being understood as labelling the elements of 'beliefs and believing' (the theological claims and theological thinking) of common religion alone. In fact, I mainly use the phrase ordinary theology with reference to the theology of those *churchgoers* – the great majority – who remain innocent of academic theological education, although it also includes others who do their theological reflection outside the church.

Robert Towler's distinction between official religion, in which beliefs and practices are 'prescribed, regulated and socialized' by a religious institution, and common religion where they are 'not under [its] domination' (Towler, 1974: 148), is perhaps less helpful than it appears. We have already noted Hornsby-Smith's argument for a *tertium quid* of customary religion, so as to accommodate those beliefs and practices that originated in official religion but have now escaped its institutional control. There is clearly a continuous spectrum here, as we have found with regard to my category of ordinary theology. Some beliefs (and practices) of ordinary believers are identical to the beliefs (and practices) of the corresponding official religion, whether that official religion is able to 'control' them or not; whereas others are profoundly at variance with the official religion and its theology (or, in the case of ordinary theology, at variance with academic theology). On my definition, however, ordinary theology is not necessarily a *deviation* from the norm of official or academic theology since it is defined, quite neutrally, as the theology held by those who have little or no academic theological training. I would argue that definitions of common or popular religion are similarly best understood in a neutral and content-free manner (cf. Schreiter, 1985: 125).

We might now revisit Richard Toon's diagram (see above, p. 91). My account of ordinary theology locates it primarily as a theology that relates to 'actual religious areas' on the left of the diagram, rather than to the 'religious areas in a metaphorical sense' that are represented by invisible, implicit and surrogate religion on the right-hand side (Toon, n.d.: 8). In using it for my purposes, my only complaint with Toon's diagram is that his horizontal axis is rather restrictively labelled *supernatural referents – empirical referents*. In writing of common religion, Towler refers to beliefs and practices 'of an overtly religious nature' (Towler, 1974: 148) and this may hint at a more useful dimension: that of the *explicitly religious – implicitly religious*. I say this because a religious belief (or practice or account of experience) may make an explicit reference to a religious figure, ritual, community or scripture without referring to anything transcendent. Hans Küng's attempt to delineate Christianity broadly, to the effect that 'everything can be called Christian which in theory and practice has an explicit, positive reference to Jesus Christ' (Küng, 1976: 125), does not specify that the Jesus referred to must be taken to be a divine or supernatural figure. Ninian Smart is similarly ambiguous in his contention that it is not possible to identify Christianity's essence 'beyond saying that the faith relates to Christ, either in historical continuity or through religious experience or both' (Smart, 1979: 128; cf. McFague, 1982: 331–4; Sykes, 1984: 255–61).

Perhaps the key to this discussion is the word 'explicit'. It is often used to qualify 'religious' and 'religion' so as to direct our attention to that which would normally be taken to be religious (as in Ninian Smart's dimensions of explicit religion: see Smart, 1996). By contrast, Edward Bailey defines implicit religion in terms of 'an investment of a religious dimension in concerns which may not usually be called religious' (Bailey, 1995: 234; cf. Hamilton, 2001).

I have so far concentrated on locating the category of ordinary theology within explicit religion. Recalling a point made earlier (pp. 71–2), readers may still wonder whether we cannot also find ordinary theology in what is only implicitly religious – that is, within invisible, implicit or surrogate religion. The answer may partly depend on the range recognized for the word 'theology' and therefore for the phrase 'ordinary theology'. Complexes of attitudes, experiences and practices that are only religious in a metaphorical sense are likely to contain beliefs and believing processes, and their linguistic expressions, that are theological in a metaphorical sense also. (This is presumably one excuse for politicians and journalists applying the term 'theology' to certain – usually their opponents' – beliefs, and to over-elaborate or ideological systems of thought in general.)[25] In that metaphorical sense, invisible, implicit and surrogate religions may be said to have a 'theology' and it will be possible to speak of 'the theology of the pub' or 'the theology of football supporters'. 'God-talk' would then be understood *very widely* to cover the lesser 'gods' to which people ascribe worth, and the beliefs associated with them.

In this book, however, I have kept to an explicit and non-metaphorical usage of the concept of theology, and have consequently limited the denotation of my term ordinary theology to *the ('non-academic') theological assertions and theologizing dimension of conventional, customary and common religion.* My preference for a phrase incorporating the word 'theology' rather than the word 'religion' fits my emphasis in this essay on three areas:

1   religious language as it is used by ordinary believers (and, indeed, unbelievers) to speak descriptively or expressively of God, Jesus and other transcendent categories such as salvation;
2   the overtly religious beliefs (beliefs-that and beliefs-in) that are manifested in or implied by such language;
3   the processes and forms of thought and argument that are employed in people's theological reflection on and discussion of explicit religious concepts.

To concentrate on theology rather than religion also serves my purpose of encouraging a *theological* appraisal of this language, and of these beliefs and processes of reasoning. A focus that included the attitudes, experiences and practices that make up so much of religion (either 'folk/common' religion or 'institutional/

---

[25]   Dictionaries have begun to incorporate such phrases as 'impractical or rigid ideology' within the more extended uses of the term theology: see COD, 1995.

conventional/ecclesiastical/organized' religion) is likely, in my view, to discourage such a theological critique. Theological evaluation can best evaluate the language and beliefs of theology, and has a more problematic function when it is applied to other dimensions of religion.

Nevertheless, I must repeat that I should not be understood to be denying the significance of these other religious dimensions, either for ordinary theology or (even) for academic theology. To the contrary, it is my strong conviction that all real theology arises out of, and is best contextualized within, religion. I have argued in this book that ordinary theology is, in many ways, more deeply earthed in certain religious phenomenon (such as spirituality and values) than is the majority of academic theology. Ordinary theology is therefore more obviously a *religious* theology (see above, pp. 72–7).

We should pay one final visit to Toon's diagram (p. 91). It should be acknowledged that the variety of human religiosity that he maps there constitutes a continuous phenomenon, and that each category – 'invisible religion', 'conventional religion' and so on – itself labels a broad spectrum that overlaps into the other categories. Hence no study of the beliefs of either conventional or common religion should treat them in isolation from the other, nor as strictly separable from and unrelated to the adjoining territories of surrogate and invisible (broadly, implicit) religion. Although maps in physical geography may distinguish highland from lowland and forest from moor, the boundaries marked by the map-makers will be a great deal sharper than the blurred margins identifiable on the ground, and (in this example) will include no reference either to any deeper levels of continuity (by rock types or water table, for example) or to the more superficial and culturally imposed social entities represented by political and administrative areas.

Map-makers routinely impose clarity and portray distinctions which will serve us, when we eventually find ourselves 'on the ground', as no more than rough approximations of the real terrain. The present author recognizes that such a criticism may also be directed to his own cartographic accounts of the messiness that is ordinary theology.

Chapter 4

Studying Ordinary Theology

The word 'theology' is frequently employed to cover not only having a theology and doing theology, but also studying other people's theology. As I have complained more than once in this text, an academic course or module under the title of theology might comprise nothing other than the scholarly and critical study of the usual suspects from the biblical traditions, the history of Christian thinking and the ranks of contemporary theologians. Such a study *should* never just be a 'description' of their theological views, but include some critical assessment of these thinkers. Parts of *that* assessment *may* incorporate theological thinking ('doing theology') on the part of the student, as she or he explores some aspect of Christian theology and makes judgements as to its meaning and truth, as an integral part of commenting on another theologian's views. Courses on 'systematic', 'philosophical', 'foundational', 'dogmatic' or 'doctrinal' theology are more likely to encourage this first-order theological activity, although even here the second-order scholarly study of others is likely to bulk fairly large.

As I have used the phrase ordinary theology it includes the first-order activity of theologizing on the part of ordinary believers, but it is perfectly possible for the same term to be applied to the study of (other people's) ordinary theology. Although I shall argue that it is very important to employ academic and scholarly disciplines to describe, study and critically and theologically reflect on the theology of ordinary believers, this task is mainly a matter of studying ordinary theology rather than doing it. To avoid confusion, therefore, I shall always refer to this second task in full as 'the study of' – or 'research into' – ordinary theology. In this chapter I shall attempt to say something about what is involved in such a study.

Researching ordinary theology, if it is to be done at all adequately, will need to draw on a range of disciplines and fields of study in order to furnish it with the requisite theoretical insights and procedures, and empirical methods and data, along with the appropriate sensitivity concerning relevant practical – particularly pastoral and educational – considerations. Two areas of original research are of particular importance: one is empirical and social-scientific, the other is philosophical and theological (that is, conceptual).

Empirical Research

Methods

An adequate empirical study of ordinary theology will need to employ a range of appropriate tools from the armoury of the social sciences (for overviews, see Madge,

1953; Oppenheim, 1992; Bailey, 1994; Heitink, 1999: ch. 12). The application of these methods in educational and counselling contexts may be particularly illuminating for our purposes (see Borg and Gall, 1983; McLeod, 1994; Cohen, Manion and Morrison, 2000; Wellington, 2000 for overviews).

The techniques of participant observation and unstructured or semi-structured interviewing that are so central to ethnographic research (broadly conceived, cf. Hammersley, 1998: 9) may best provide us with the necessary full description and depth of understanding for the study of ordinary theology (cf. Towler, 1974: 158; Ahern and Davie, 1987: 36–7; Hopewell, 1987: chs 6 and 9; Jenkins, 1999: introduction and *passim*). On such *qualitative* research in general, see, for example, Patton, 1987; Ely *et al.*, 1991; Moustakas, 1994; Gillham, 2000.

These qualitative methods can provide rich data. But because the gathering and analysis of these data is so time-consuming, such research can inevitably only draw on small samples (cf. Towler, 1974: 158). Questionnaire surveys, by contrast, can work with much larger samples and provide data that are open to *quantitative* statistical analysis, thus enabling us to test hypotheses about the relative influence of different variables and possible causal relationships between them. Their 'survey instruments' are also more easily assessed in terms of reliability (the extent to which they are consistent measures, yielding repeatable results) and validity (the extent to which they are actually measuring what they purport to measure).[1] On quantitative methods see, again among a vast literature, Marsh, 1988; Ary, Jacobs and Razavieh, 1990; Bryman and Cramer, 1992; Oppenheim, 1992; Kay and Francis, 1996: 168–80.

Where qualitative research adopts what has been described as an 'inner perspective' on the phenomena being studied, quantitative research facilitates an 'outer perspective'. I believe that each has its own contribution to make in the study of ordinary theology.

Problems and Controversies

However, we cannot ignore the fact that the employment of such methods is regarded by some theologians as extremely problematic. Many will resist, for theological reasons, the attempt to study religious faith by *any* social-scientific methods, or at all events by those that are thought to be dependent on 'secular' social theories perceived to be 'theologies or anti-theologies in disguise' (Milbank, 1993: 3). Admittedly, there is a great deal of work in the social-scientific study of religion that needs to be questioned and criticized, not least when it is too uncritical of (or naively ignores) its own ideological perspectives. But it would be foolish to dismiss the hard-won methodological developments and substantive insights of the social scientists forged through their attempts to understand the nature of religion. Used intelligently, their methods can be powerful and revealing. Read critically, their explanations and interpretations are often compelling.

---

[1]   Hill and Hood, 1999 is a valuable handbook that brings together over 125 such scales in the psychology of religion, and provides a critical introduction to each.

The social-scientific study of religion is most vulnerable in its a priori conceptualizations, rather than in its a posteriori appeal to experience. As Callum Brown argues in his perceptive study *The Death of Christian Britain*, the problem (in his case, of secularization studies) often lies with social science's definition of religion. Brown finds social science reductionist in its account of what religion 'is' and what it 'does', and advocates that we concentrate on a form of religion that is more fundamental than, and a prerequisite of, the different roles of religion in society that social science has traditionally studied. He calls this form of religion *discursive Christianity*. Discursive Christianity may expect, imply or prescribe certain forms of behaviour as necessary for Christian identity (churchgoing, rituals and so on); but it is also (and more clearly?) discerned 'in the "voices" of the people'. In justifying his use of the testimony of autobiography, oral record and the popular media that have captured this religious culture, Brown writes, 'We reconstruct an individual's religious identity from how they in their own words reflected Christianity' (Brown, 2001: 13). Although Brown sees this emphasis on the study of discursive Christianity as one that involves 'the relegation of social science as a method of inquiry', it is clear that he is thinking here of quantitative and statistical studies rather than of sociology's ethnographic methods (cf. Hammersley, 1998: 1–6). Against his view, I would contend that quantitative studies, where they are properly (that is critically) used, are an important complement to qualitative methods.[2] Nevertheless, I believe that Brown has adopted the right focus and methods of research, and provided a useful cautionary emphasis in his comments about the danger of a priori restrictive definitions of a topic. In both respects Brown points the way for our (rather different) study of ordinary theology.

Although ordinary theology may benefit from both qualitative and quantitative studies, both need to be approached with appropriate circumspection. Qualitative data are often difficult to handle and report on, and the researcher who adopts this approach will frequently feel swamped by her data. Qualitative studies are not only highly selective, they are also inevitably less objective than quantitative studies. This is an issue that I shall attempt to address, at least in part, below. But quantitative research has its own problems and limitations. For one thing, it cannot really stand alone since in-depth qualitative work is needed before valid research instruments can be devised. I am also wary of limiting an empirical approach to theology to a methodology in which particular hypotheses are tested against empirical facts. While recognizing the value of such an approach, particularly in quantitative studies, I would argue that its demand for a specification of a research question prior to the collection of data can blind us to the relevance of much of that data. In addition, Hans van der Ven notes that hypothesis-testing requires a substantial existing body of knowledge about empirical relationships relating to the matter in question, and in

---

[2] Brown offers a critical analysis of relevant statistical data in his own text (Brown, 2001: ch. 7). (Brown's book presents a fascinating, if controversial, thesis about the fundamentally *gendered* nature of religious discourse in Britain and the key place of women in the abrupt collapse of discursive Christianity – that is, the 'secularization' of British culture – in the 1960s. For a summary, see Brown, 2001: 195–6.)

its absence much empirical theology will be descriptive or explorative in form, relating to broader research questions (van der Ven, 1993: 125–6).

Qualitative research allows for very open and 'loose' empirical procedures. Some researchers call their main tool of research a 'research conversation' rather than an in-depth interview, arguing that they are interested primarily in understanding what people have to say rather than testing a hypothesis (Hay and Hunt, 2000: 9). The champions of 'grounded theory' notoriously argue that the research should be allowed to revise and adapt the research question as it proceeds. Again, the model of a conversation may be appealed to. 'Creating categories triggers the construction of a conceptual scheme that suits the data. . . . At its most useful, the process of establishing categories is a very close, intense conversation between a researcher and the data that has implications for ongoing method, descriptive reporting, and theory building' (Ely *et al.*, 1991: 87; cf. Glaser and Strauss, 1967).

Richard Pring has complained of a 'false dualism' between quantitative and qualitative approaches, or rather between the epistemological and ontological *assumptions* that are frequently associated with these two kinds of research. Much theological criticism of social-scientific research is directed to these more theoretical 'implications' or 'presuppositions', rather than to the research methodologies themselves. According to Pring, the assumptions that should be resisted from the quantitative approach are the *naive* realism of a picture or correspondence theory of truth, together with the equally naive and *inappropriate* extension to aspects of personal and social life of a form of quantification that ignores qualitative distinctions between people's attributes (such as feelings, attitudes, knowledge, understanding, behaviour). But Pring argues that we must also resist any *wholly* constructivist, idealist and relativist account of notions of truth and explanation that may accompany the qualitative research perspective (Pring, 2000: 43–55, cf. ch. 5). He writes:

> How we conceived the world . . . is different from social group to social group. Such 'social constructions' are constantly reconstructed as new experiences force us to reshape how we understand things. Hence, the need for that interpretive and hermeneutic tradition in which we seek to understand the world from the perspective of the participants, or to understand a set of ideas from within the evolving tradition of which they are part. However, such differences in how we understand reality are possible because there are stable and enduring features of reality, independent of us, which make such distinctions possible. . . . There are features of what it is to be a person which enable generalizations to be made and 'quantities' to be added or subtracted. . . . The qualitative investigation can clear the ground for the quantitative – and the quantitative be suggestive of differences to be explored in a more interpretive mode.
>
> (Pring, 2000: 55)

This balanced view of the qualitative/quantitative debate, and of the philosophical prejudices that often go along with these two different approaches, may serve as a useful prolegomenon to developing proper methods for studying ordinary theology.

Asking the Right Questions

In both areas of research, the nature of the questions that are asked is crucial. Many questionnaire studies in religion continue to suffer from a lack of intelligence and discrimination in posing their questions, a weakness that frankly sometimes renders them incapable of supporting the sophisticated interpretative structures built on their foundations. The excuse that is often made here is that questions need to be simple and straightforward, so that they are capable of being understood by respondents across a wide range of intelligence and linguistic ability. But a wooden application of these maxims can sometimes lead to worthless data, even nonsense-on-stilts. I hazard some examples.

The figure of approximately 70 per cent of adults who 'believe in God' is still routinely reported (especially by the churches) from surveys of the general population of Britain. It surely must be glossed by some reference to the fact that more sophisticated surveys reveal that over half of this group understand 'God' to be some form of impersonal spiritual force or power, rather than interpreting it as the traditional conception of a personal God (Gill, 1999: 69–72; Kay, 1997). It is extraordinary that it has taken so long for many researchers themselves to appreciate the significance of how they ask this particular question.

It is a question that poses a further, general problem. Purists may also object to the way that the majority of questionnaires conflate the very different notions of 'believing in' and 'believing that'. I argued in Chapter 2 that a belief-in incorporates a factual or propositional belief into an affective context of pro-attitudes, especially those of trust, commitment and devotion, often understood as *active* trust, commitment and devotion. There is no doubt, however, that a common usage exists that appears to confuse belief-in with belief-that. Philosophers have called these states 'reducible beliefs-in', and have conceded that the language of a 'minimal or merely factual belief-in' is commonly employed in the case of doubtful beliefs such as the belief that fairies or ghosts exist (Price, 1969: 431–7). This might provide some sort of justification for the indiscriminate use of belief-in language in questionnaires.

Unfortunately there is evidence from interview studies that respondents also use belief-in language in ways that support a different analysis. Thus some of Edward Bailey's interviewees confessed that they 'believed in' such objects of belief as Christianity, a sense of humour, honesty and the ultimate goodness of human beings. They also expressed the wish that other people would not believe in Powell-ism (the racist views of Enoch Powell) and materialism (Bailey, 1997: 70–71; cf. 1998: 67). With reference to a confession made by one interviewee that 'I do believe in Christmas', Geoffrey Ahern comments, 'The word "believe" here relates to practice, not faith' (meaning by 'faith', presumably, supernatural beliefs-that) (Ahern and Davie, 1987: 99). These respondents are not just affirming the existence of these entities; they are saying – in essence – that each of them is a Good Thing.

The MORI poll on which the book *We British* was based drew on a research interview that poses the present problem most acutely. It asked, 'Which, if any, of the things I'm going to read out do you believe in?' The interviewer then recited the list: 'God, life after death, a soul, the devil, hell, heaven, sin, astrology and opinion polls'

(Jacobs and Worcester, 1990: *Appendix 2*, Q29, cf. ch. 6). Surely the question, 'Do you believe in the devil or in sin?' is one that should properly give religious believers pause. Are some not likely to want to reply, 'I believe that they *exist*, certainly; but I don't believe *in* them.' William Temple's quip, 'I believe in one Holy, Catholic and Apostolic Church but regret that it nowhere exists' captures the issue; as does the old joke, 'Do I believe in baptism? Dammit, I've seen it done . . .'. Since many people seem to appreciate the humour of both of these anecdotes, I conclude that the distinction *is* quite widely recognized.[3] Students of ordinary theology will do well to keep their theological wits about them, including their academic theological wits, when phrasing their research questions about religious beliefs.

A more general problem that will inevitably face the student of ordinary theology is the classic debate over the relative advantages and disadvantages of 'open' (or open-ended) questions, which allow the respondent to answer in his own words, compared with various species of 'closed' (closed-ended) questions that offer only a limited number of carefully formulated responses from which to choose (cf. Bailey, 1994: 118–22). If interview studies are envisaged, open questions are more feasible. They are also more likely to encourage honest replies. (These may then be used to build up a list of closed responses for a questionnaire study.)

But even open questions can pose difficulties. Robert Towler has argued that, given the pragmatic, concrete ways of thinking of many people, we would be foolish to force responses out of them on topics that they have never thought about before, by using 'highly specific questions which admit of only one interpretation'.

> Questions should be so phrased that a respondent does not feel constrained to reply. It should be clearly implied that the respondent may well have no opinion on a question, or that it is a question which may never have occurred to him, and that either of these responses would be perfectly acceptable. Obviously such responses are not failures to respond, nor different ways of saying 'don't know': they are vitally important negative responses.
>
> As a general rule we may say that responses should be interpreted as reactions to stimuli, and treated accordingly, not naively accepted as rationally thought-out answers to simple questions.
>
> (Towler, 1974: 159–60)

Edward Bailey has tried to tackle this problem head on in his own research:

> As the interviewees were told at the start that the purpose was to discover what they already felt and thought, and not to think up answers to questions on which they had no views, they had in fact been positively encouraged to decline to answer anything if they so wished.
>
> (Bailey, 1998: 46)

---

[3]   The situation may be compounded by the fact that some non-realist theologians treat 'believing in God' as expressing approval of a commitment to certain character ideals and actions, without any implication of the real existence of God: that is, they believe in God but they have no belief-that God exists (cf. Astley, 1994b: 154–6). This usage is employed by Don Cupitt (cf. Cupitt, 1980: 54, 69; 1989: 55; 1997: 83–4).

Although this is an important issue, it can be overemphasized. Many respondents appear to be quite willing to say that they have no opinion about something, whether or not they are encouraged to do so. There is also some evidence that being provoked to think about a topic for the first time often evokes a deep, but hitherto unarticulated conviction that they *already* hold, rather than some superficial non-answer that masquerades as an answer. Many people will find themselves, whether in public discussion or private reflection, saying in effect, 'Now that I think about it, I realize that I do believe *a* and *b*, and I don't believe *c* and *d*.' David Hay and Kate Hunt make a similar point about one of their interviewees, who 'discovers her beliefs through reflecting on her life' in conversation or in response to questions (Hay and Hunt, 2000: 15–16).

Certainly, the study of ordinary believers' believing must take us beyond a research methodology that depends on the impressionistic and the anecdotal (despite some of my examples in the last chapter). Serious 'looking and listening' are needed to test the intuitions that we all have about what and how people believe and feel. A number of elements in my account of ordinary theology would be prime candidates for testing through such serious research. I offer two further examples, from other writers. I share David Martin's view that liturgical changes such as gathering in a circle round the altar can communicate some bad theology along with the good, and may even evoke unintended psychological trauma since 'a person pulled into a circle is exposed. . . . His defensible space is overwhelmed' (Martin, 1980: 98). Likewise, John Drane may well be right that the baptismal practice of those churches that choose to dribble small quantities of water onto the heads of their baptizands may serve 'as a symbol of a God who is tight-fisted' (Drane, 2000: 98). In both cases, however, these interpretations need to be tested out through an empirical study of what, and how, Christians learn in worship (cf. Astley, 1992). In order to do that, there is no real alternative to organizing some careful empirical research into the ordinary theology of ordinary believers.

Conceptual Reflection

The study of ordinary theology needs the best sort of empirical research, then. But empirical study is not all that is demanded; we also need conceptual work. Gerben Heitink's principle should be applied here: 'If practical theology really wants to be theology, it cannot be content with only an empirical approach. . . . It must also deal with the normative claims embedded in the Christian faith tradition' (Heitink, 1999: 221). As 'critical practical theology', our study must also ask how far ordinary theology is faithful to the Christian norms, and whether it is true (Kelsey, 1992: 206–7, 211). Theology must always be open to reflective theological and philosophical analysis. The ordinary theology of adult believers and the 'atheology' of non-believers are not immune from such study; I am not proposing any exemption in their case. I *am* proposing, more controversially, that this area is worthy of such efforts. Ordinary theology deserves its share of the same careful analysis and critique that is routinely bestowed on the reflections of professional theologians and scholarly critics of theology. It is certainly the case that only by taking their theology seriously can we discover what ordinary people really believe and why, and begin to evaluate the strengths and weaknesses of the content and form of their believing. But if, as I shall argue in the next chapter, ordinary theology is important not only to those who own it but also to the enterprise of academic theology, it needs to be taken more seriously for wider reasons.

The fact that ordinary theology is usually not well formulated is not an adequate excuse for not studying it. This fact only means that we need to be particularly sensitive in offering a description, analysis and critique of the language and forms of argument that people use when speaking of God and religion. This aspect of the work is essentially a *philosophical* task, and it is one that is central to much of academic theology. But a *theological* study of ordinary theology cannot be confined to a philosophical theology. As well as employing the tools and standards of rationality of the philosopher, therefore, it must also embrace the evaluation of theological beliefs from the standpoint, and using the resources, of the normative theological criteria derived from Christian scripture, doctrine and ethics. What I am advocating here, therefore, is a *full* theological study *redirected* to the belief system of the everyday believer.

Anders Jeffner has distinguished between *descriptive* and *constructive* investigations into religious language (Jeffner, 1972: 17–19). He understands the former as an empirical study of how the language is actually used, in the sense of how other language users understand that it is being used ('descriptive 1') and of how the language user herself thinks she is using it ('descriptive 2'), within a given culture and context. These understandings may be explored through surveys of the linguistic intentions and expectations that people have when they employ language. (Jeffner suggests that appropriate techniques here might include asking people 'what other sentences have the same meaning in this situation', and enquiring how other people react to such language.) He insists that this descriptive task must be distinguished from any constructive study that 'aims to make the language better than it is', by the application of certain evaluative criteria.[4]

This distinction parallels to some extent Don Browning's contrast between *descriptive theology* and *systematic theology*. He defines descriptive theology as the task of describing 'the contemporary theory-laden [religious and cultural] practices that give rise to the practical questions that generate all theological reflection'. According to Browning, systematic theology involves a critical dialogue between the questions and answers of contemporary experience and practice and those of the normative Christian texts: a dialogue that generates a 'new horizon of meaning' that must be tested and justified by critical reasoning and on practical grounds (Browning, 1991: 47–54). This task of systematic theology seems to incorporate

---

[4]   Cf. below, pp. 119–22. Some have distinguished between 'descriptive research', concerned with categories of facts and their mutual relationships, and 'explanatory research' that explores the direction of causal relationships between the facts (van der Ven, 1993: 82). From the point of view of this discussion, however, both may be thought of as descriptive – that is, as describing the empirical facts of the case.

Jeffner's 'constructive' study, while Browning's descriptive theology is a broader version of Jeffner's descriptive study (see also below, pp. 109–10).

One sense in which Jeffner's concerns are narrower than those of Browning is that the former are mainly focused on distinguishing the different functions that religious language serves: for example, making statements, expressing and prescribing emotions or perspectives and performing certain acts.[5] The way that language functions is of considerable interest in the study of ordinary theology. I agree with Jeffner that it should be possible, for example, to design empirical studies so as to reveal the extent to which, for example, ordinary religious language users both actually employ, and think of themselves as employing, their religious beliefs as beliefs that are subject to criteria of reasonableness and evidence similar to the ones that they recognize for the other beliefs that they hold (cf. Wittgenstein, 1966: 53–72). We may also be able to discover how far their theology can properly be described as 'expressivist' or 'non-cognitive'.

But there is more to conceptual reflection on ordinary theology than this, of course. Theology is interested in the content as well as the form or function of religious discourse and has normative concerns that are not reducible to those of the philosopher. Nevertheless, Jeffner's argument for a descriptive empirical element in the study of the *language* of religion is important, and is consonant with the 'looking and listening' theme of the present book. This is the sort of 'looking and listening' that theology should welcome, and I would argue that ordinary religious discourse is one place where it needs to be practised.

Empirical Theological Research

My account of an empirical and a conceptual study should not be taken as specifying two activities that never meet or interact. At one level, it has become routine to argue that all data are 'theory-laden' and that empirical study involves a great deal of 'thinking research', under the guise of conceptual analysis and interpretation, in the very framing of the research instruments and methods that generate empirical data. Empirical studies will therefore need the conceptual reflections of the theologian and the philosopher from the outset.

It is not as widely accepted that a comprehensive Christian theology should also be knowledgeable about the findings and theories of empirical studies, and willing to think through their theological implications. The prejudice against this move is assuredly not limited to the study of ordinary theology. The general assumption behind my position is that truth claims about empirical reality, particularly the empirical reality represented by human beings and their individual and social behaviour, have some relevance for truth claims in theology and therefore must be

---

[5]   Jeffner's addition of a third category of *explanatory theories*, which represent the attempt to 'provide an explanation of the function which a sentence has . . . or ought to have', extends this study to a meta-level.

taken account of in theological discussion. This will not be true of every area of theology, but it ought to be accepted for those parts that attempt a theological account of the nature of human beings and of human society (including the church). This should be no more controversial than arguing that the doctrine of creation needs to take account of scientific claims about evolution and cosmology, and that the doctrines of sin and eschatology should take account of scientific claims about the causes of and constraints on human behaviour.

Even if theology does insist on ignoring scientific claims in these areas, it will be very hard to continue this resistance when it attempts a *practical* theology. In order to reflect on human practice, human practice needs to be studied. And in order to suggest modifications in that practice, it cannot be enough to draw on a priori norms of what should happen and what the result should be. In the case of practical disciplines, we need a theory, and therefore a theology, that can make practical connections with practice. Practical theology therefore needs to frame empirically testable hypotheses, and to revise them in the light of empirical findings. This is how practical studies are done.

It is in this context that people have begun to speak of 'empirical theology': a phrase that is attractive to some, a contradiction in terms to others, and the subject of suspicion by many. For the leading figure in this field, Johannes van der Ven, empirical theology refers to 'the direct use of empirical tools and methods in theology' (van der Ven, 1993: 27). Its historical roots may be traced back to an early 'Chicago School' of scholars with empirically oriented and socio-historical concerns, including process theologians (cf. Inbody, 1992), which was itself related to the clinical pastoral education movement and to American pragmatic philosophy (van der Ven, 1993: 3–7). The extent to which practical theology has incorporated an empirical dimension has varied considerably. Some models of practical theology have paid little serious attention to empirical research, despite their emphasis on practice and experience. By contrast, van der Ven's approach, which he describes both as 'empirical theology' and as 'an empirical approach to practical theology',[6] has extensively incorporated social-scientific research studies. Van der Ven argues that this inclusion of the social sciences works best as an *intra-disciplinary* enquiry, in which theology provides an overall framework that incorporates the appropriate techniques and methods of the social sciences to further its own work. The central requirement here is that 'theology itself become empirical, that is, that it expand its traditional range of instruments . . . in the direction of an empirical methodology' by borrowing empirical methods, concepts and techniques and integrating them into its own procedures (van der Ven, 1993: 101).

Empirical research helps theology to study contemporary society, the contemporary church and its current practice, through a multi-phase procedure (van der Ven, 1993: 112–14, ch. IV, 225). In this procedure, the theological problem and its goal are first posed and a theological question formulated which is then

---

[6]   The approach has also been described as 'empirical-theological' and 'empirical-analytical' (Heitink, 1999: 131, 173; but cf. van der Ven, 1993: 154).

operationalized in empirical terms.[7] Empirical testing then follows by utilizing the usual procedures of social-scientific research, with the results being subjected to theological interpretation aimed at answering the original theological question and explaining the meaning and relevance of the study. The focus throughout is on human experiences of and communication with God, that is on *faith*, which is always the direct object of theology (cf. 30, 103).

The earlier work of van der Ven's own department at the Catholic University of Nijmegen in the Netherlands operated with a different 'two phase' or *multi-disciplinary* approach, in which empirical description and analysis was followed by theological reflection.[8] In his 1993 publication, van der Ven rehearses the reasons for abandoning this and replacing it with the *intradisciplinary* model, in which empirical research is *applied* to the problems and issues of theology so as to further their *theological* description and reflection. He lists the following weaknesses of the earlier way of working: first, theology becomes highly dependent on data from the social sciences; secondly, the theological reflection on the data tends to be 'haphazard and arbitrary', because the theological themes appealed to are usually too abstract; and, thirdly, the difference between the social sciences and theology leads to 'a discordance of registers provided by shifting unchecked back and forth between two differently-tuned linguistic "pianos"' (van der Ven, 1993: 2, 93–7).

Kay and Francis (1985) favour a rather different, *interdisciplinary* approach (cf. also van der Ven, 1993: 97–101). They agree that the contributing disciplines must be rigorously applied to the topic or field of concern in such a way as would satisfy the practitioners of each of the disciplines. Empirical theology must always therefore conform both to theological and to social-scientific criteria. However, the connection between theology and social science is looser on their account than on the intra-disciplinary model, and the starting point might be a sociological or psychological model which is then applied to theological issues, or the testing of existing theological assumptions, rather than developing new theological accounts. Practitioners of this approach also argue that there is 'no obvious methodological bridge back from the results of empirical test to the uncertain conditions or assumptions that had first generated the theological model' (Kay, forthcoming).

Either of these models of empirical theology might be employed in the study of ordinary theology. They will best fit hypothesis-driven and carefully specified research questions, which I have argued should not be the only approach adopted. Such methods must also recognize the challenge posed by the explicitly *hermeneutical* approach to descriptive theology that I discuss below. Van der Ven's model certainly acknowledges that empirical study is to be set in a hermeneutical frame of reference (van der Ven, 1993: 20, 32, 87). 'Empirical facts are meaningful only when they are placed within a hermeneutic context of theological concepts and theories and evaluated from within that context' (153).

---

[7]   To 'operationalize' is to translate a theory or theoretical term into, or to link it with, publicly verifiable measurements or manipulations.

[8]   This is said to have developed from suggestions in a five-volume handbook of pastoral theology edited by Karl Rahner and others.

Description and Prescription

One of the more common responses from professional theologians to my tentative *apologia* for ordinary theology is that I am not describing a *theological* activity at all, but (as one professor of theology put it) 'mere sociology'. How might this criticism be met?

I assume that what was worrying my critic was whether ordinary theology is merely a descriptive exercise and is in no sense analytical, corrective, reconstructive or (particularly) *normative*. Hans Frei distinguishes two main parts of the notion of Christian theology within the Christian community (Frei, 1992: 2): (a) 'first-order statements or proclamations made in the course of Christian practice and belief'; and (b) the 'second-order appraisal of its own language and actions under a norm or norms internal to the community itself'. Under category (b) Frei discusses two further aspects: (i) a *descriptive* endeavour 'to articulate the "grammar", or "internal logic" of first-order Christian statements', and (ii) a *critical* endeavour 'to judge any given articulation of Christian language for its success or failure in adhering to the acknowledged norm or norms governing Christian use of language'.

On this account, a large part of the study of ordinary Christian theology will be a descriptive exercise that portrays its God-talk in detail, as well as providing an account of the depth logic or grammar of ordinary faith as a form of 'Christian self-description' (Frei, 1992: 33). The criticism reported above is that my concerns go no further than this: that is, that ordinary theology only describes beliefs, it does not itself engage in critical theological judgements about them. But Christian theology proper, it is argued, should always be involved in the exercise of testing beliefs against doctrinal norms and rational standards. It should not just tell us what people happen to believe, but also what they *ought* to believe. In other words, we need a little of Frei's category (b)(ii) as well.

Now the question as to whether people's *ordinary theology itself* contains such a self-critical dimension is one that I have already touched on, and will discuss at greater length in the next chapter. It is, however, irrelevant to this particular outburst of friendly fire aimed at the ordinary theological enterprise, for I take it that this is a criticism of ordinary theology as a topic for research.

In face of this attack, my defence is to surrender. I wholly accept that the *study of* ordinary theology should not just involve 'description' or empirical research. Theological work is also, and often largely, normative. This particular study needs to 'transcend the informative' in this way (see Smart, 1968: 105, cf. 106) and therefore must employ theological as well as social-scientific approaches (cf. Kelsey, 1992: 155–6). We should perhaps note that academic theology itself has a very extensive descriptive ('textual', 'exegetical' or 'historical') dimension, which it builds on with (rather less sizeable) evaluative discussions about the reasonableness, truth and 'Christian worth' of the beliefs it describes.[9] If the study of ordinary theology is to

---

[9]   This second task requires some different skills from those of scholarly description; as I shall detail in Chapter 5, there is even a position that reserves the term 'theology' for this critical, second-order task.

be modelled on other fields of theological study, such as the study of the theology of the biblical traditions, of historical figures and movements, or of contemporary theologians, it also requires an element of critical evaluation. Point (already) taken.

Description and Interpretation

I wish to reflect further, however, on the nature of the descriptive task in the study of theology. As we have seen, Don Browning is one author who is happy to use the term 'descriptive theology'. For Browning, descriptive theology describes the contemporary practices that give rise to the practical questions 'that generate all theological reflection'. He argues that descriptive theology is the proper *first* moment in a theology that *then* proceeds to relate its findings to the normative texts of historical theology, and the critical and philosophical questions of systematic theology. But 'it would be a great mistake', Browning writes, 'to believe that descriptive theology is simply a sociological task' (Browning, 1991: 47). At all events, it would be a mistake *unless* sociology is itself recognized as being 'hermeneutical' – that is, as involving an interpretive dialogue between the researcher and the subjects being researched, both of which must be regarded as social or communal (cf. Tracy, 1981: 118–19, 120–21). 'Description takes place within a dialogue or conversation' (Browning, 1991: 64, cf. 78, 86–91).

It would indeed be naive to assume that ethnographical or sociological 'description' and 'discovery' is ever 'a simple reflection of what exists', rather than 'the product of complex processes of understanding, as well as of social interaction' between the researchers and those who are being studied (Hammersley, 1998: 26). The alternative view would be a 'doctrine of immaculate perception' (van Maanen, 1988: 74) which needs to be tempered by a more hermeneutical and critical approach to description and explanation.

The point is this: even in *describing* your theology I am implicitly engaged in a conversation between my theology and yours, at least to some extent. My perspective influences what comes to my attention as I listen to you talk about, and see you practise, your faith; indeed it influences what it is that I am capable of seeing and hearing, and what I take seriously in what you say. 'Listening is never perfectly neutral'; it is itself a theological act – 'an act of descriptive theology' (Browning, 1991: 286). We must, of course, seek to hear what the other is really saying and not fill our ears with what we ourselves want to hear. In an important sense, we must attend to what *they* find significant rather than what *we* do (Jacobs, 1982: 29). But we cannot wholly leave behind our own framework of presuppositions and structures of understanding, for to do that would be not to understand the other person *at all*. Some researchers suggest that it is best to acknowledge the interviewer's preconceptions by bringing those presuppositions into the conversation with the subjects, without imposing ideas on them, so that an explicit dialogue can result (cf. Bellah *et al.*, 1985: 304–5).

In hermeneutical theory it is said that the interpreter inevitably operates like a translator, using his or her own understanding and frame of reference as a vantage point from which 'the text' is surveyed, but then finding that this original understanding or interpretation is transformed by the perceived meaning of the text. Thus the text 'reads us' as we read it, and our understanding moves in a circle or spiral from our 'horizon' to that of the text and back again (either with or without some critical corrections to prevent a systematic 'distortion' of meaning), bringing the two horizons ever closer (Gadamer, 1982: Second Part, II and Third Part; Thiselton, 1980: *passim*).

The problems that this situation gives rise to have been aired even outside of the hermeneutical conceptualization, particularly with regard to the social sciences. Can there be a sociology and anthropology that is not 'culture-bound'? Alan Ryan has summarized the view of Peter Winch and others on this issue.

> The key point is that the classification of activity as activity of a certain kind essentially relies on an appeal to its significant features; and the claim is that their significance is lent them by the social organization of the community from which the investigator comes.
>
> (Ryan, 1970: 153; cf. Winch, 1958)

The sociologist's understanding might then be seen, paradoxically, as 'a participant understanding'. Ryan goes on:

> It is not just a matter of our being able to make sense of what we are told – and between an account of what *we* would be doing in their shoes and an account of what they in their shoes *say* they are doing, there seems no room for a simple, objective, culture-neutral account of what *as a matter of fact* they are doing.
>
> (Ryan, 1970: 153–4)

This general point connects with some of the more plausible concerns of a sociology of knowledge, which Ryan articulates with reference to the activity of selection. 'Because in any understanding of the world we have to select some aspects and ignore others, we are necessarily vulnerable to the preselection of significant detail which the existing social organisation of our society involves' (226).

Translated into our present concerns, we might say that the description of another person's (ordinary) theology will always be *partly* dependent on the describer's own theological presuppositions. We notice and select 'significant' themes and concepts from *our* theological standpoint, at least to some extent. All description involves selection, and all selection is *our* selection, even if we decide to select everything that a person says. In giving an account of another's thinking, however, our selection will never be that wide. But does this mean that it can never truly represent the other person?

Phenomenological and Hermeneutical Research

If we are listening to a person respectfully and closely, or reading the transcript of an interview in the same way, we shall hear and see more reliably the beliefs and the believing of the person we are studying. The phenomenological (or 'transcendental phenomenological') tradition of research takes this concern very seriously. Indeed, it argues for an approach that *sets aside* prejudgements about the phenomenon under investigation, so as 'to be completely open, receptive, and naïve in listening to and hearing research participants' (Moustakas, 1994: 22). But what might be involved in such a procedure and how realistic is its aim?

The phenomenological approach to the study of religion adopts Edmund Husserl's concern with the methodological virtue of *epoché*, a Greek word meaning 'to stay away or abstain', which is construed here as a matter of 'bracketing', 'restraint' or 'suspension of judgement'. Husserl's interest was in 'bracketing out' particulars so that the universal could be directly perceived and involved the adoption of a 'strictly contemplative' attitude (Habermas, 1970: 40). Developing this theme, the phenomenologist of religion Gerardus van der Leeuw wrote that epoché:

> implies that no judgement is expressed concerning the objective world, which is thus placed 'between brackets' as it were. All phenomena, therefore, are considered solely as they are presented to the mind, without any further aspects such as their real existence, or their value, being taken into account; in this way the observer restricts himself to pure description systematically pursued, himself adopting the attitude of complete intellectual suspense or of abstention from all judgement, regarding these controversial topics.
>
> (van der Leeuw, 1938: 646)

As personal biases, values and prejudgements are to be set aside in this 'Epoché Process', after conscientious self-examination on the part of the researcher, phenomenologists now usually write of *these* elements as the ones that are to be 'bracketed off' or 'bracketed out', in a procedure that entails 'setting aside voices, sounds, and silences that so readily tell us what something is' (Moustakas, 1994: 60, cf. 88). But there is something to be said for retaining the original sense that it is the *phenomena* that are bracketed and therefore placed out of court – immune from our criticism and evaluation – so that they may be allowed to be themselves, as mere phenomena. 'This implies the absence of presupposition which would influence resultant understanding. In other words, bringing to one's study the concepts and constructs of one's worldview is seen as a distortive influence upon the results' (Erricker, 1999: 77). Exponents claim that this method leads to an 'openness, seeing just what is there and allowing what is there to linger', and they describe the process as 'a way of genuine looking that precedes reflectiveness, the making of judgements, or reaching conclusions' (Erricker, 1999: 85–6). Ninian Smart has therefore called the phenomenological approach a form of 'bracketed expression': it is 'a bracketing of all that is being presented'. But he insists that any good description of religion will also need to bring out the feelings and beliefs of the religionists themselves, so that the study of religion needs to be 'evocative as well as descriptive', employing the capacities of imagination and empathy to understand 'what it is like' (Smart, 1973a: 31–4).

All this demands some hard work on the part of the researcher. In the Epoché Process we must be aware of our preconceptions and prejudgements, open and receptive to them so that they can be 'labelled' and 'written out' prior to the interview (Moustakas, 1994: 89, 116, 180; cf. Jackson, 1997: 27). Even so, those who espouse and practise a phenomenological approach admit that 'the problem of language and habit still exist' and that their own 'rooted ways of perceiving and knowing still enter in' (Moustakas, 1994: 61). The Epoché is rarely achieved totally, although the claim is made that the influence of preconceived thoughts and judgements can be reduced by entering into the process (Moustakas, 1994: 90).

It is important to recognize that what underlies the phenomenological approach is primarily the attempt 'to justify the study of religion on its own terms rather than on the terms of the theologian or the social scientist' (Erricker, 1999: 83). But any such attempt at a purely 'descriptive', value-free study of religion has long had to face the criticism of hermeneutical naivety (Erricker, 1999: 82). The utopia of a value-free and wholly 'objective' enquiry is simply not realizable; our understanding of the other will always be *our* understanding of the other, as this is the only sort of human understanding that there is. And if an intersubjective consensus obtained through discussion is all that can count as objective truth, the purity of the phenomenological approach is put even more into question. Further, as Robert Jackson has argued, sensitivity and a capacity for empathy, although necessary to understanding another's way of life, are not on their own *sufficient*. We also require the ability to grasp the grammar of someone else's discourse (Jackson, 1993: 151). Jackson asserts that 'even though ethnographers can get close to the insider's view, they cannot be insiders, and must be interpreting' (154). Jackson therefore advocates a version of a hermeneutic methodology, proposing this as the only realistic alternative to the naivety of any 'descriptivist' approach in which the researcher seeks to bracket out her own understanding in order to identify another's viewpoint (Jackson, 1997: 21–2).

This alternative, hermeneutical-phenomenological framework recognizes the irreducible significance of the interpreter:

> The hermeneutical task is to find justifiable modes through which my experience and comprehension of the phenomenon being researched can serve as a bridge or access for elucidating and interpreting the meaning of the phenomenon.
>
> (Titelman, 1979: 188)

The hermeneutical approach that has developed from the work of Hans-Georg Gadamer rejects the Romantic tradition of interpretation which equates the discovery of the meaning of a text with discovering the author's *intention*. By contrast, Gadamer focuses on *what the author has said*, for 'the meaning of a text goes beyond its author' and hence 'understanding is not merely a reproductive, but always a productive attitude as well' (Gadamer, 1982: 264). The interpreter is now no longer to be seen as an individual isolated from history who is trying to get into the mind of the author, but as a member of a community bound historically to the tradition that it is seeking to interpret: 'history does not belong to us, but we belong to it' (245).

This analysis, of course, is most often invoked to give an account of our interpretation in the present of the *writings* of authors from the *past*. In what sense is it relevant, then, to understanding what an interviewee says in an interview or writes on a questionnaire?

Anthropologists have a similar question to face. Jackson appeals to the *interpretive anthropology* (or 'ethnography') of Clifford Geertz as a model for understanding religion. Ethnographic research is particularly relevant to the study of ordinary theology in that it presents religions as they are perceived and lived by their adherents, rather than as abstract systems of beliefs. Geertz views the work of the ethnographer as more akin to that of a literary critic: 'What we call our data are really our own constructions of other people's constructions of what they and their compatriots are up to' (Geertz, 1993: 9). He nicely captures the sense in which our study of the other is inevitably a 'translation' of the others' ways of putting things – not because their language is recast in our terms, but because our account displays the logic of their ways of putting things in language of our own. The student of culture is therefore more like a critic illuminating a poem, than a scientist or even a 'cipher clerk'. She must adopt what is clearly a species of hermeneutical method.

I agree that, despite the potential weaknesses of that approach and the ever-present dangers of its abuse, it is our most valuable method for understanding religion and a necessary condition for empathy in the study of religion (Jackson, 1997: 46–7, cf. ch. 6). As we have seen, accounts of empirical theology may also appeal to some sort of hermeneutical framework in which 'continuing theological reflection, i.e., a process of ordering and interpretation, . . . [modifies] the perspective within which the "facts" are perceived' (van der Ven, 1993: 121).

Taken to extremes, a purely phenomenological approach leads to an unrealistic view of the process of understanding others and of the study of ordinary theology as well (cf. Browning, 1991: 94). Even our account of what other people take to be significant in their faith and life depends not just on what they say and believe, but also on what *we* believe. This is because we have to take their expressions of significance as being expressions of *significance*, as having that meaning for them; in particular, we must take their ordinary theology *as theology*, as having theological significance and theological meaning for them. Failing to recognize this, many academic theologians dismiss the ordinary believer as someone who simply does not have a theology or is not really engaged in doing theology.

I wish to persuade the academic, or at least his clerical equivalents and any researchers who are willing to undertake the study of ordinary believers, to adopt a different view of theology. It is only when we adopt a broader concept of what theology is that we shall recognize the ordinary believer's talk as theological talk. We cannot do this by emptying our minds, eliminating all conceptual categories that relate to our understanding of theology and firmly suppressing *all* our evaluations of what is meaningful, or indeed what is true. This is, in any case, psychologically nearly impossible and epistemologically counter-productive. If we stop thinking for ourselves in this way we shall cease to perceive anything or at least cease to notice anything. Our recognition of what is meaningful to others is dependent on our prior conception of what it is for something to be meaningful. We have to hold on to this, whatever else we 'bracket out' of our thinking. This is the essential evaluative dimension of the researcher's perspective.

It is often said that what students of society select for study is determined, at least in part, by their conception of what has 'cultural significance'. Max Weber, who argued vigorously for 'value free' social science, nevertheless recognized that:

The concept of culture is a *value-concept.* Empirical reality becomes 'culture' to us because and insofar as we relate it to value ideas. It includes those segments and only those segments of reality which have become significant to us because of this value-relevance. Only a small portion of existing concrete reality is colored by our value-conditioned interest and it alone is significant to us. . . . Perception of its meaningfulness to us is the presupposition of its becoming an *object* of interpretation.

(Weber, 1949: 76)

This is the situation in which the researcher finds herself, in describing her interviewee's beliefs. She is listening and looking for his ordinary theology and therefore for something that may count as *theological* or *theologically significant.*

Perhaps the difference between the phenomenological and hermeneutical approaches to research, when fully unpacked, will again prove to be a difference of degree rather than a difference in kind. In trying to hear and describe another's beliefs, the researcher of ordinary theology must certainly not be engaged at the same time in evaluating those beliefs against the whole range of the researcher's own theological presuppositions, either overtly or covertly. But that does not mean that some very basic presuppositions are not needed on the part of the researcher before ordinary theology can be heard *as theology* and therefore correctly heard at all. Such presuppositions concern the meaning of theology and the meaningfulness of a person's life – together with the attitudes, values, beliefs, actions and relationships that constitute that life. These are the 'theological presuppositions' and 'theological standpoint' that the researcher *must* employ to do her research properly.

Wittgensteinian Methodology

I have subtitled this book, 'Looking, listening and learning in theology'. Interestingly, it is a philosopher who stands at the forefront of those who have argued that we need to look and listen to people's language much more seriously than we do. Ludwig Wittgenstein's 'pedagogical turn' in philosophy also drew our attention to how people learned and are taught the (often implicit) rules for the use of concepts. 'One thing we always do when discussing a word', Wittgenstein insisted, 'is to ask how we were taught it' (Wittgenstein, 1966: 1).

Wittgenstein's approach in general is of signal relevance to our theme. It underscores the importance of taking 'our lives and our practice seriously' (Putnam, 1992: 135). It celebrates ordinary tasks as the proper, unconfused workplace for language and emphasizes 'the primacy of the everyday over and above the speciousness of philosophy' (Clack, 1999: 22). As Wittgenstein himself put it (quoting Goethe), 'in the beginning was the deed' (1980: 31). Meaning is therefore grounded in something as public and social as acting. Despite his focus on language, therefore, Wittgenstein insisted that language must be seen not just as a form of words, but in terms of the contextualized, public use that is made of those words. 'Language is a characteristic part of a large group of activities', he wrote, and we must concentrate not on the words 'but on the occasions on which they are said'. 'We don't start from certain words, but from certain occasions or activities'; 'our talk gets its meaning from the rest of our proceedings' (Wittgenstein, 1966: 2–3; 1974: §229). Wittgenstein does not argue that understanding is itself to be identified with these practices, but that 'it presupposes them, so that it is not possible without them' (Hamlyn, 1989: 218). This concern for our customs and practices, these 'deep contingencies about the human condition', explains why Wittgenstein's approach is frequently described as an attempt to shift philosophy in an anthropological direction (Scruton, 1994: 266–7) – that is, back to *us*.

In the context of a discussion of theology, this shift is towards religion – that is, towards working religious language, the lived religious perspective, and human religious conduct and experience – and away from any second-order, intellectual theory. 'Those who speak of such things [sin, despair and salvation through faith] (Bunyan for instance) are simply describing what has happened to them, whatever gloss anyone may want to put on it.' 'Predestination: . . . It simply isn't a theory. . . . It's less a theory than a sigh, or a cry' (Wittgenstein, 1980: 28, 30). Unquestionably, then, Wittgenstein saw religious belief as a personal commitment to a way of life and not merely as an intellectual commitment. Unlike some of his followers, however, he did not *reduce* such belief to religious practice (Barrett, 1991: 257).

A person's belief in God is, or includes, an 'attitude to all explanations', according to Wittgenstein. In this case, it is 'manifested in his life' by that person's 'taking a certain matter seriously and then, beyond a certain point, no longer regarding it as serious, but maintaining that something else is even more important'. Here it is not the words that are of significance. '*Practice* gives the words their sense' (Wittgenstein, 1980: 85). Thus Wittgenstein's main emphasis can be said to be neither on feeling nor reason, but on action as 'the foundational thing' (Kerr, 1986: 158).

Theology has, of course, always been wary of moves to the personal, to the religious and to practice, but in this area at all events we should take them seriously. Wittgenstein's position is germane to a number of my arguments in this book. As we saw in Chapter 2, it is natural for someone who adopts this approach to argue that religious concepts are 'learned within the Christian community where they have instituted ruled uses' (Martin, 1994: 185): 'they learn to think about God in these terms and in this way. . . . [they] learn a theology when they learn how the word "God" is used' (Rhees, 1969: 125–6). Religious learners will also recognize that these rules for the proper use of concepts in religious language, the 'grammar' of the language-games operating within religion, are closely related to certain forms of life or ways of acting. 'Language-games', or rule-governed uses of language, always grow out of and define 'forms of life'. Our religious practice may therefore be seen as such a form of life or, at all events, as inextricably linked with it.[10] D. Z. Phillips writes that 'it is impossible to imagine a religion . . . without imagining it *in* a form of life' (Phillips, 1986: 79), which he specifies as the 'larger context of human life

---

[10]   Brian Clack argues that both language-games and forms of life have a small scale, and that neither term was applied by Wittgenstein to denote a category as wide as religion. Clack defines a form of life as 'an instinctive human way of acting, part genetic, part nurtured' (Clack, 1999: 89, cf. 116–24).

in which we see how a language-game is taken' (Phillips, 1993: 88). (A 'language-game', according to Wittgenstein, consists of 'language and the actions into which it is woven' for 'the *speaking* of a language is part of an activity, or of a form of life': Wittgenstein, 1968: §§7, 23.)

Hence we need to look at how people live and behave, as well as looking at and listening to what they are saying, if we are to grasp the meaning of their theology. Religious belief, according to Wittgenstein, 'is shown by what we do rather than by what we say, in *praxis* rather than in dogma, theory and theological speculation. And, of course, it is shown in our attitudes, which are a part of *praxis*' (Barrett, 1991: 208). So the *observer* will be required to observe the forms of life of their religion in order to understand people's religious beliefs. Phillips comments, 'What we need is not to look at the sentence, but at what [they] do with it. . . . As elsewhere, to see whether the "acting out" is confused or not, we must not think – impose our *a priori* assumptions – but look' (Phillips, 1993: 115). Wittgenstein himself writes, 'the *words* you utter or what you think as you utter them are not what matters, so much as the difference they make at various points in your life' (Wittgenstein, 1980: 85). This suggests that just interviewing people will not reveal their theology in a way that we can understand, *unless* we can get them to talk about what this theology means in their practice, in their lives and in their culture. Better still, we should also seek to observe that behaviour, life and culture, as far as we are able. 'What is called for in understanding religious language . . . are the virtues of patient observation, a certain degree of participation and empathy, and a talent for "thick description"'[11] (Stiver, 1996: 200).

Post-Wittgensteinian Models

A currently influential understanding of theology that is sympathetic to many of Wittgenstein's concerns, and therefore open to a similar empirical approach, is *post-liberalism* (Lindbeck, 1984: 24, 33). George Lindbeck attacks liberal, experiential, revisionist theology for locating the core of religion in common pre-reflective religious experience and existential concerns, and for demoting the status of religion's external features – including its culture, tradition and language. Instead, he would have us understand the Christian religion as a cultural-linguistic system and interpret Christian doctrine as the rules of the grammar of that religion. Being religious is to be modelled on learning and speaking a language, since 'a religion can be viewed as a kind of cultural and/or linguistic framework or medium that shapes the entirety of life and thought' (33). To become Christian, on this view, is to acquire proficiency in the specific 'Christian language and form of life'; it involves 'learning the story of Israel and of Jesus well enough to interpret and experience

---

[11]   Anthropologists and sociologists use the term 'thick description' (originally coined by Gilbert Ryle) to denote a multidimensional, nuanced and complex account of a situation in its context, utilizing different standpoints and interpretations (Geertz, 1993: ch. 1; cf. West, Noble and Todd: 1999: 37–9).

one's self and one's world in its terms'. For Lindbeck, the appropriate educational methodology to ensure this result will not involve instruction in or inculcation of beliefs, nor will it be oriented to the exploration or evocation of the learner's experience. Rather, the form that Christian education should take is to concentrate on developing strong communities that 'cultivate their native tongue and learn to act accordingly', by being faithful to the Christian narrative and its performance (34, 132–4; cf. Higgins, 1996). This 'faith community' approach to Christian education is currently widely endorsed (cf. Astley, 2000c: 17–20 and literature cited), although it is not the only educational procedure that will effect the result that Lindbeck seeks. Lindbeck's concern with learning the grammar of religion and his recognition of the centrality of language to religious identity tie in with major emphases of this book.

Unfortunately, however, Lindbeck's account reduces doctrine to a regulative role. For Lindbeck, doctrines are second-order rules that regulate – 'recommend and exclude certain ranges of' – the belief statements and symbolizing activities of ordinary believers (Lindbeck, 1984: 19, cf. 107 and ch. 4). Doctrines interpreted as rules are not statements, and therefore cannot be judged either true or false. Logically, this is to construe the language of doctrine as 'formal' rather than 'material' mode discourse: that is, as rules for consistent talking about God, rather than as talk about God (cf. Ramsey, 1973: 46–7, 54). While this may be a useful analysis and interpretation in the case of many doctrines, even rules need some justification, unless they can be shown to be fundamental to our cognitive processes or our essential human practices or natures. And the usual justification for doctrinal rules is that they guide us in the production of a theology that adequately represents the nature and activity of God. It is considerations such as these that discourage some theologians from drinking too deeply from post-liberal wells.

Among the many scholars who have been influenced by Wittgenstein's approach to religion, there are others who may provide us with helpful pointers to its implications for our study. One such is the Dominican Gareth Moore. Moore takes a Wittgensteinian line when he asserts that 'religious language . . . gets its meaning from being embedded in what people do' (Moore, 1988: 131). 'Conversion of life', he writes, includes 'conversion of language'; it is a matter of learning a 'new . . . way of speaking as part of learning a new way of life'. In his 1988 essay *Believing in God*, Moore offers many insights into what Wittgenstein calls the 'depth grammar' of the concept of God.[12] The book also illuminates the logic of religious trust, prayer and spirituality; as well as the notions of rewards in the spiritual life, miracle and God's activity.

There is a strong empirical focus to this study: 'We actually have to *look* at how our language about God works, how it is used, if we are to get any real understanding of what it is for God to be a person, an agent' (Moore, 1988: 102). Moore uses the fiction of Otto, someone who knows nothing at all about Christianity (or any

---

[12]   The 'surface grammar' of a word or sentence is its appearance, which can often mislead us; the 'depth grammar' is its real significance – as shown in its usage (Wittgenstein, 1968: § 664).

religion) but who visits churches, reads the Bible and observes how religious people act and speak (2–5). Although he reports no direct empirical research data, Moore's concern to understand what it is that people are actually doing and saying when they pray to and speak of God is frequently exemplary. It is also much more nuanced and intelligent than a great many empirical studies. Moore's work therefore encourages a careful and sympathetic analysis of the depth grammar of ordinary theology. He also lays great stress, as I have in Chapter 2, on religious understanding being taught rather than being discovered by the individual. Such an understanding, he writes, 'belongs to what we are taught when we are taught about God. It is part of the concept of God' (188).

The postmodernist Christian theologian Don Cupitt presents another, more radical, model. For Cupitt, the human world is the world of language and 'everything is what it seems to be; that is, what the common language says it is' (Cupitt, 1997: 47). This high view of ordinary language allows him to assert that 'ordinary language is the best radical theologian, and significantly sharper than the professionals' (Cupitt, 1999a, 'Foreword'); it embodies a vision of the human condition that is 'more substantial and even *formidable* than we have supposed' (Cupitt, 1999b: 103). Cupitt even claims that 'if we are to make any progress in religious thought, we should begin by studying the philosophy of life and the religious and moral ideas that belong to us because they are built into our language.' We should also ask ourselves 'whether our special creeds and systems of thought really do much better, in *practice*, than ordinary language – and I suggest that in the majority of cases the answer is humbling' (Cupitt, 1999b: 102–3). If this is true, it is a powerful incentive for the study of ordinary language.

In his own research, Cupitt has adopted a very wide perspective. His trilogy of books about the theology of everyday speech explore, for example, a range of idioms about 'life' and 'living' (cf. Cupitt, 1999a: 91–6) and about 'it', 'it all' and 'everything' (Cupitt, 1999b: 107–18). Much of this is not technically *God*-talk, a fact that should not surprise us as Cupitt draws his evidence not from religious believers but from common usage as described in dictionaries and collections of idioms, proverbs and slang (cf. 1999b: 'Sources'). Nevertheless, in Cupitt's view this language certainly counts as *religious* discourse and we may think of it as implicitly theological. In the light of its broad, secular origins, Cupitt may be correct in detecting in such popular parlance a radically immanentist, relativist and non-realist faith 'embedded in ordinary language and in everyone's life experience' (2001: 27). He calls it 'language's own philosophy' (2000a: 4; cf. 2000b: vii). It is no longer supernatural and it is certainly post-ecclesiastical, but Cupitt asserts that it is not post-Christian because it can still be understood in terms of Jesus' kingdom theology.

We do not need to embrace all Don Cupitt's conclusions in order to acknowledge the importance of his method.[13] Cupitt has certainly brought together some valuable data and provided some perceptive reflections. He has begun to call his method *ordinary language theology* – 'a descriptive study of the common religious

---

[13]   On Cupitt's theology, cf. Cowdell, 1988; White, 1994; Crowder, 1997.

philosophy' (2000a: 1) – and asserts that this study, which pays close attention to 'the way words move in ordinary language', is worthy of the title 'democratic philosophy' (2000b: ix). This is to use the word theology (and philosophy) of a 'field of religious enquiry' and a 'study of' the expression of a religious, philosophical or theological position, pattern or trend. I have preferred, however, to reserve the word theology for the activity of *having* and *doing* theology, including ordinary theology, and to distinguish this from the empirical or conceptual *study* of that theology.[14]

Leaving Everything As It Is?

Does such a descriptive theology 'leave everything as it is', as Wittgenstein proposed as the only appropriate outcome of the work of the philosopher (Wittgenstein, 1968: §§ 124–8)? According to Renford Bambrough, philosophy itself both does and does not do this. In presenting what is there, in all its complexity and with all its differences, philosophy does leave everything as it is. But in exposing fallacies, clearing minds, contrasting assertions and practices, and reminding us (in a religious context) what we count as 'prayer' or 'conversion' or 'god', it does not (Bambrough, 1989: 235–6).

There is an educational truth here, for description itself can be a powerful engine for learning change. I have found when working with adult Christians that a good place to start in the task of exploring a particular religious belief or value is to get people to fill in a questionnaire on the topic under discussion first, and then to feed the results back to them; or, when working in 'tutorial-mode' (at a one-to-one level), to start with a listening or interview format that elicits the other's views. But starting somewhere is not the same as finishing there, even in this case and even in those cases where no educational input follows. For what almost always happens is that the group or the individual, in articulating their own beliefs, slides naturally and easily into assessing them critically. Show a person his beliefs clearly and it is very likely that he will want to begin to modify them or feel himself forced to do so. There is nothing like looking in the mirror for unsettling our satisfaction with ourselves as we are. 'I ought to be no more than a mirror, in which my reader can see his own thinking with all its deformities so that, helped in this way, he can put it right' (Wittgenstein, 1980: 18). Unearthing a person's ordinary theology is therefore itself part of the critical task.

Vincent Brümmer's account of the relationship between philosophy and theology may be relevant here. He also argues that 'philosophy does not necessarily leave everything the way it is, but can also generate improvements in our thinking.' Philosophers do not just reflect on empirical data about ordinary language usage in order to describe how people in fact talk; they also do so 'in order to recollect the way conceptual skills should be exercised correctly' (Brümmer, 1992: 9). This may

---

[14] Cupitt forgoes any evaluative perspective in his study of ordinary language theology. I agree with Hyman (2001) that such a perspective is necessary to avoid an unqualified cognitive or moral relativism.

involve innovative work on the part of philosophers, in reflecting on possible conceptual forms in addition to the actual ones they discover in practice – including their own practice. Brümmer writes:

> Perhaps we should rather say that philosophers reflect on *possible* conceptual forms and not merely on their own *actual* concepts. The latter form only a small part of the possibilities to be considered. The form of a philosophical problem is not: 'Is this the way I think?' nor: 'Can you share this sample from my conceptual horizon?' but rather: 'Imagine what it would be like if we thought thus . . .'.
>
> (Brümmer, 1992: 19)

Innovative philosophy thus goes beyond the description of the depth grammar of language to test the adequacy of 'these conceptual games' to the (often new) demands of life, and to propose modifications to them. In this way, theology can learn 'to extend the rules . . . of Godliness over the ever-changing circumstances' (Holmer, 1978: 23).

This innovative work seems to me to be close to what many people mean by 'doing theology' or 'thinking theologically', where they understand this in terms of new and creative thinking rather than just exploring the applications and implications of traditional theological formulations. Ordinary theology also engages in these attempts at conceptual innovation, and – in so far as it is self-critical – it also tests the adequacy of its own new theological thoughts. The critical *study* of ordinary theology will further share in and develop this task 'from the outside', as it were. At both levels, appeal will be made to criteria of evaluation.

In discussing these criteria, Brümmer is not only concerned with the work of the philosopher; he also wishes to specify the roles undertaken by different sorts of theology. He concedes that one of these, philosophical theology, must restrict itself to a very basic level of *logical criteria* for conceptual innovation, testing the adequacy of our religious language against the norms of reasoning. Other types of theology, however, will be able to operate with criteria at rather different levels of reflection: that is to say, *confessional* criteria, which measure adequacy against the norms of a church, and *person-relative* criteria, which assess its adequacy to the demands of a person's life and her own sense of 'intelligibility'. In summary:

> The most general level of reflection here is that of *philosophical theology* which tries to determine which conceptual forms can be accepted without contradiction. The next level is that of *confessional theology* (church dogmatics) which goes a step further by involving confessional criteria and trying to determine which conceptual forms can be accepted without becoming untrue to the community of faith (or the religious tradition, or the ideological group, and so on). A final level of reflection is that of *personal faith* in which each person must determine for him- or herself which conceptual forms he or she can accept without losing his or her integrity.
>
> (Brümmer, 1992: 28; cf. Mitchell, 1991: 19)

For our purposes, this discussion is useful both in distinguishing logical criteria from more theological and spiritual norms of evaluation, and for introducing person-relative criteria into the evaluative framework. Too often the theological task of evaluating a person's theology as a 'good theology' is done solely at the level of the church's norms of faith. But Brümmer suggests that we should recognize a further level of appropriate evaluation that is much more personal and individual. It is this personal level that brings us back again to the level of a person's ordinary theology, while providing us with criteria that may sometimes conflict with the more objective theological norms of faith.

D. Z. Phillips robustly asserts that his own philosophical reflection on religious language is a matter of description rather than prescription, construction or revision (Phillips, 1993: 242; against Sutherland, 1984: 7). Phillips claims that, like Wittgenstein, he is not tampering with ordinary religious beliefs; he is engaged in mirroring practice, not changing it (1993: 244–5). But we should note again that the touchstone here is *practice*, for a person's practice shows the actual conclusions he draws. Wittgenstein likewise insists, 'I don't want to say anything he himself wouldn't say. I want to say that he draws these conclusions.' To understand the believer we therefore have to know the conclusions that the believer draws. 'Are eyebrows going to be talked of, in connection with the Eye of God?' (Wittgenstein, 1966: 71).

We can discern and describe a person's beliefs from what that person says and does, but this is not the same as always accepting at face value *his interpretation of his own beliefs*. We listen to the account and we look to see how it is lived out. But we do not necessarily accept 'whatever gloss anyone may want to put on it' (Wittgenstein, 1980: 28), including the believer himself. We must look and see what conclusions he draws in his practice and not be misled by any philosophizing he (or anyone else) engages in concerning it. Phillips calls this a matter of 'trying to give perspicuous representations of the practice' (Phillips, 1993: 243). The practice referred to here again includes both linguistic practice and behaviour – what people do as well as what they say.

How then should we take up our empirical tools when looking and listening for ordinary theology? I think that the best way to put the matter is that an accurate description of what people are *really* saying will be based on the evidence of the *implications*, both implicit and explicit, that they actually draw and adopt in their discourse and their lives from the language they are using (that is, its 'logic'). Usually they will be conscious that they are using theological language in this way, and conscious that they are drawing these implications, accepting these particular entailments and incompatibilities. Under those circumstances, they will agree with our account, which is an account of what they *actually mean* by what they say and do. But if they do *not* consciously recognize that they are drawing and accepting these implications of their theology, they will not accept our account of what they are 'really saying' either.[15]

In either case, what they are saying can still be *criticized*. It is important, however, that the criticism be directed to what people actually mean, its depth grammar, and

---

[15]   Thus my interpretation of the nature of this empirical study does not at first sight quite fit either Jeffner's 'descriptive 1' or his 'descriptive 2' investigation (see p. 104).

not to what they might on a superficial listening appear to mean, its surface grammar, or to the (usually second-hand) interpretations and glosses on what they mean that they have picked up and now repeat, but do not really believe (as their practice reveals). But none of this suggests that people's language and behaviour cannot be confused, and therefore properly subject to criticism. According to Phillips, 'taking a pragmatic attitude to religious practice does not condone superstition', nor does it mean that believers 'can say what they like' (Phillips, 1993: 251–2). Studying a person's ordinary theology is *not* the same as agreeing with it.

Chapter 5

Debating Ordinary Theology

If anyone is going to look seriously at and listen carefully to ordinary theology, they must first swallow their contempt for it (cf. Barth, 1975: 279). Such disdain is very widespread. However, I should not locate myself too quickly on the high moral (or self-righteous?) ground in this respect, for I vividly recall complaining, not that long ago, that the trouble with theology is that 'everybody thinks themselves an expert in it'. It is only now that I repent in dust and ashes, having come to appreciate that, even though only relatively few are true experts in *academic* theology, each person is the expert in his or her own theology at least in the sense that it is almost certain that no one knows more of their *own* theology than they do themselves.

Censuring Ordinary Theology

I begin this chapter with a review of other criticisms that have been made of the phenomenon that I have described as ordinary theology, together with some attempts at responses. First, the basic question: Is ordinary theology truly theological? Some years ago, in an unpublished paper, George Pattison seemed to suggest that it was not. Referring to the use of the word 'theology', he argued:

> there was [once] a fashion amongst theologians for extending the use of the word in such a way as to argue that every Christian, every user of religious language, symbols and practices is in a sense a theologian. I would prefer to go in the opposite direction and distinguish sharply between the way in which 'ordinary' believers use religious language, symbols and practices and what professional theologians do.
>
> (Pattison, 1995)

Pattison seems to be distinguishing here between ordinary *religion* and academic *theology*. However, he accepts that the priority should be given to the religion rather than the theology:

> What the theologian does essentially is to reflect on, to organize and to work towards a coherent interpretation of the language, symbols and practices that constitute the religious world of the believer. The theologian does not have access to any information or experiences that are not available to the believer and the theologian's work is entirely dependent on the primary world of religion itself.
>
> Theology does not generate religious meanings: it sorts, clarifies, organizes and appraises – logically, historically, hermeneutically, etc. – the meanings that are already in circulation in the religious community.
>
> (Pattison, 1995)

Now, I certainly accept the claim about priority. But I would argue that ordinary theology is still theology. If, as I have argued, the difference between ordinary theology and academic theology is only a matter of degree, then we may describe ordinary theology as being closer to religion – learned and embraced religion – and therefore more connected with our spiritual concerns and our life concerns, and with our emotions. For those who wish to *analyse and justify* beliefs, these connections can often appear to be contaminating factors, making theology more difficult to explore. But for those who wish to identify the *point* of belief, their presence is a mark of authenticity. Religion is the point of theology. Ordinary theology is never likely to forget that; it seems to me that academic theology can forget it all too quickly.

In his later writings, Pattison appears much more willing to apply the word theology to those outside the academy. He writes of the 'existential dimension' and 'soteriological motivation' of theology, and complains:

> I have heard a leading teacher of philosophical theology assert that most theology is done in the context of academic teaching. If this were true, I would find it highly depressing. Theology, at least, should have deep roots in human beings' actual attempts at living the religious life, their searching for salvation, their efforts of praise.
>
> (Pattison, 2001: 137)

In another book, Pattison concedes that, since 'practice' involves putting into practice a kind of understanding, it *is* appropriate:

> to speak of 'theology' even at what might be regarded as quite low levels of intellectual culture in the life of the church. . . . The language of even the simplest, most unlettered believer is always going to involve some element of reflection, judgement and interpretation and is, thus far, 'theological'.
>
> (Pattison, 1998: 104–5)

Such reflection may be limited to that which is prescribed by 'the requirements of the practical art of Christian persuasion' (or 'rhetoric'), a factor that distinguishes it from theology in the secular university. Nevertheless, even theology in the church will be open to the 'rigour of disciplined self-reflection', unless that church has withdrawn entirely from the world (Pattison, 1998: 106, 110).

In a recent personal communication (October 2001), Pattison identifies, as the consistent thread in his thinking about theology, a desire 'to resist any attempt to see the theologian as some kind of "expert" in relation to the issues of church life and, indeed, spiritual/religious life outside the church', or as having an 'answer' to the questions of the world or the church. While theologians do have certain kinds of expertise (linguistic, historical, etc.), it is often at a level other than the theological, and there is always a danger of their defining issues and imposing closure. He writes that the theologian must recognize the 'primacy of the existential' and be bound to what is 'outside of and prior to the academic discipline as such' (including reaching into what he refers to, in another unpublished piece, as 'our general human discourse concerning what it is best for us to be and do'). 'If I have changed', Pattison writes, 'it is in the direction of being less hung-up on words!' All of this is well said, and a very welcome attempt to put academic theology in its proper place.

But we should not allow the concept of ordinary theology off the hook too quickly. I recognize that there is a danger in yielding to a sort of democratic soft-heartedness when faced with the theological views of ordinary believers. Has Robert Towler given in to this when he applauds David Martin's use of the term 'subterranean theology' for restoring 'dignity' to those beliefs that exist apart from conventional theological ideas (Towler, n.d.: 5)? Am I in the same danger? Many of my readers, having borne with me thus far, may still be asking themselves, 'Is this stuff worthy of the name theology?' Many will argue that the 'theology' that a study of ordinary believing is likely to reveal will fall foul of a number of criticisms. In particular, the subject will be regarded by many as too superficial, naive, anthropomorphic, incoherent, confused, over-personal, superstitious, uncritical and varied to warrant our attention.

Too Varied?

I shall take the problem of variety first. At first sight, this is a strange criticism. Surely all serious scholars accept the view that the Old and New Testaments each contain a wide spectrum of different theologies (cf. Dunn, 1977: 373–4 and *passim*; Barr, 1999: ch. 4 and *passim*)? Historical theology is also primarily an account of variety, as is any study of the dogmatic pronouncements of the church (cf. Pelikan, 1971–89; Cunliffe-Jones, 1978; Leith, 1971). So the classic Christian tradition is pretty varied but that does not stop it being taken seriously and, indeed, endorsed as a norm against which to test other theology. Therefore variety alone cannot be the problem.

But perhaps variety is allowable in past tradition but not in a theology for today? Yet contemporary theology is confessedly varied. Any entry of sufficient length in a dictionary, encyclopaedia or handbook of modern theology will survey a wide range of different positions. In a series of influential studies, David Kelsey, George Lindbeck and Hans Frei have charted, respectively, the variety of uses of scripture by theologians, the variety of 'theories of Christian doctrine' and the variety of 'types of Christian theology' (Kelsey, 1975; Lindbeck, 1984; Frei, 1992). These scholars find quite as much variety in their surveys of recent work in academic theology as is revealed in many published studies of ordinary theology. In fact, traditional and academic theology sometimes appears *more* diverse than ordinary theology. Studies of ordinary theology do not always overwhelm us with the diversity they have discovered: for example, James Hopewell's typology of the world views of congregations identifies just four categories,[1] and Robert Towler has found five ideal types of Christian religiosity.[2]

---

[1]   The four are 'canonic', 'gnostic', 'charismatic' and 'empiric' (Hopewell, 1987).
[2]   They are 'exemplarism', 'conversionism', 'theism', 'gnosticism' and 'traditionalism', to which he adds, although they are unrepresented in his data, 'mysticism' and 'millenarianism' (Towler, 1984). The study is based on a content analysis of (of all things) over four thousand letters sent to John Robinson after the publication of *Honest to God*.

I do not doubt that qualitative and quantitative research studies in ordinary theology will reveal both an internal variety in each sample studied, and a variation between different individuals, groups, congregations, denominations, genders and cultures that reflects their different backgrounds and contexts, among many other factors. I do not suppose that there is *one* account to be given of ordinary theology. But this is hardly a reason for ignoring the phenomenon. Social scientists deal all the time with variety, and I would argue that it is a central feature of much of the work of the academic theologian as well.

Too Confused, Incoherent and Unsystematic?

What of the related criticism of *incoherence*? Towler himself has criticized other sociologists for the 'vulgar stereotype' that official religion comprises a logically coherent set of beliefs and practices, whereas what he calls common religion (see Chapter 3) is dismissed as an incoherent amalgam. He cites as contrary examples the thematic nature of the oral tradition behind the New Testament and the fragmentary nature of early Christian belief (Towler, 1974: 153).

It must be admitted that a lot of ordinary theology is *confused*, even self-contradictory, although sometimes less so than it first appears. It is not surprising that one finds confusion and unsystematic thinking among a population who have had no careful induction into the 'proper' use of theological terms and methods of theological discussion, and often precious little development of their skills of critical appraisal and argumentation in any field, despite the enthusiasm in some educational contexts for 'discussion'. But, as Wittgenstein argued, sophisticated reasoning itself can lead to a particular sort of confusion that can only be resolved by tracking discourse back to its home in more ordinary language (Wittgenstein, 1968: §§ 38, 123). As he and many others have shown, language is a complex, many-sided thing, which can easily lead us astray. At the root of much of the confusion in everyday speech lies the fact that people do not always recognize or spell out the actual *implications* of their language. Because of this, ordinary God-talk often contains unacknowledged inconsistencies and contradictions.

But such failures are not the sole prerogative of the unscholarly; academics often miss these implications as well. In truth, there is something slightly ironic in directing these charges of intellectual inadequacy against ordinary theology, for academic theologians feed on their colleagues' and rivals' intellectual deficiencies. Is that not why academic theology continues and is it not the main way in which it *develops*? Once again, the difference between the academic and the ordinary reasoner is not a difference in kind, but a difference of degree.

Perhaps the criticism that ordinary theology is not sufficiently *systematic* should be revisited. Martin and Pluck's comments on their interview data from 13- to 24-year-olds made much of the fact that their subjects' belief was 'very amorphous and inchoate indeed' (Martin and Pluck, 1976: 20). The 'incoherence of the phenomenon' of ordinary belief was also noted in the chapter in their report that drew on evidence from the wider literature: 'it does not add up to a consistent theological position' (44). With reference to Berger and Luckmann's account of our human tendency to construct a meaning system, 'meaningful order' or 'nomos' that will help us order the flux of our experience and ward off a sense of meaninglessness, chaos and terror (Berger, 1973: 28–37; cf. Berger and Luckmann, 1967; Luckmann, 1967), Martin and Pluck write:

> First the attribution of meaning is a pragmatic activity: it is only *partly* intellectual and it may well be that articulated intellectual *coherence* is only infrequently a feature of 'nomos' construction. . . . Something approaching an intellectualisation of a meaning system often takes place when ordinary people unexpectedly confront the marginal experience – bereavement, divorce, a child's rebellion or whatever. Even here they may only ponder one or two of the items in their meaning system and leave the rest alone. . . . So long as people have group support, or conventional, shared assumptions to make sense of their world, they seem able to tolerate without noticing them all sorts of hiatuses and contradictions. They behave in fact *as if* life were underpinned by beliefs but they do not work them out in coherent verbalised philosophies. In short, *system*, if by that we mean logically coherent pattern, may be exactly the wrong word to use of the phenomenon: it is more like a patch-work quilt or much-mended net than like a system. And it operates most of the time as an *implicit* attribution of 'sense' to the way things are in the world, and only very seldom orders itself into formal propositions about what things 'mean' and why. Even when something approaching formal propositions has a part to play, it may not take the form of a consistent *single* system of meaning.
>
> (Martin and Pluck, 1976: 47–8)

Academic theology draws on religious traditions and experiences and seeks to make systematic that which is unordered and not yet consciously related together. There is great value in an approach that brings together in this way different beliefs, acknowledges logical relationships and pursues consistency. But there are also some dangers. Fowler's faith development theory provides an interesting account of (the mainly adult) Stages 4 and 5. At Stage 4 (the 'Individuative-Reflective' stage) we think for ourselves, choosing and endorsing our own belief system. This is a stage of autonomy and cognitive responsibility, features that are usually applauded in a person's meaning-making. But it is *also* a stage when we can develop an unrealistic sense of independence and an arid over-intellectualism, which is much more problematic. As a result of these developments, at this stage people may be rather dogmatic and defensive in their thinking, seeking the tidiness of clarity at the expense of complexity and adopting an 'either/or' stance that caricatures the faith of others so as to justify their own truth (Fowler, 1981: ch. 19).

The minority of adults who later move to Stage 5 ('Conjunctive' faith) will be more willing to hold together tensions and acknowledge paradoxes in their world views, without collapsing them (ch. 20). Their 'both/and' faithing will also be confident enough to allow themselves to be more open to, and welcoming of, the outlooks and convictions of others. Cognitively this is a less rigid stage, at which definition and conceptual clarity have become qualified and their roles circumscribed, in an acknowledgement that truth is many-sided, complex and ambiguous and needs insights from other perspectives and other ways of knowing reality (particularly intuition). *Understanding* is now being sought, rather than any reductionist *explanation* that forces facts and interpretations into a pre-existing conceptual framework.

It is significant that Fowler claims that the individual's transition from Stage 4 to Stage 5 recapitulates the development in western thought from Enlightenment ideals of rationality to the less tidy, multi-perspectival (and often feminized) modes of consciousness of today's postmodern world (Fowler, 1992; 1996: 172–6). As is well known, postmodern approaches to meaning give an account of its fragmentary nature that is not dissimilar to Martin and Pluck's analysis, as a form of thinking that resists appeals to any single, unitary world view, especially one that claims to be the only 'rational' option (cf. Lyotard, 1984; Lyon, 1994; Tilley *et al.*, 1995).

Unlike Stage 4, where 'ideological purity and consistency are major concerns, as is defending one's own ideologically held perspective against the threat of relativity', the individual at Stage 5 'does not reject this plurality [of multiple meanings and perspectives] as a source of confusion nor seek to reduce it to a simpler scheme, but will embrace this feature of reality as a possible source of deeper understanding, allowing reality to present different aspects of itself to awareness'. This is not the naive relativism that affirms that one view is as good as another, but a more sophisticated perspectivism that is open to, but not swamped by, the plurality of world views (Moseley, Jarvis and Fowler, 1986: 148, 153).

Both postmodern perspectives and a more normative view of faith development theory reflect the claim that coherence and consistency are not always a good thing. These intellectual virtues can be overdone, especially where a rush to a tidiness of judgement fails to capture the complexity and ambiguity of reality. A maturer mind may be willing to hold together in tension apparently conflicting thoughts. I am not, however, asserting that the rather chaotic disorder of beliefs and argument that we often hear in interviews is a mark of any thought-through postmodern perspective (nor of a Ricoeurian sophisticated, post-critical 'second naïveté'). It is often just unrecognized confusion, rather than a willed embracing of post-Enlightenment plurality (cf. Walker, 1996: 175–6, 180; Astley, 2000b). However, we may still argue that the sophisticated postmodern thinker should be less willing than is his modernist opponent to dismiss ordinary theology on the grounds that it does not hold things together very coherently.

It is not just postmodernists who are sceptical of the value of metaphysical schemes that purport to give an overview of all truth. Many academic students of religion share with ordinary believers a wariness of the move from religious practice and expression to metaphysical conceptualization and speculation. Thus D. Z. Phillips endorses Paul Holmer's endeavour 'to get theology back from its metaphysical to its proper, ordinary use' (Phillips, 1988: 236). Holmer wrote:

> The point is that the language of faith is not an artificial and contrived tongue. . . . *Faith, hope, grace,* and other words become internal to one's life and its vicissitudes. . . . The difficulty with the technical and artificial theologies is that they all sooner or later propose a special vocabulary. The sense that they then have depends on the amount of work that one can get the terms to do. But philosophies, and lately the theologies, can get such special terms to do no more work than their surroundings themselves provide.
>
> (Holmer, 1978: 199)

What really needs to be understood, according to Holmer, is the ragged primary language of faith.

Too Concrete and Anthropomorphic?

Another frequently voiced criticism is that ordinary theology is 'too concrete', frequently in a way that is naively anthropomorphic. Proper theology, by comparison, should be 'abstract' and its language understood as figurative or at least analogical. Naive literalism, and hence naive realism, are after all *naive*.

There is no doubt that ordinary theological discourse is much more likely to employ concrete images, and even concrete ways of thinking, than its academic equivalent. I am not convinced, however, that this is as disabling as many scholars suppose. Even a concrete theology can hold great religious insights. John Hull has argued this point with regard to the theology of young children.

> If the concrete thinking child cannot easily appreciate God as the abstract generalisation 'ground of being', that without which there would not be anything at all, that which absolutely all things have in common and so on, not much is lost; God can still be appreciated as 'the friend of Moses', or as being a Mother or a Father. . . . The concrete thinker arranges things in concrete ways, no matter whether the things are available to the senses or are based upon generalisations. There is no reason why the concrete or the pre-concrete thinking child should not think of God in ways which are perfectly adequate for the needs of that child although they will naturally not include all of the ways in which God can be thought of, nor all of the meanings of the word God. Because children cannot understand everything, we must not conclude that they can understand nothing.
>
> (Hull, 1991: 9)

Hull is writing of children up to the age of about 10. But adults will also think and speak concretely about God. I refer again to Fowler's work, which builds on the Piagetian sequence of cognitive stages (perhaps too uncritically, but that is another matter). Fowler claims that his research interviews have revealed a proportion of adults who remain in the stage of concrete operations that is typical of Stage 2 Mythic-Literal Faith. In the sample of 359 interviewees reported in *Stages of Faith*, six adults over the age of 20 were either still at Stage 2, or in transition from Stage 2 and still showing some Stage 2 characteristics (Fowler, 1981: 318). Such adults may well be incapable of more abstract thought. Undoubtedly, however, many other adults will regularly utilize concrete thinking in their theology, although developmentally they are able to operate at a more sophisticated level. If they choose not to do so in thinking about God, is much lost?

I would argue that it is more important that Christians endorse the personal metaphors, analogies and narratives that are employed by the Christian tradition to render the 'moral' and 'personal' character of God, than that their non-literal or mythic status be appreciated. To affirm that God is human – or even male – is certainly to make a theological mistake; but it is not as big a mistake as denying that God is *in any sense* a 'father' (creator, provider, carer, guide) to us. Many literal entailments of the word 'father' may appropriately be predicated of God. We may cite other examples in theology. To think that Jesus is literally 'seated at God's right hand' is as likely (perhaps more likely) to evoke worship and to fire piety as any more abstract representation of the same theme. If 'God's eye is upon me' then I am open to his judgement and my deeds are not hidden, as would be the case if God could literally see my behaviour. The literal misconstrual of such theological language does matter; but it is not as disabling to theology as the refusal to apply any analogies or metaphors to the deity, particularly when speaking of the *character* of God (God's 'moral attributes'). That way total agnosticism lies.

Furthermore, even those who insist on taking religious figures of speech literally know that the tradition has provided us with a bewildering collection of such images, and many will acknowledge that each image puts a qualifying pressure on every one of the others. So God is 'father', but also 'midwife' and 'mother', and 'rock' and 'light'. There is a mutual qualification built in to the variety of such concrete religious language (cf. Thiselton, 1992: 580–81).

In any case, does the criticism of anthropomorphic, concrete theology not also apply to the founding documents and classical liturgical and hymnic expressions of the Christian tradition? Where ordinary theology utilizes a primary religious language that is replete with metaphorical talk, it reveals how close it lies to the literary forms of scripture, prayer and the poetry of hymns (TeSelle, 1975; Caird, 1980). Academic theology needs to take such imaginative, figurative language much more seriously than it usually does (Avis, 1999). Dare we deny the title of 'theology' to the early traditions of the Pentateuch or the prose story of the Book of Job: narratives in which God walks in the garden in the cool of the day and converses with, even boasts to, his court? Are these stories not 'perfectly adequate' for many of the *religious* and *spiritual* needs of their readers, even *when* they are taken at their anthropomorphic face value?

Theology does not have to be so very sophisticated in order to communicate religious truth. In the radio play *Spoonface Steinberg*, the handicapped, terminally-ill young girl asks about the source of her cancer, directing her enquiries to the cleaning lady, Mrs Spud. She muses, 'I think I might have caught it off God.' Mrs Spud eventually answers, 'If *God's* got cancer we're all in trouble.'[3] Despite the anthropomorphism, does that remark not capture very well one of the central insights and concerns of Christian theodicy? And does it not also illustrate the truth that, very often, 'the image is more capacious than the concept' (Ahern, 1984: 24)?

Ian Ramsey's writings on religious language gave considerable space to analysing 'the less sophisticated and self-conscious language of religious experience, worship and commitment', as expressed in the language of hymns, prayers and scripture (Astley, 1978: 262–3; cf. Ramsey, 1957: ch. III; 1965b: 6–8, 72–3). Although Ramsey described theology as 'a kind of second order language, reflecting on [religion's] first order language' and attempting to systematize its 'riotous mixture of phrases' (Ramsey, 1969: 50; 1957: 156), he recognized that the basic evocative

---

[3]   *Spoonface Steinberg*, written by Lee Hall, first broadcast on Radio 4, 27 January 1997 (London: BBC Radio Collection, © 1997; 2BBC 2058).

and representative functions that he had come to identify in religious language were shared by doctrinal and credal discourse. Although Paul Holmer sees a different relationship (a 'parasitic' one) between academic theology and the language of faith, and therefore makes a different point, it is one that is equally relevant to my thesis. Holmer would have us value most highly the wisdom of faith's 'primitive and plain kind of theology' (Holmer, 1978: 112, cf. ix, 9). It is, he insists, the task of all theology 'to move towards such simplicity'; if the academic theologians cannot do this they are 'actually changing their subject' (16).

Many will find my defence of anthropomorphic language ill-judged, however, arguing that, on the contrary, there is less of it about than I am assuming and that many ordinary theologians are themselves highly critical of it. David Hay and Kate Hunt write that their research (admittedly among non-churchgoers) suggests 'a widespread suspicion about the adequacy of traditional theological language to describe our experience of God', as evidenced in people's unwillingness to say anything more about their spiritual experience other than that there is 'something there', and in their recognition that 'anthropomorphic ideas of an old man in the sky are inadequate' (Hay and Hunt, 2000: 26, 35). Hay and Hunt remark that these concerns are not too remote from the apophatic tradition in theology (cf. also Slee, 2001), although in the case of less articulate respondents they may be more related to a lack of familiarity with the use of metaphor in religion. Ironically, therefore, at the same time as the educated God-talker is disparaging the concrete anthropomorphisms of the less articulate, the less articulate *may* be dismissing the theology of the sophisticated credal formularies and the vicar's sermon (carefully worded so as to avoid controversy) for their crude anthropomorphic accounts of descents, ascents and heavenly seating arrangements. This is an area that is ripe for research by the student of ordinary theology.

From the other side of the divide, the views of many academic theologians carry some quite positive implications about concrete theological language, in that they argue that Christian thinking is *irreducibly* metaphorical and narrative in form (Stiver, 1996: chs 6 and 7). What they mean by this is that metaphor and myth are no mere ornamentations in theology. When they are employed with some sort of control, rather than indiscriminately, they are features of considerable cognitive significance and have the power to represent or describe reality (Ramsey, 1957, 1965b; Soskice, 1985). Like non-linguistic symbols, they may be said to 'structure' our lives and carry the significance of things 'we live by'. And what is more, they are natural to us.[4]

> Metaphorical thinking constitutes the basis of human thought and language. From the time we are infants we construct our world through metaphor; . . . we constantly ask when we do not know how to think about something, 'What is it like?' Far from being an esoteric or

---

4   The indispensable role of metaphor in understanding reality, and its origin in the common sense (*sensus communis*) of a society, were both affirmed in the challenge to narrow Enlightenment rationality presented by the Italian philosopher Giambattista Vico in the early eighteenth century (cf. Louth, 1983: 18–20).

ornamental rhetorical device superimposed *on* ordinary language, metaphor *is* ordinary language. It is the *way* we think . . . we always think by indirection.

(McFague, 1983: 15–16)

Peculiar moments in ordinary lives, saturated by metaphor or personal symbol-making, are the stuff of religion.

The sacred quality of our lives is fabricated from the metaphors we make.

(Sexson, 1982: 3)

Too Biographical?

A person's ordinary theology is often expressed in an autobiographical mode, for reasons that were rehearsed in Chapter 2. We noted Barth's reference to this phenomenon above (p. 77). Some are suspicious of the salience of elements of biography and story within ordinary theology, but it is hard to justify their misgivings.

Some highly successful exercises in theological education encourage the development (usually by a group of learners) of stories, as well as images and metaphors, that illuminate and express the learners' own experience, so as to capture 'the heart of the matter'. 'Entering the space of the image', or 'exploring the world of the metaphor' or story, can enable people to make correlations between their own lives and the theological tradition by generating insights about and perspectives on their experience that bring to mind relevant elements of the tradition (Bairnwick Staff, 1984: IR5–12; Buttitta, 1995; Killen and De Beer, 1995: chs 2 and 3).

What James Fowler has called 'master stories' – stories by which we live – are a significant part of the 'ultimate environment' which represents the content of human faithing. His anecdote of the playwright-lawyer is an arresting one. During a brief acquaintanceship, this man told Fowler the tale by which he lived *his* life: 'We can stir the pot while we are here and try to keep things interesting. Beyond that everything runs down' (Fowler, 1978: 21–3; cf. 1981: 277–9). From a very early age – and, according to Fowler, an early faith stage (Stage 2, appropriately titled the 'Mythic-Literal' stage) – humans are inveterate storytellers. Most of us cannot stop talking about ourselves, about our social, historical and even physical worlds, and about our gods. As Stephen Crites argued, human experience is inherently narrative in form, patterned by time. Our experience 'is itself an incipient story' (Crites, 1971: 297). Therefore 'stories are the most fitting way to tell of human experience because human experience is essentially durational' (Tilley, 1985: 26; cf. de Certeau, 1984: ch. VI).

Christianity comes to us largely in story form and thus appears to some extent isomorphic with our own lives. Both come together in Christian learning, in what Thomas Groome calls 'present dialectical hermeneutics'. The conjunction it generates lies at the heart of both Christian religious education and doing theology (Browning, 1991: 218). It involves a conversation between, on the one hand, our experience of our own engagement in the world, our expression of ourselves and hope for the future (our own 'story' and 'vision') and, on the other, the Christian story and vision (Groome, 1980: chs 9 and 10; 1991: part II). It is in this interpretative dialogue between our own biographies and hopes, and the stories and promises of the tradition, that Christianity truly confronts 'the human limit situation of our lives' (Groome, 1978: 12). Here the past story affirms some parts and condemns other parts of our own stories, and pushes us towards action that is more faithful to it; but it is here also that our own stories affirm, condemn and move us beyond the past story (Groome, 1978: 28).

The power of story in promoting religious learning is undeniable. Stories invite participation and evoke response. They take us up into themselves. 'It is not possible to read or hear a story without it impinging on our own story, or even becoming our story' (Drane, 2000: 140). Drane appeals for support to William J. Bausch, who writes, 'Doctrine is the material of texts; story is the stuff of life. . . . Theology is a secondhand reflection of . . . an event; story is the unspeakable event's first voice' (Bausch, 1984: 28). Symbolic narrative language is primary in religion, and cannot be reduced to conceptual theological reflection. Stories reach places where (academic) theologies do not and cannot reach.

The category of story is regarded as fundamental in much current academic thinking about religion (cf. Hauerwas and Jones, 1989; Thiselton, 1992: 566–75; Stiver, 1996: ch. 7; Sauter and Barton, 2000). In particular, theologians have argued that the identity of Jesus and of God are given in the biblical and mythological narratives in an irreducible way (cf. Frei, 1975; Kelsey, 1975: 48–9; Sykes, 1979; Astley, 1981). Although there is a danger here of seeing theological meaning solely as a function of the text itself, it is possible to emphasize the role of the narrative and yet leave room for a 'reader response' within the interstices of the text that is guided but not fully determined by the text (cf. Thiselton, 1992: ch. XIV). Here meaning arises in the interaction between text and reader in a way that provides an illuminating account of what is going on when ordinary theologians respond to story.

Among those for whom narrative theology is central, some also emphasize that human biography is often shaped by religious convictions. For them, 'theology must be at least biography' (McClendon, 1974: 37). The lives that James McClendon explores, as serving as 'data for the Christian thinker', are 'singular or striking' ones. But theological convictions may be apparent in and derivable from more ordinary life stories too. For McClendon and Smith, such convictions are persistent beliefs which are always of signal importance to the person who holds them. 'Convictions are the beliefs which make people what they are. They must therefore be taken very seriously by those who have them. This means that to take a person seriously we must take that person's convictions seriously, even if we do not ourselves share them' (McClendon and Smith, 1975: 8, cf. 91). To lack all such persistent and central beliefs, these authors argue, is to lack character, 'not just laudable or virtuous character, but any character at all' (111).

Whatever else ordinary theologians do not possess, they each have a biography and they all have convictions. As in the case of everyone else – even scholars – their own life story is of far greater personal significance to them than that of any other person. They would not be sane human beings if this were not so. According to one understanding of theology, therefore, ordinary believers suffer no disadvantage when reading the Christian narratives, for Christian identity, theology and Christology are not only *best* expressed in story, but also most effectively encountered and appropriated when that story (or, rather, those stories) is heard from within the story of a 'lived life'. Ordinary theologians are the ones who are *least* likely to forget and ignore their own lives as they do their own theology. While our concerns remain at the descriptive rather than the normative level (see later), ordinary biographies may be said to provide us with highly significant data. For most ordinary theologians, theology is to be found within life, rather than books.

> 'Being religious' or 'reflecting theologically' in the parabolic mode means reading the ordinary events of one's life and times as a parable, that is, seeing those events within a surprising and new context, the context provided by the gracious God. It means starting with where one is and what one has at hand to move beyond that place.
>
> (TeSelle, 1975: 179)

Too Personal, Subjective and Relative?

This brings us back to the personal and to the criticism that is routinely voiced that ordinary theology is 'too personal'. What might this mean and why should it be a problem?

The personal and 'subjective' tone of much ordinary theology indicates that people are here *doing* theology first-hand, thinking through and thinking with their own beliefs, expressing their own feelings and reflections in their own language. Far too much academic theology, by contrast, remains in a second-hand mode: thinking and writing *about* Paul or Schleiermacher, rather than being some sort of Paul or Schleiermacher oneself.[5] 'Personal' is often only intended as a pejorative epithet when it is applied to someone else. But it ill behoves the Christian scholar to be snooty or high-brow about other people's faith. As Phillips puts it, we must find room for 'the ugly, the banal and the vulgar for these, too, may be forms of religious belief' (Phillips, 1993: 250). He recounts a telling incident:

> I recall an elderly widow asking me why God had called her two sons home before her. She proceeded to provide her own answer. She said that if she went into a garden to pick flowers, she would not choose weeds, but the best blooms. In taking her sons to himself, God had picked the best blooms. Does this picture imply that the longer one lives, the less one counts in the eyes of God? Obviously not. She does not push the picture in that direction. She is saluting her sons, that is all. Her practice is decisive. It need not be confused or superstitious. On the other hand, I do not find the picture very helpful. It sustained her, but it would not sustain me. Here, she and I have to speak for ourselves.
>
> (Phillips, 1993: 248)

---

[5]   While the student of philosophy is mainly engaged in philosophizing, 'it is not true in the same way that the theologian spends much of his time theologising' – as opposed to being engaged in literary or historical criticism (Mitchell, 1991: 8).

Reactions to religious beliefs '*must* be personal', Phillips insists. Faith is a matter of personal reaction, in which we all speak for ourselves. This is not a cause for regret or an occasion for contemptuous dismissal. It is, rather, the mark of authentic God-talk.

As I have argued in Chapters 2 and 3, there is an inevitably subjective, personal dimension to our beliefs and values, in so far as these are salvific for us. This is one aspect of the insight that John Locke offers: 'I cannot be saved by a Religion that I distrust, and by a Worship that I abhor.' We may express this truth by saying that a person's theology must be *at least subjective*. It is at this point that we are confronted by a form of relativism that we may allow, indeed welcome, for in this personal dimension we encounter again that species of truth that is inevitably and unavoidably relative to the person who holds it. This is spiritual truth, faith truth or ordinary theology truth; it is salvific truth (cf. Hodgson, 1999: 99, 103). What salvation is for you is not necessarily what it is for me. The same objective God, engaged in the same objective activity, may save us both; but I am saved in *my* context from *my* stains and chains. Whatever that salvation is, I must recognize that *God* did it '*my* way'. And what is true of our salvation is also true of what is spiritually strengthening and illuminating for us. People are just different.

To take but one (personal!) example: humour is a very important part of my life and an important part of my spirituality and faith. I therefore feel a kinship with such sweeping theologies as those articulated by John Irving's character Garp, who claimed that 'laughter is my religion', and by the caricaturist Ralph Sallon, who contended that 'humour is what saves us all'. What I perceive as the wit and sometimes wicked humour of Jesus serves me as a very powerful medicine. But our appreciation, even our recognition, of humour is a very personal thing. I do not just mean that people vary in the sense of humour they have; I mean that their sense of humour has a different significance for different people. I have and I need a theological sense of humour; my theology must be in some way a humorous theology.[6] But I have learned to my cost that many other people do not need this and many more do not want it, or not in the form that works for me. In a real sense, therefore, my religion and my theology will not do for them. Different people respond to different things. At this level, at all events, a 'hundred flowers' must blossom, and many more theologies.

'It sustained her, but it would not sustain me', Phillips writes. 'She and I have to speak for ourselves.' I do not see how a person's theology can avoid being personal in this way. In theology, as in many other areas of life, one size simply will not 'fit all' – nor one style, colour or type of material. The manufacturer, retailer and advertiser will always try to persuade us that their single product will do; but they are not as concerned with our (subjective, personal) comfort, happiness or well-being as we are, and we should not be as concerned with their (objective, impersonal) sales figures, profit margins and market penetration data as they are. In religion we are allowed to be rather suspicious customers; and our suspicion should particularly be aroused when someone tells us that our theology is 'too personal'.

---

[6]   On the theology of humour, see Evans, 1979: 115–16; Sutherland, 1986a; also Kuschel, 1994.

I must admit, however, that there is a rather different version of the 'too personal' criticism that does not originate in academe but in a more ordinary locale. In England anyway, front doors are regularly shut on the evangelist or clerical visitor with the excuse that religion is 'a private and personal matter', or words to that effect. Much has been written on the so-called 'privatization of religion' that is now endemic in western culture. But there also exists a peculiarly English version of the disease, which has a longer history.

The eighteenth-century essayist Joseph Addison remarked that there is in England 'a particular bashfulness in everything that regards religion'. There still is. Roger Scruton, who quotes this passage from a 1712 edition of the *Spectator*, puts this embarrassment down to the English understanding that the veneer of religion was 'a human invention' and 'a conscious artefact', which 'like good manners . . . did not bear too close an interrogation' (Scruton, 2000: 94). But there are other factors at work here. One of them might be expressed by saying that for many people in our culture religion 'works' at the level of a set of commitments and assumptions which, like all moral and spiritual values, are difficult to justify and therefore inherently *fragile*, a situation that Scruton elsewhere describes with some brilliance (cf. Scruton, 1998: 15–16, 30–31, 38–9, 84, 115). We hold our values as 'givens' or not at all. We may recall that Hans Mol defined religion as 'the sacralization of identity', understanding sacralization as a process involving a system of symbols coming to acquire a 'taken-for-granted, stable, eternal, quality' (Mol, 1976: 1, 5). People sense instinctively that the values they hold must have this quality of 'givenness', but we sense a problem: contemporary culture no longer sustains or protects them as it did. Everything is now open to criticism and up for sale to the highest bidder, and we are complicit in this commodification of the holy. We have, in the colloquial phrase, 'lost the plot'. And some of us, conscious of what we have lost, are ashamed.

The decline in conventional churchgoing suggests that unless religious evaluations can be endorsed by us as 'givens', and endorsed with a degree of passion, they will rapidly lose their significance as social conditions change. Ordinary theology itself might well then appear 'too personal' to those who do not really share much affective commitment to its value system. But where there is no passion there is no true commitment, and therefore no community of commitment, and thus no real community at all. Closing the door on someone else's religion is one way of hiding from the embarrassment of the personal commitment that I do not share, but which I half acknowledge would alone support a value system worthy of the name – and therefore a real identity.

Perhaps some such account might explain the resistance of many people to talk about their lack of belief, and the corresponding eagerness of many believers to reveal their ordinary theology. For the first group it is 'too personal' to talk about, because they have a sense of their own lack or loss of the personal passion that they instinctively feel could give them an identity and a value world to embrace. In the case of the second group, however, their theology is too personal *not* to talk about, because in talking about it *they are* talking about their identity, their value world and themselves. No 'impersonal theology' could possibly adequately fulfil the needs of either group.

Too Superstitious?

Superstition has been defined as 'the age-old handy term for flawed, futile or false religion – as judged by the defining centers of normative religion' (Braun, 2000: 8). Phillips raised this issue in the passage quoted above (p. 134). In a number of his writings, he has worked energetically to distinguish between superstition and true religion, claiming that 'the distinction between religious belief and superstition is extremely important' (Phillips, 1993: 73). His rejection of traditional understandings of 'answers to prayer' illustrates his view. Where prayer is treated as a way of getting things done by influencing God, he calls it superstitious; construed in this way it does not reveal a dependence on God, only a dependence on the prayer (Phillips, 1965: 115–24; cf. 1970b: 127–30). Superstitious prayer involves 'trust in non-existent, quasi-causal connections'. In such a case, the devotional act itself is seen as a means to an end and its religious character is 'reducible to its efficacy *as one way among others* of securing certain ends' (1993: 74). By contrast:

> The prayer of petition is best understood, not as an attempt at influencing the way things go, but as an expression of, and a request for, devotion to God through the way things go. . . . When deep religious believers pray *for* something, they are not so much asking God to bring this about, but in a way telling Him of the strength of their desires. They realize that things may not go as they wish, but they are asking to be able to go on living whatever happens.
>
> (Phillips, 1965: 120–21)

Phillips follows Wittgenstein in taking to task those anthropologists who viewed the beliefs and rituals of primal peoples as incorporating elements of 'magic' that should be understood in quasi-empirical, manipulative and pragmatic terms. On their interpretation, a rain dance is to be thought of as an impersonal, causal inducement of rain and is therefore to be understood as scientifically erroneous (Phillips, 1976: chs 3 and 7). Dismissing the views presented in Sir James George Frazer's *The Golden Bough*, to the effect that both magic and religion seek to provide 'an explanation of nature' and have been 'displaced by science' because they have failed in this role (Frazer, 1922: 712), Wittgenstein rejects any functional and 'primitive science' account of magic and religion. He treats both phenomena as essentially symbolic, rather than explanatory. And in an insight that is more sensitive than that of some pastors, he writes that perhaps 'someone shattered from love will be little helped by an explanatory hypothesis – it will not calm him' (cited in Barrett, 1991: 213). Rituals have effects on those who perform them; they do not aim beyond this, or at all events they do not do so by aiming at any scientific, causal effects. Where superstition is to be distinguished from religion it is on these grounds: that one is trust and the other 'results from fear and is a sort of false science' (Wittgenstein, 1980: 72).

Yet scholars caution us against interpreting Wittgenstein as simply advocating an expressive view of ritual, resulting from the need to express emotion. The important feature to grasp is Wittgenstein's rejection of Frazer's view that magic and ritual are both *theories*. 'No theorising is necessary before we tear to pieces pictures of those we hate, . . . ritual actions . . . are not the products of thought but . . . spring spontaneously from human beings' (Clack, 1999: 65). The essence of Wittgenstein's purpose, then, is to put a full stop to the urge for any *explanation* of ritual. 'A man does not smash the portrait of his beloved *in order* to express his anger. This is the form his anger takes' (Phillips, 1993: 94, cf. ch. 7; see also 1988: ch. 22).

All of which suggests that we should not be too quick to spot – and then to condemn – superstition in ordinary theological discourse. Having said that, some empirical studies have claimed a positive correlation between holding religious beliefs and holding superstitious beliefs, at least under certain circumstances. However, their data also show that regular churchgoers are less superstitious than other believers, suggesting that 'the church exercises a genuinely counter-superstitious influence among its adherents. . . . reinforcing the distinction between beliefs which are theologically acceptable, and those which are not' (Abercrombie *et al.*, 1970: 112–14, cf. 124).[7] Yet there is no doubt that superstitious beliefs, which many would describe as 'unreasoning', 'irrational', 'unjustified' or at least 'misdirected', are fairly well represented in the general populations of western nations. For example, over a quarter of the British population (between 26 per cent and 37 per cent) claims to 'believe in' astrology (Gill, 1999: 70, cf. 80; Krarup, n.d.: 38–9). Even 'lucky charms' attract the support of some 18 per cent of the population (Gill, 1999: 70). But these data again show that lower levels of such beliefs are associated with more regular churchgoing (42, cf. 135).

Some scholars explain superstitious beliefs as the result of mistaken empirical learning or a reversion to infantile beliefs (cf. the accounts in Jahoda, 1969: ch. 1, 102–8), and others either as ways of coming to terms with the harshness and injustice of the world, or as representing metaphysical 'gods of the gaps' of scientific and other explanations – explanations that are intended to help us to predict and 'control' events and thus allay anxiety (Abercrombie *et al.*, 1970: 122–3). Richard Hoggart's non-cognitive analysis of such beliefs in terms of expressions of social solidarity should also be noted. He writes that while these 'largely unexamined and orally transmitted tags' are elevated into the status of maxims, they are often little more than an idiom of speech (Hoggart, 1958: 103, cf. 27–33). Where such beliefs appear within ordinary theological discourse we may have to examine them quite closely to discover exactly how important they are as a part of that theology.

Too Uncritical?

Christian theology has been described as 'faith asking questions' and the work of theology as 'a continuing search for the fullness of the truth of God made known in Jesus Christ'. As an enquiry, it never merely repeats traditional doctrines but 'continually calls in question unexamined assumptions about God, ourselves and our world' (Migliore, 1991: 1–2). It is in this sense that it may be described as 'thoughtful faith' (6). This sort of questioning is not something that ordinary

---

[7]   While these researchers found a significant positive association between frequent private prayer and superstitious belief, this was reversed for regular churchgoers (Abercrombie *et al.*, 1970: 117).

believers can exempt themselves from. Karl Barth writes, 'no one is excused the task of asking questions or the more difficult one of providing and assessing answers' (Barth, 1961: 498).

There is a species of Christian minister who sees his ministry (and it usually is a he) as a response to Milton's challenge that 'the hungry sheep look up, and are not fed', while complaining throughout that it appears to him rather that the sheep just look fed up and fail to realize they are hungry. He is the type of clergyman most likely to be patronizing about his congregation's ability and readiness *to think*. I have often listened patiently to his complaints. But on those occasions when I have attempted to pursue the matter further, I have rarely been impressed by his depth of knowledge of his congregation – or of his other parishioners.

It is true that few people are trained to argue, analyse and criticize in the way that academics prefer. But 'thinking can never be the monopoly of any self-defining cadre' (Pattison, 1998: 116). I accept that religious beliefs should not be called 'theology' unless they are to some extent articulated and reflected upon. But most believers engage in some measure of articulation and reflection; they *do* think about and 'think through' their faith, in their own way. And most people do see the problems, especially the 'intellectual' problems, in their faith; and they also care about having consistent beliefs and being able to justify them to themselves and others. Further, people can and do work out 'theological solutions' for themselves. Even children do this. Unlike official religion and theology, with their organizational and institutional supports, if ordinary theology survives it is for the same reason that Towler cites for the survival of common religion: 'because it remains credible' (Towler, 1974: 149).

Moreover, the intellectual challenges that people face up to are real ones: questions about the nature of God ('Why can't God be seen?'), about the activity of God ('Why doesn't God do something?'), and about the nature of the world and of life ('Why do we suffer so?'). These are the same 'intellectual challenges' to faith that most 7-year-olds come up with. Everyone has thought of them, even if they have later been deliberately suppressed because the 'answers' do not come easily, or in fear that convincing answers are not to be had. After all, these are very difficult questions. And academic theology is not as impressively superior as it sometimes thinks it is in coming up with acceptable responses, when compared with the more ordinary sort of God-talk.

Academic theology also has its own versions of avoiding the questions. John Hull has reviewed a number of ploys that adult Christians use to reduce the discomfort of religious learning that involves facing up to the cognitive challenges of religious belief. He includes among them the psychological defence of *objectifying* Christian belief, which ensures that it keeps its distance even as it is approached. 'There will be a readiness to take notes on the historical and exegetical aspects of biblical texts', he writes, but not to discuss personal reactions to a passage or problem in question (Hull, 1985: 141). The academic version of this avoidance technique is to work on some more peripheral issue, rather than the serious critical, intellectual and spiritual demands and problems that Christianity poses: perhaps a piece of historical scholarship, or a scholarly exegesis of a little-known and long-dead thinker. Don

Cupitt wryly comments that the academic remains cool and works 'at one remove' from the real subject, for 'we are too sophisticated now to be able to cope with big, simple questions' about the human condition (Cupitt, 2000b: 47–8). The 'big, simple' and more obvious issues and problems of human life, and of religious belief too, are those that are more closely related to a person's spirituality and faith than is such recondite displacement activity.

Critical theology for all? But I am being too uncharitable and (worse) unfair to my friends in the groves of the theological academy. As the differences between the two types of theology are mainly differences of degree rather than of kind, and if (as I have also allowed) many academic theologians share the positive characteristics that mark out the ordinary theologian, it is not surprising that some professional theologians will be found who speak quite highly of ordinary theology's self-aware, and even of its self-critical, features. In what follows I shall survey a number of supporters of this view.

Edward Farley's position has already been explored in Chapter 3. His account stresses that 'existence in the world before God requires a wisdom that is not merely spontaneous but self-consciously interpretive' (Farley, 1988: 90). This (ordinary) theology is what Farley calls 'reflective wisdom'; he does not deny this reflective status to the theology of ordinary believers. David Kelsey is more explicit about its critical dimension. His book *To Understand God Truly* has a chapter on Christian congregations, which the author sees as the concrete embodiment of 'the Christian thing', the place where it may be concretely encountered. By way of introduction to this theme, Kelsey rehearses some objections to it, including the claim that congregations are 'faithless'. In a section entitled 'self-critical congregations', he argues that any group that never engaged in critical reflection on its own faithfulness to the Christian norm (of meeting and worshipping 'in Jesus' name') would not understand what this involves, nor therefore what is involved in being a Christian congregation (Kelsey, 1992: 139–40). For Kelsey, congregations are 'constituted by a practice that is inherently *self-critical*' (187). Faithfulness to Jesus' name involves faithfulness to Jesus and faithfulness to the truth. Kelsey argues that 'the practice of worship of God inherently requires critical examination of whether and why we should engage ourselves in the Christian thing at all' (141), and therefore in questions about its truth. Congregations are therefore committed *as Christian congregations* to a continuing self-critique in the light of Christian and other norms (cf. 206–7).

Richard Osmer argues something similar. He declares himself unhappy with Lindbeck's analogy between theology and grammar on the grounds that, although it works for systematic theology, it does not fit historical or practical theology. In particular, practical theology needs a more hermeneutical account in which the 'rules' are starting points for reflection, but are themselves 'confirmed or disconfirmed as the situation unfolds'.[8] All Christians, Osmer writes, are engaged in this sort of

---

[8]   Cf. above, pp. 116–17. Treating doctrines as rules shows us that we do not *own* theological language (Lash, 1986: 264). We do, however, need to *endorse* it and Osmer's criticism may usefully be fed into a discussion of the normative nature of theology (cf. below, pp. 154–62).

theological reflection 'as they attempt to interpret their present existence in relation to God'. Christians are never totally non-reflective; for while they do not strive for 'the logical coherence of a systematic treatise', their reflection does attempt a deeper understanding of their situation. In identifying relevant theological and ethical issues within these situations, it both considers how to act and reflects on the consequences of such action (Osmer, 1990b: 226). Hans Frei might also be interpreted as accepting that ordinary Christians exercise a critical function, in his account of the Christian community's engagement in a normative, critical 'second-order appraisal of its own language and actions' using norms that are internal to the community and given in its beliefs and practices (Frei, 1992: 2).

Among the questions that even ordinary theology must face, then, are questions about what is truly Christian, and therefore about how far and in what sense ordinary theology can itself be called Christian; along with the more general sort of 'critical questioning' about the coherence of its concepts, the validity of its arguments and the role of supporting evidence.

For Dietrich Ritschl, as for these other scholars, theology has an essentially critical function that is shared by all believers. In Ritschl's view, however, theology is *limited* to this function. He reserves the term for that (small) part of the thought and language of believers that regulates, examines and stimulates that thought and language, along with their actions. It thus has a regulative function, and constitutes the grammar or logic of the responsible thought of faith. In fact, Ritschl distinguishes two sense of theology (cf. Kelsey, 1983: 363). In what he calls the 'broad sense', theology is rational discourse about matters of faith generally or explanations of material from the biblical tradition. (It is this broader understanding that has been largely assumed in this book, a sense that includes the narrower one.) In his 'narrow sense', however, theology is reflection that tests the function of 'implicit axioms' that regulate the thought, speech and action of believers, in a critical examination of their statements. Examples of such regulative statements include, 'Jesus Christ shows himself both as Lord and as Servant' and 'God wills good even for evil people' (Ritschl, 1984: 85; cf. Williams, 2000b: 19–20).

But even in the narrow sense, Ritschl claims, theology 'is in no way limited to professional academics'. As 'oral theology', it takes place 'in the conversations and the heads of any of those who examine ideas and actions, statements and prayers from the story of Jesus and Christians and from the present in terms of their own statements and actions' (Ritschl, 1984: 92). In a quite direct and straightforward sense, this involves the adoption and application of regulative statements. It also always involves a testing that aims at clarification and coherence, and raises the question of the degree to which statements may deviate from biblical and traditional ways of talking. By applying the regulative statements, ordinary believers as well as scholars test the comprehensibility, coherence and permissibility of their discourse. It is for these reasons that Ritschl can insist, 'All believers can do theology and in principle also teach it' (99).

Charles M. Wood is equally generous about the place of theological thinking in the life of the ordinary believer. Wood lays a greater stress than Farley appears to do on critical reflection, arguing that *theological* education 'is not to form Christians, but to form the habit of critical reflection on one's formation . . . to equip one for theological reflection on the Christian tradition' (Wood, 1996a: 310). As we saw in Chapter 2, Wood argues that an aptitude for theological judgement is something that must be formed in *oneself*. Theology cannot just be a second-hand thing; doctrines such as the Trinity and the Incarnation must somehow function as 'working judgements in one's thought and conduct' (Wood, 1996b: 345). Wood describes this view of theology as 'a critical enquiry into the validity of Christian witness', 'a reflective moment within the Christian life, when that life is examined and when judgements are reached bearing on its past and future' (1996b: 352; 1985: 21, 24). It is a critical enquiry that asks three questions: whether a belief is truly Christian, whether it is true and valid, and whether it is fitting to its context. This enquiry is indispensable for church leadership, Wood insists, but he also affirms that it is a task that is performed – albeit at a different level – by many ordinary believers as well. The thinking-for-themselves that this involves is surely necessarily more significant than any other person's (or any community or tradition's) theological self-reflection.

Wood agrees with Farley that theology may be defined as a *habitus*. He understands this, however, not as a mode of consciousness but as a disposition for *activity* – 'the activity constituted by a type of inquiry, which engages the whole person as an agent, a doer' (Kelsey, 1993: 201). Theology in the primary sense is theological enquiry, and the *habitus* for theology is 'the capacity and disposition to engage in theological enquiry' (Wood, 1985: 34). This is not only defined in terms of, but acquired through our participation in, theological activity. Wood writes:

> Some aptitude for Christian theology is requisite to Christian life itself. This does not mean that every Christian must be a theological scholar, not even that she or he must be cognisant of what theological scholars are up to. It only means that every Christian, under normal circumstances, inevitably is called upon to make judgements as to what constitutes valid Christian witness.
>
> (Wood, 1996a: 307)

If these scholars are correct in their portrayal of ordinary Christians and ordinary congregations, ordinary members of the church are also committed to a normative self-criticism of their faith, which in this case includes a critical dialogue with Christian sources and some reflection on practical situations and their own actions within them.

Actually it would be strange if ordinary theologians were *not* both reflective and critical. All human beings are concerned about the plausibility or 'believability' of their beliefs. Our beliefs need to be believable to us. A critical ('judging', 'assessing', 'evaluating') element is crucial if people are to *own* their faith. For most people, particularly in our culture, this will involve some reflective, rational examination of their religious beliefs. It will not be an evaluation 'at arm's length', as the academy expects, but at least ordinary theologians will sometimes get up off their knees to do it; the passionate embrace that clasps religion to their hearts will usually allow for some such element of evaluative self-criticism (cf. pp. 74–6). Despite all I have said elsewhere about the importance of formation in religion, and despite my insistence on recognizing the *a*rational dynamics that support it (Astley, 1994b), I gladly acknowledge that we must be very chary of any formal Christian education procedure that does not also normally induct adults into the attitudes, skills and dispositions of critical reflection. I am also suspicious of any Christian community that seeks to squash the reflective, questioning element in its faith. For most adults anyway, if not perhaps for all, formation in the faith must go along with 'Christian criticism'.

I would make a similar point about spirituality. Spirituality is the engine that drives not only religion and morality, but all fulfilled living. I continue to insist that, although they serve to express, articulate and sometimes to evoke spirituality, religious beliefs and practices are secondary. They are not the most important elements of the religious life or outcomes of religious formation. Nevertheless, I again allow the need for some critical element, in this case for a *critical spirituality*. Here the relationship between beliefs and spirituality is important. While acknowledging the subordinate status of beliefs, we should also recognize a symbiotic relationship between beliefs and spirituality, which includes a feedback loop that gives our beliefs an influence on our spirituality. That relationship is not then to be interpreted as all one way, as if beliefs were epiphenomena with no control, power or significance of their own. If our beliefs are malformed or diseased, the spirituality that they connect with is also very likely to go into decline. And it is the belief dimension of faith that is particularly subject to our critical reflection and evaluation. Thus religious people should, and mostly they do, think for themselves for spiritual reasons; adults must engage in critical reflection if they are to hold adult beliefs that can express and inform an adult spirituality. Hence, ordinary believers must also engage in a theology that involves, in Barth's phrase, 'taking rational trouble' over the mystery of God.

On critical breadth, embodiment and theological reflection All of this points to elements within ordinary theology concerned with questions of Christian normativity, and elements concerned with questions of truth and with other aspects of 'appropriateness' (cf. Wood, 1985: ch. III). These critical dimensions should not, however, be understood too narrowly. Being critical is a character trait that incorporates and promotes a range of virtues and attitudes (Astley, 1994b: 86). Wood includes within theological judgement such affects and affect-driven activities as 'imaginative grasp', 'attention', 'sensitivity' to context and situation, and 'a readiness to deal with the unforeseen' (Wood, 1996b: 350, 355). This more inclusive understanding of 'criticism' and 'judgement' is not as intellectually elitist as its usual construal.

It has been said that systematic theology requires, in addition to the tools of the philosopher, 'qualities of imagination and judgement in spiritual matters' (Mitchell, 1991: 19). If this is the case, then many 'ordinary people' may fulfil this part of the job description very well, and often much better than the academics. Those with spiritual wisdom and imagination, and even perhaps what psychologists have described as 'interpersonal', 'intrapersonal' or 'emotional intelligence' (Gardner, 1993: ch. 10; Goleman, 1995), may offer reflections and critiques that are as valuable within theology as is hard-headed, critical cognitive reflection.

A reflective, critical response need not be presented in the usual coin of intellectual discourse, either. It has been well said that 'perhaps the keenest response to an image . . . is to pose a counter-image' and that 'poets also respond to poets' (Pattison, 1998: 133–4). Just as the expression of our beliefs and believing is not limited to prose (theology), but can take place through other media – art, dance, music, poetry and especially lives – so the critical and evaluative response to belief can take a variety of forms.

I have more than once defined theology in terms that include some element and some degree of *reflection*. I have argued that ordinary believers are certainly involved in what has variously been called 'doing theology', 'thinking theologically', 'theological thinking' or 'theological reflection'. Although the verb 'to reflect' can mean either 'to meditate on' or 'to think about', academic theologians have tended to settle for its more cognitive connotation – hence 'reflective theology seeks to understand, clarify and explain the faith' (McGrath, 1993). But theological reflection need not and should not be understood solely in intellectual terms.

The phrase 'theological reflection' has become popular in English-speaking adult Christian education circles to designate 'a process of relating experience of the contemporary world and the Christian heritage of faith so as to discover God's presence and action in a way that leads to new or renewed attitudes and action' (Durston, 1989: 35). Richard Osmer defines his notion of 'practical theological reflection' in a parallel way, as 'an interpretive process which takes place in the midst of unfolding situations and seeks to understand and shape those situations according to the discernment of God's will' (Osmer, 1990b: 227).

This process has been spelled out many times as a formal exercise of theological education (see Groome, 1980: part IV; 1991: part II; Green, 1990; Killen and De Beer, 1995; Whitehead and Whitehead, 1995). But it is also a process that is engaged in without the intentional facilitation of any educator. In both cases, certain elements are integral to it. As we have seen, these include an interpretative, dialogic, 'conversational' relationship of correlation or 'resonance' between, on the one hand, contemporary experience and praxis (reflective action) and, on the other, the Christian heritage of faith (which is more than, but includes, the Christian 'theology' of the tradition). This process, sometimes described as 'faith translation' (Wingeier, 1994), has as its intended goal both new insight and action guided towards 'social and individual transformation' (Browning, 1991: 36; cf. Groome, 1991: ch. 10). The conversation that is engaged here is essentially *critical* and, in many versions, the criticism is mutual, cutting both ways so that the tradition is critiqued by our contemporary experience as well as vice versa, and there is mutual correction and mutual enrichment of the conversational partners (cf. Tracy, 1975: ch. 3; 1981: 453; 1983: 76; Browning, 1991: 44–7, 220–21).

My point here is that Christian educationalists have usually recognized that this reflective process needs not only a cognitive skill or dispositions, but also certain imaginative skills and affective dispositions (Groome, 1980: 186–8; Green, 1990: 80–83, 91–6). As with the conversation on which it is modelled, there is more going on in this process than can be mapped on to our cognitive faculties alone. This feature, together with the 'practical goal' of theological reflection, means that it is 'ultimately intended for every believer; it is not a theological speciality reserved only for experts' (Kinast, 2000: 64).

However, despite its importance in theology and its relevance to ordinary faith, the critical approach must not bulk too large in the religious life. Nor should academic theology, which by definition is an activity of people with strong intellectual interests and cognitive skills, succeed in defining criticism – or religion – solely in terms of argumentation and knowledge claims. Most discussions about theology pay little more than lip-service to the more affective, volitional and imaginative aspects of being in faith. It is as tragic as it is tempting to forget that 'receiving the gospel is not a matter of having brains but of free personal response where imagination, thought and emotion are integrated' (Tinsley, 1996: 94). Ordinary theologians can help to remind us of this truth.

Others have criticized academic theology for encouraging a view of theology, and indeed of Christianity, 'as a purely intellectual . . . pursuit', undertaken by disembodied minds whose thoughts were little affected by their social, political and cultural (and, I would add, psychological and educational) contexts. In voicing this criticism, Linda Woodhead argues for 'a recognition of the fuller, embodied reality of Christianity' (Woodhead, 1997: 11–12). Whatever else we may find fault with in ordinary theological thinking, at least it does not present itself as a purely intellectual pursuit *or* a species of disembodied Christianity. As I argued in Chapters 1 and 2, the learning context of religion is very much to the fore in ordinary theology and is a feature about which ordinary theologians often explicitly comment. Further, the personal nature of ordinary theology means that ordinary theologians are forced to recognize the significance of their own particular contexts, backgrounds and concerns. The response, 'I think like this because of . . .' is commonly heard in interview studies, as people acknowledge and confess the formative elements, not just of their religious believing, but particularly of the affective and praxis (or 'lifestyle') dimension of their Christianity. Non-academics on the whole do not need to be told that they are not disembodied minds, and are often genuinely puzzled when they meet intellectuals who seem blind to the significance of their own (that is, the academics') embodiment, contextuality or feelings. Ordinary theology is an expression of a holistic, embodied faith.

Justifying the Study of Ordinary Theology Pragmatically

I shall conclude this book with a defence of ordinary theology at a rather different level. Instead of responding to particular criticisms of the 'untheological' nature of ordinary theology, I will attempt to answer the more general query as to why anyone should concern themselves so far as *to study* it. There is surely enough for theologians and social scientists to do in their different scholarly and academic territories, without wasting time with ordinary theology. Why bother with it? There are, I think, two main sets of justifications for engaging in the study of ordinary theology. In this first section I shall propose an essentially pragmatic justification for researching ordinary theology.

Pastoral and Communicative Ministries

Here I will brook no opposition; I feel utterly sure of my ground. In order to preach to you I must not only know something about the gospel, I must also know something about you. This principle applies quite generally.

Educational theory and practice, particularly in the field of adult education, encourage us to lay great store on the present beliefs, attitudes, values and dispositions of the learners. Educators need to know, it is said, 'where people are' and 'where they are coming from'. These metaphors of location are ways of expressing our need to know *who* these learners are. Those engaged in Christian religious or theological education need to know about the religious beliefs and thoughts of their learners, and the processes of their religious believing and thinking. Pastoral theology would make the same point with regard to those who receive the church's care and helping ministry.

The church therefore needs to study ordinary theology so that it may properly exercise its ministry of pastoral care, worship, Christian education, apologetics, preaching and evangelism, and indeed every other form of Christian conversation, leadership, concern and relationship (cf., for example, van der Ven, 1993: 158, 160–61). And the church needs to know *far more* than on the whole it currently does about the beliefs of those adults to whom it ministers.

I remain puzzled that this fact is not universally recognized as blindingly obvious. I have taught in theological colleges and on theological courses now, both regularly and occasionally, for nearly thirty years. This makes me bold enough to express publicly what I first strongly felt privately when I went through ministerial training myself. What clergy really most need, and what they usually most lack, is a large dose of careful, reflective experience of *people*, and of a wide variety of people. Along with academic theological content, insights from other disciplines, and training in skills of care, communication and leadership, they need to *meet* people in their own context and to *listen* to them. This sort of experience should not and cannot be left until after ordination because by then the barriers will have come down on both sides. While there is still hope, then, while they are still regarded as human and have a chance of regarding themselves as human – and perhaps while they are not so far inducted into academic theology that they have forgotten what it was like before, students for ordained ministry need to look at people and their lives, and to listen to them. Among all the things that they will receive in this process that will be of benefit to their future ministry, I rank as the first and foremost achievement that they will see and hear ordinary theology.

None of this is difficult. It does not require a whole new module injected into an overburdened degree programme. Parish/congregation/circuit and other placements, and hospital and other sorts of visiting, can provide the sorts of experience I am advocating. But that experience needs to be taken seriously as a (admittedly, special form of) *theological educational* experience, and in particular it needs to be structured and commented on with an eye to elucidating and making explicit the ordinary theology that they will see and hear along the way. And if we care at all about their future ministerial activity, someone will need to keep an eye on how well the student is doing in his or her looking and listening and learning. Discussing other research into ordinary theology will also be helpful.

Listening and Respecting

This is another area in which the process is as significant as the product. Listening is a mark of *respect*; listening is a deeply pastoral, affirming act; listening tells people that they matter (cf. Browning, 1991: 284; Richter and Francis, 1998: 149). Some clergy are brilliant at it; others, to be candid, are appalling. Ministerial education should develop in ordinands the skill and habit of listening, and of listening for ordinary theology, as it should develop the virtue of respect for other people – even the lay members of the church! Listening is an essential skill for ministry.

The less theologically educated are saying to us, usually very softly, 'I am like this. I believe this; I value this; I hold it all together like this. I speak of God like this; I talk religion like this. And all this means a lot to me.' It is very important that 'applied', 'pastoral' and 'practical' theology, subject areas which inform the tasks of Christian education, preaching and mission as well as those of Christian care and concern, should take note of the ordinary language and logic of the religious believer (and also of those who reject religious belief). Only those with the ears to hear will hear it. We must all work hard to listen and learn.

I believe, in particular, that the general communication of the Christian gospel in the contemporary context, as well as the specific activities of Christian nurture, formation and education of the church itself, are greatly hindered because we do not listen hard enough or skilfully enough. Part of the reason for that is that we do not take seriously enough the everyday theology of ordinary adult Christian churchgoers and Christian believers, both that which is explicitly articulated and that which is more implicit and inarticulate. Nor are we sufficiently concerned about the nature and structure of the beliefs (particularly the beliefs about Christianity) that are held by non-believers and by non-churchgoers. Ministers and others who are engaged in Christian education, apologetics and evangelism, as well as those involved in the church's pastoral ministry, need to listen far better to – and to know far more than they do about – the beliefs that are held by the adults for whom they exercise this ministry of teaching and care, and the ways in which these ordinary believers speak, think and reason about religious and theological matters.

This is especially true if, as I would argue, communicative and even pastoral ministry can only be truly effective if it is partly founded on a *dialogue* between the minister and the one being ministered to. Those who attempt to pastor, preach, teach or offer counsel as an entirely one-way process create a relationship that will be ultimately ineffective as communication or as care. In practice, and also in theory, 'we simply have to take others as seriously as we take ourselves' (Pattison, 1998: 43; cf. Graham, 1998).

> This listening [in research conversations] has been an important part of our spiritual re-education. . . . Ideally what we discover together is a non-oppressive, mutually respectful mode of dialogue across the cultural divide . . . that increasingly separates the secular and

religious worlds. . . . We suggest that the development of this dialogue is the work of mission.
(Hay and Hunt, 2000: 39–40)

Justifying the Study of Ordinary Theology Theologically

We need, then, to listen to people for their sake. And we need to listen to them for our sake as well. Understanding the *nature* of ordinary theology, especially by tracing better its origins as a learned and learning theology, will help us know more about what it is about ordinary theology *that works*. Ordinary theologians are saying something worth our hearing. They also say this in a whisper, sometimes *very* hesitantly: 'I think I have found this truth, this strength, this power, this vision. I think this works . . .'. Other people's ordinary theology can in this way serve our needs also.

Additionally, just as children teach adults about themselves, so ordinary theology can help us understand some of the more hidden dimensions, motivations and connections of our own, more academic, theology. Inside every extraordinary theologian is an ordinary one that he is usually trying to keep hidden in there, or that she just hasn't yet noticed. We shall understand our own scholarly and academic theology much better if we attend to our own ordinary theological background and origins with more sympathy, more respect and more self-understanding.

Are there any further *theological reasons* for engaging in the study of ordinary theology? Could it, perhaps, contribute to the health of its more academic cousin? I offer here a variety of suggestions of ways in which a study of ordinary theology might offer such a contribution.

Theology and Experience

Theologians sometimes claim that all theology arises, at least partly, from our experience, albeit in conversation with the Christian tradition. Others claim that it is ultimately to be tested against our experience. For most theological systems, experience has some part to play in the framing or assessing of Christian belief. But whose experience do we have in mind here?

Inside and indeed outside the churches there exists a huge living experiment of people struggling to find and make meaning in their lives, from a vast variety of different standpoints, personality types, social and cultural perspectives, and across an enormous range of different contexts. I am reminded of Douglas Adams' image in *The Hitch Hiker's Guide to the Galaxy* of the earth as a computer designed to calculate the 'Question to the Ultimate Answer' (Adams, 1980: 182). To appeal to a related, but less bizarre analogy, one may note the way that much computer software undergoes its final testing by being put on the market and waiting for the customers' computers to crash! The church as a part of contemporary society offers a vast user-base for our academic theological code, which should be able to check how, when, where and to what extent it works. The results of this testing process, however, will only be expressed in – and therefore only available to – the student of ordinary theology.

This great resource of experience, including the experience of reflecting on and testing its theology against its experience, is too significant to ignore. If experience is the grounding of theology, should we not try to tap some of this? Academic theologians should be more curious about what ordinary believers have come up with. They should be willing to look and see whether there is some theological *wisdom* out there, often forged through experiences that they may never share – as well as those that they too shall suffer or celebrate. If academic theologians believe what many of them say about the relationship between theology and personal experience, they ought to take the experience of non-academic theologians more seriously.

Ian Ramsey was one theologian who insisted that theology's connection with experience should be acknowledged at both ends, as it were: both in its genesis and in its justification. With regard to what he called the 'empirical anchorage' of theology, Ramsey encouraged us 'to read theology backwards', back into a disclosure of God. Ordinary theology, which lies so close to human spirituality, faith and all our human religious impulses, is a type of theology that can be read back more easily than the more distanced forms of academic theological reflection. Much academic theology has departed a long way both from where it started and from *any* sort of experience that can 'anchor' it in people's lives.

Ramsey also insisted on theology's 'touching down' on human experience and its having some sort of 'fit' to empirical events, to the experienced experience of a life. Ordinary theology is being tested every day for just this 'empirical fit'. Ramsey likened it to the fit we need with our footwear. Like a 'preferred and selected' shoe, our theology is repeatedly tested against the slush, rain and forced-walks-on-account-of-missed-buses of our human life experience (Ramsey, 1964b: 17; 1965a: 58). This is not the knock-down, instant verification of an 'exact fit'; 'such a fit is pragmatic in the widest sense; but it is not given by experimental verification in a strict scientific sense' (Ramsey, 1966: 90). If an element of checkability against experience is expected of their religious discourse, it must be the case that people find reality reliable and trustworthy after all – or salvific, or meaningful in some other way. Their religious perspective must somehow 'fit' their experience, or they would not be willing or able to sustain it.

Ramsey himself parallels the testing of theological claims for empirical fit with the testing of wide-ranging generalizations, such as those expressed in the everyday questions: 'Is this a genuine case of love?' or 'Is this man trustworthy?' In principle, the beliefs underlying the answers to these questions are open to the possibility of falsification, although they may be quite resistant to it because of the wide-ranging nature of the claims, and particularly if there has been a sufficiently powerful and convincing originating experience. In all such cases, 'the test of whether [the claim] is or is not reasonable, will be . . . whether the resulting loyalty and pro-attitude can remain when confronted with a larger and larger picture, and when the empirical canvas broadens' (Ramsey, 1964a: 214). But note that this falsifiability of our trusting commitment is a matter not only of logic but also of our psychology.

Shoes are certainly put to the test and often rejected too. This pair looked snazzy enough – and watertight enough – in the shop, but what about out there, down the muddy lane? In the real world we may eventually realize that we shall need something tougher, something that will last better. This suggests a rather different sense in which ordinary theology can count as a form of 'empirical theology': that is, as an empirically tried-and-tested theology. Ordinary theology may lay claim to this status more convincingly than can many proposals of theological scholarship.

But I should remind myself of my earlier claim that one size does not 'fit all' in religious matters. In discussing Ramsey's analogy, I have argued elsewhere that many different theological schemes may be said to fit the same ambiguous empirical facts. How, in practice, do we choose between them?

> The answer to that question is likely to be a highly personal one, dependent on the answers to questions like: 'Which facts do you think it most important that a . . . scheme should fit well?' The answer here might be 'the facts of evil', or 'the facts of goodness', or 'my personal autobiography', or 'the history of Israel', or 'the person of Jesus'. But this is all a matter of personal choice, as is our choice of a 'good' shoe. For we all have different feet (differently 'shaped' worlds – i.e. different perceptions of what is significant in the world), and therefore the same shoe will fit different people to different extents. This aspect of the fit of a shoe or a theory is prior to its being tested more widely against the slush and rain of the world; a theory that fails this (personal) text is never 'adopted' and therefore never tested further.
>
> (Astley, 1984: 429)

This personal dimension continues to function even when the selected shoes are tested in more 'objective' conditions. As a matter of empirical fact, some shoes will never 'do' for some people in some situations, however watertight they may prove to be, because they do not fit their *other* needs (style, colour, appropriateness to their personality). Hence the familiar family dispute: 'For goodness' sake put something more robust on before you go out.' 'Mother, I am not turning up at the nightclub (party, date) in my wellies.' A compromise between fashion/image-fit and fitness-to-the-elements/terrain may be negotiable; but the personal appraisal will never be wholly trumped by impersonal meteorological data.

For not dissimilar reasons, there can be no such thing as a neutral, and in that sense purely 'objective' and 'impersonal' account of what falsifies religious belief. Religious beliefs are also held by believers, and they are the people who decide what *in fact* will count as falsifying evidence for their own beliefs. (To this extent, religion and science must always remain very different activities.)

Nonetheless, the great *variety* of ordinary theology can provide us all with a rich database of the forms of theology available, and how they perform and are viewed when lived out and tested out in this personal manner by other people.

Revisiting Revelation

Christianity's holy texts are always being re-read, re-assimilated, re-imagined and elaborated by the Christian tradition (cf. Brown, 1999). 'Revelation', Avery Dulles wrote, 'rather than being presupposed as fully known from the start is progressively elucidated as theology carries out its task' (Dulles, 1983: 283). Tilley comments that this is a matter of elucidating 'the living practice of faith': that is, revelation as understood in the traditions as those traditions change and 'the culture in which the traditions flourish . . . change'. This is done, we may hope, 'in fidelity to our forbears and in responsibility to our present and our future fellow-travelers' (Tilley, 2000: 176).

It is arguable that this particular 'task of theologians' need not, in practice is not, and for the good of the church *should not*, be limited to academic theologians. We should recognize that ordinary theologians are also engaged in delivering this crucial theological service. Thus all God's people are 'enabled to translate and interpret biblical texts again and again: as a reflex of the divine abundance and creativity'; and the fulfilment of biblical interpretation may be located in proclamation through 'a sermon which enables the listeners to explicate new ideas concerning the interpretation of the text' (Maurer, 2000: 76). In particularizing the gospel in its own life and culture, the congregation continually reinterprets the normative beliefs and practices of the church in a manner that provides important innovations for the church as a whole (cf. Osmer, 1990a: ch. 9). The study of ordinary theology can make these innovations and elucidations available to theology in general.

Incidentally, it is often assumed that the average churchgoer is some sort of biblical or doctrinal fundamentalist, wedded to an understanding of orthodoxy that implies an unchanged transmission of some perceived primordial revelation that has been once and for all time delivered to the saints. It is, of course, difficult to generalize, and empirical studies in this area are in any case fairly sparse, but my own reading of what evidence there is shows that *biblical* fundamentalism is a minority position in mainstream denominations. A study of 445 adults across ten Anglican parishes in Northern England, while it certainly revealed some confusion in their attitudes to scripture, also showed that only a very small percentage of respondents endorsed the inerrancy of scripture overall (including what it says about history and nature), with over a quarter accepting that the Bible is not always accurate even in its theology and nearly 23 per cent taking the same view of its ethical teaching (Fisher, Astley and Wilcox, 1992). In Leslie Francis' more recent survey of 409 churchgoers across four English denominations in one town, an average of only 17 per cent of the sample accepted the fundamentalist option (Francis, 2000: 182–3).

Aiding Understanding

It is now widely accepted that our current context and understanding, the perspective from which we see things which incorporates our biases or 'legitimate prejudices' (*die Vorurteile*: Gadamer, 1982: 246), is the *condition* of our understanding the Christian past and its classic texts, rather than some insuperable barrier to it. An associated assumption is that our conceptual prejudices are themselves 'inherited' from the past through a process of socialization that forges the links that place us in the same cultural tradition as the writings or history we are studying.

These preliminary and provisional 'pre-judgements' constitute 'the horizon of the particular present' of the interpreter. In order for us to understand the past, our horizon must be consciously fused with the horizon of the past (the 'text'). This fusion involves applying the past to the present in a new creative, fruitful way, rather than allowing the tensions between and the distance between past and present to be covered over or to swallow us up, resulting in the latter case in our merely repeating or reproducing the text (Gadamer, 1982: 273). Thiselton calls our present horizon a 'horizon of expectation'; it is a horizon that represents our practical, behavioural and pre-conceptual *background* (Thiselton, 1992: 44–5).

Our *Vorverständnis* – our 'assumed' or 'preliminary understanding' – is conditioned by our context. In the view of liberation theology, this pre-understanding is shaped by our praxis, including our religious praxis; but it is also shaped by theological assumptions within the tradition in which we live, think and act (cf. Thiselton, 1980: 111, 315; 1992: 65, 330). The first step in understanding is to employ it in a pre-judgement that raises questions, anticipates answers and guides us in our search for knowledge. This can only lead to genuine understanding when present and past then come into a true dialogue, through this 'fusion' from which new truth (an 'advance') emerges. In the process of interpretation our horizon is transformed and restructured by the horizon of the text.

Gadamer insists that two things are necessary on the part of the interpreter for understanding a text. One is a properly sensitive openness, for our pre-understanding must be corrected and revised by the influence of the text itself, as it speaks what is new to us. But as interpreters we must also become aware of the nature of those pre-judgements that we bring to the text, 'to make them conscious, in order to assess them against the text itself' (Thiselton, 1980: 305). Thus: 'We do not come to know the past by eliminating these conceptual prejudices that constitute our horizon of understanding, but precisely by trying to achieve an explicit awareness of them' (Brümmer, 1992: 11). It is this form of critical consciousness that allows the theologian self-critically 'to challenge and transform their own pre-understandings and interpretative horizons' (Jeanrod, 1994: 174).[9]

It might appear, then, that helping people to recognize their own 'ordinary theology' is a necessary preliminary to their proper self-critical understanding of the past as well as the present. Therefore even if you really want ordinary theologians to study the Bible or John Henry Newman, you will also need to get them to study themselves. Correlatively, people's confrontation with an alien horizon will help to make them aware of their own deep-seated assumptions, so that they come to notice – often for the first time – what it is that they really believe. At whatever point on the hermeneutical spiral this happens, therefore, the process of understanding another's theology will involve people in a new self-awareness of their own ordinary theology.

---

[9]   Jürgen Habermas' critique of Gadamer mainly centred on the claim that the notion of the fusion of horizons is too conservative, not sufficiently critical of received tradition and ignores the possibility of ideological distortion. A truly 'uncurtailed communication' should be more concerned with this critical dimension, transcending hermeneutics in order to find a truth acceptable to any rational person 'in the intersubjective mutuality of reciprocal understanding' (Habermas, 1979: 3). Yet Gadamer does allow for critical interaction in his notion of the fusion of horizons; the claims of the text (the other) *may* be challenged and checked. Gadamer insists that 'our human experience of the world, for which we rely on our faculty of judgment, consists precisely in the possibility of our taking a critical stance with regard to every convention' (Gadamer, 1982: 496; cf. Warnke, 1987; Thiselton, 1992: 329, chs X and XI; Stiver, 1996: 90–107).

A study of ordinary theology, undertaken by ordinary theologians themselves, may therefore be defended as a significant step on the way to their understanding every other theology.

Correcting the Grammar of Faith

Although ordinary theologians are not usually thought of as having theological expertise (least of all by themselves), according to George Lindbeck even those who have a less 'active theological ability' may still have a 'passive competence' to recognize religious mistakes, in that they are capable of noticing when theology goes astray at a fundamental level. Not only are ordinary theologians capable of this, *in the end* they are the ones who *must* do it, for 'corporately and in the long run, those who have internalised a communal tradition are the final judges of its theology' (Lindbeck, 1996: 293). It is the language users, Lindbeck argues, not the grammarians (that is, the official theologians), who are often in the best position to recognize the crucial touchstones and criteria of correction; just as it is the scientists, rather than the philosophers of science, who make the advances in scientific understanding.

> The spiritually mature may have only the most meagre ability to articulate and describe their patterns of belief and practice, but they can recognise misdescriptions. They may have no talent in assessing differences between the second-order accounts which theologians formulate, but they can sense . . . when the usages authorised by these accounts violate the deep grammar of the faith.
>
> (Lindbeck, 1996: 292–3)

I imagine that many academic theologians, and even more clergy, would resist such a claim. But on a post-liberal, or more broadly faith community or 'traditional' account of Christian theology, it ought to be taken seriously. We may be reminded here of Paul Holmer's account of the situation. In so far as 'theology tells us what faith is', it does so by articulating the 'structure and morphology' of the life of Christian belief, its logic and grammar, which is 'what we all have access to already' (Holmer, 1978: 19–21). But does this really mean *all* of us?

Gareth Moore's account of Christian spirituality may be instructive here. He offers a very striking interpretation of the meaning of Jesus' *logia* concerning seeking a reward in heaven (as a matter of not seeking a reward), and of laying up treasure in heaven ('the treasure you acquire by not being interested in acquiring any treasure'), and of spiritual success and greatness (as not being a species of success and greatness) (Moore, 1988: ch. 5). But Moore's account is not in any way an 'expert' or 'scholarly' interpretation, for which much study is a prerequisite. It is simply a matter of seeing the point of, reading the grammar and discerning the logic of, what every Christian has read in the scriptures and what every Christian 'knows'. In ways such as these, real theology tells us what we know already. Ordinary theologians are frequently quite as capable of seeing the point in this fashion as their academic cousins.

We should anticipate a significant criticism, however. As Lindbeck notes, 'most Christians through most of Christian history have spoken their own official tongue very poorly.' It is, after all, 'the spiritually mature' of whom he writes. But according to Lindbeck their maturity in these matters can be *assessed*; the ordinary theologian's linguistic competences are 'empirically recognizable'. What are their characteristics?

Those who can speak Christianity rightly are 'not tied to fixed formulas', they do not come from 'isolated backwaters or ingrown sects uninterested in communicating widely' but are truly 'ecumenical', they are 'flexibly devout'. Above all, perhaps, 'they are likely to be saturated with the language of scripture and/or liturgy' (Lindbeck, 1984: 100). Such people presumably are often *generally accepted* by others in their congregations and communities as those who know of what they speak. As Augustine would recommend, they will have a deep familiarity with, and a proper approach to, scripture (cf. Louth, 1983: 83). But we might suggest that they will also need 'a sensitivity to context, an extraordinary capacity to listen, and an immersion in . . . the experience of other churches' (Schreiter, 1985: 18). As competent speakers of the Christian language, they may truly be said to *represent* the community that is the locus of Christian truth and the final court of appeal for questions about what it is and what it means. They are truly *Christian* theologians, but they are *ordinary* Christian theologians. And these are those who should judge and correct substantive academic theology.

Enlarging Ecclesiology and Normativity

This brings me to a final argument for the study of ordinary theology and its radical theological implications. Such a theology can furnish us with a wider understanding of doctrinal norms, by providing a wider concept of what the church believes as a norm for doctrine. In this last section I shall contrast ordinary theology not so much with academic theology as with received, official, *ecclesial theology*, which is 'extraordinary' in a rather different way.[10]

'Doctrine' is usually taken to be a narrower category than 'theology' (Lash, 1986: 260–61). 'The views of theologians are doctrinally significant, in so far as they have won acceptance within the community'; this is the factor that turns theology into doctrine (McGrath, 1997: 11, 46). But this raises three questions: What and where is this 'community'? Whose church is it anyway? And isn't it now time for a lay theology?

If critical theology includes some testing of beliefs against the norms of Christian belief, it is appropriate to ask where these norms come from. They originate, of course, in *other people's* beliefs, particularly the beliefs of the Evangelists and Apostles, and the Fathers, Doctors and Councils of the church. In other words, they originate in the Christian tradition. They are themselves beliefs, accepted as 'normal'.

We should first recall a dilemma that was touched on earlier (pp. 42–3). We can only accept these beliefs by adopting them as our own; their 'givenness' depends on *our* accepting them. My concern now is not one about who is judging what in this

---

[10]   Connections between ecclesial and academic theology are forged wherever the latter views itself as confessional theology, adopting ecclesial norms for its 'Christian-ness' (see pp. 77, 120, cf. 140–2), or the former imports its theology from the academy.

relationship, but about the centrality of our autonomy. However much biblical or doctrinal fundamentalists strive to diminish their own significance by adopting a theology of obedience that places all truth and authority in the text of scripture or tradition, even they cannot escape this dilemma. As in moral decision-making, people cannot deny some measure or moment of autonomy. It is always true that 'those who accept the authority of a priest or a church on what to do are, in accepting that authority, deciding for themselves' (Nowell-Smith, 1999: 405). In this sense, *we* always decide what the norms of belief should be.

The question of the nature of theological norms is one that cannot easily be separated from questions of the nature of religious authority and of the identity of the church, topics that I shall say more about shortly. I wish to introduce these topics in a rather particular way, however, by trying to develop a parallel with the debate about *rationality*.

Donald Hudson has argued that our criteria for the rationality of our beliefs may include the criterion of conformity to 'the rational system of beliefs', along with such other criteria as lack of self-contradiction or support by relevant evidence (a rational belief does not need to fulfil *all* such criteria). This rational system of beliefs comprises generally accepted beliefs about what is the case and what we should do or choose, and regulates 'what it makes sense to say or do' (Hudson, 1980: 80–81). Hudson contends that our accepted rational system of belief includes not only propositions that are fundamental to our world view or to certain disciplines of thought (for example the principle of the uniformity of nature), but also 'propositions . . . which are very widely and consistently taken for granted in our society',[11] together with generally accepted moral principles. He comments that beliefs that fall into these last two categories *may* sometimes change through 'fortuitous' factors, in addition to many changes related to the application of other criteria of rationality. Thus *some* generally held beliefs just become outmoded or people simply lose interest in them (80–85). As Robert Frost put it in his 1914 poem, 'The Black Cottage':

> Most of the change we think we see in life
> Is due to truths being in and out of favour.
> (Frost, 1951: 79)[12]

To summarize: in listing the criteria of *rationality* that actually hold in our society, Hudson's main point is that *conformity to the rational system of beliefs* (that is, the system of beliefs that are widely held to be rational and regulative of our talk and action) is *one such* criterion of rationality. On this account, beliefs may be adjudged rational simply and solely because they conform to the rational system of beliefs (as do those beliefs contained within it); they are not necessarily first judged against

---

[11] Hudson gives as possible examples the beliefs that no one has visited Mars and that dogs feel pain.

[12] 'The minister' who is speaking in the poem (from the collection *North of Boston*) is arguing, however, that we should not abandon a belief 'merely because it ceases to be true'.

other criteria such as the criterion of possessing adequate supporting evidence or not being self-contradictory.

I would like to suggest now that it may be possible to apply this model more widely, to other normative systems. Let us try to develop an analogous account of the *criteria of religious orthodoxy*. We might consider the 'orthodox system of beliefs' held by a religious group as constituting a material criterion of orthodoxy, alongside such formal criteria as (in the case of Christianity) 'conformity to scripture' and 'taught by the councils of the church'. This material criterion of orthodoxy would then be constituted by conformity to the set of widely held religious beliefs. As with the rational system of beliefs, their defining feature is that people 'widely and consistently' take these beliefs for granted and use them to regulate their lives and thought, but in this case that happens only within the (admittedly different and more restrictive) context of Christianity. But within this context these beliefs are nearly universally held to be true.

These systems of belief are *sociological facts* that serve as touchstones of what is 'rational' or 'orthodox' to believe (or, if we were to develop the analogy more widely, of what is 'moral', 'scientific', 'humane' and so on to believe, depending on the particular normativity under consideration). On Hudson's account, it is appropriate to believe, and irrational to doubt, that which is in conformity with the generally held beliefs that regulate what it makes sense to believe. In a similar way, I am proposing that the notion of orthodoxy within the Christian community may also be partly based on empirical facts about the beliefs that are *actually held* (widely, consistently and regulatively) by that community. This is particularly significant for those beliefs about which scripture and tradition are silent or ambiguous. This empirical grounding may provide one explanation of how it is that what is taken to be orthodox gradually changes over time, without any explicit appeal to any of the other standard criteria of orthodoxy such as conformity to scripture. Sometimes something we take to be the 'right opinion' (*orthodoxos*) in Christianity changes in ways that are best explained by social and psychological factors, rather than by theological or philosophical ones. Some elements within Christianity just become outmoded or the church loses interest in them for no real (principled) reason. What will seem unpalatable to many theologians about this claim is the same feature that many philosophers find outrageous about Hudson's original thesis: both accounts introduce a 'sociological' or 'descriptive' dimension into our understanding of norms, both the norms of rationality and also, in this case, the norms of Christian believing.

Yet there has surely been an empirical, human component to the notion of orthodoxy from the beginning, although this has been restricted to the few rather than widened to include the many. The defining of creeds and dogmas, like the specification of a canon of scripture, are historical processes that may be reconstructed and traced. Church councils argued and there were winners and losers in these arguments. Popes and reformers came and went, and their theological influence waxed and waned with them. The basic rules have always been that the influential have had most influence and the winners have written the rule book. Much of this influence, and much of this 'winning', has been based on more 'objective' criteria of argument and scholarship, or in retrospect *could* be justified by appeal to these criteria; but it would be naive to expect that fashions do not change in argument and scholarship as well. What counts as 'the faith of the church', to which 'assent' should be given – to quote Adrian Hastings' definition of orthodoxy (Hastings, 2000a: 504) – will change with differing accounts of the connotation and denotion of the terms 'faith', 'church' and 'assent'. Similar points may be made about any understanding of orthodoxy as 'right worship' or of its alternative *orthopraxis* ('right practice or behaviour'). What is 'right' in all these cases is what is taken to be right, by some criterion or other, accepted by some group or other. As these groups change and change their minds, so the criteria change also. The question remains, however, as to *who* decides what is right, or (in my terms) just how 'widely held' do beliefs need to be to count as being orthodox? The parallel with the case of rationality only seems to work if they are *very* widely held within the church and among Christians. This analysis therefore tends to reverse the delimiting thrust of traditional accounts of orthodoxy.

Theology for all? The traditional notion of the *consensus fidelium*, the 'consensus of the faithful', was reaffirmed by the Second Vatican Council as a criterion for the authentic faith of the church (*Lumen Gentium* 12). At first sight, it might seem to offer us, if not a democratic, then at least a 'whole community' definition of the church. This appears to be how Lindbeck interprets the matter, with respect to those who are theologically 'linguistically competent' anyway (Lindbeck, 1994: 98–104).

Medieval theology recognized three sources of teaching and learning within the church. Alongside the official magisterium (teaching office) and the researches of scholars, it placed 'the discernment of ordinary people of faith'. The Roman Catholic Thomas Groome, interpreting these as three 'cooperative sources' with each of them reflecting and guiding the others, remarks boldly that even the pope 'is meant to be a witness to what is already the faith of Catholic people' (Groome, 1998: 241–2). If 'the faithful', as I have argued, are daily involved in progressively elucidating, and (especially) in continually contextualizing, the Christian revelation (see above, pp. 150–51), then they may be said to form a part of God's continuing revelation to the church.

Defenders of ordinary theology might be tempted to appeal, perhaps, to 'The Vincentian Canon': *quod ubique, quod semper, quod ab omnibus creditum est.* For Vincent of Lérins, who flourished in the fifth century and was an opponent of Augustine's theology, scripture was the final ground of truth. Yet he recognized that scripture needed to be interpreted by the tradition of the church. He therefore defined the 'norm of ecclesiastical and Catholic opinion' as 'that which has been believed everywhere, always and by all'. So far so good. Even better, for my purposes, is the fact that in glossing what he calls the principle of 'universality', Vincent allows 'the whole church throughout the world' to be the gold standard. Unfortunately, however, in the case of the principles of 'antiquity' and 'consent', he limits the testing ground quite strictly to our 'ancestors and fathers' and (in antiquity) 'all, or certainly nearly all, bishops and doctors' respectively (Bettenson, 1967: 84).

So much for going beyond the clerical paradigm. Admittedly, the focus here is on the tradition of the church and on 'antiquity' as a firm guide over against any 'novel contagion' that may be currently infecting it, so the reference to the godly predecessors in the faith is perhaps not so surprising. But even in that (past) context it is startling that the apparently democratic reference to the faith that 'the whole church throughout the world confesses', which is 'held, approved and taught, not by one or two only but by all equally and with one consent, openly, frequently and persistently', should in fact be restricted to the beliefs of 'approved and outstanding' teachers (84). For Vincent, it is the church's theologians who define theology – and they do not include her ordinary theologians.

Yet surely a strain, if not a paradox, is created when theology identifies as 'Christian doctrine' or a 'doctrine of the church' beliefs that many ordinary Christians do *not* share. And empirical evidence increasingly shows that many churchgoers are quite unorthodox when measured against the 'godly predecessors', 'fathers', and 'bishops and teachers'. I laid the groundwork in Chapter 3 (p. 48) for debating the relevance of a *statistical* norm for debates about what should be the *prescriptive* norm for the church's theology. In that context, what should the church make of the fact that, in one survey, only 44 per cent of churchgoers hold the view that Christianity is the only true religion (Francis, 2000: 181; cf. also Francis, 2001: 171); or that, in another survey, 50 per cent of churchgoers affirmed that all religions are 'equally true'? (Buckler and Astley, 1992: 399).[13] What about the fact that among the churchgoing population, at all events in one town, only 40 per cent of Catholics, 28 per cent of Anglicans and 23 per cent of Methodists said that they believed in hell as a 'real place' (Francis, 2000: 181)? What do we make of the empirical claim that 'the majority of Catholic weekly church-attenders . . . believe that the consecrated host is only a symbolic representation of Christ, rather than Christ himself' (Morris, 1997: 393).[14]

Hans van der Ven is willing to use data from empirical research to map the contours of the *consensus fidelium*. He argues that empirical theology encourages such an 'exoteric standpoint', as opposed to 'an esoteric one based on the teachings of ministers and theologians' (van der Ven, 1993: 25–6).

> Empirical methodology provides practical theology with the techniques and instruments to order, analyze, interpret and evaluate the religious convictions, beliefs, images and feelings of men and women. If the *sensus fidei* and *consensus fidelium* are not to degenerate into mere rhetoric, they must be conscientiously investigated. Only then can the dialectic, or the discrepancy, between the teaching of the church and the faith of its members . . . be clearly brought to light and explicitly presented as an inevitable subject for ecclesiastical and pastoral considerations.
>
> (van der Ven, 1993: 109)

---

[13] Even adopting the perspective of the clerical paradigm does not avoid some of these issues. In a recent study only some 47 per cent of female Anglican clergy (although some 64 per cent of their male counterparts), who were ordained in the 1990s in Britain and Ireland, agreed that 'there is only one true religion' (Jones, 2001: 366).

[14] Admittedly a disputed allegation (cf. Tilley, 2000: 70–71).

This is a cautiously expressed claim. Empirical facts about what Christians believe need to be taken account of; they are not necessarily to be read as definitive for Christian belief. Even so, we may argue that there is something unstable in any account of Christian doctrine that ignores substantial minority views (and in some areas *majority* views) within the laity, particularly if they are common among the theologically 'linguistically competent'. My attempt to develop Donald Hudson's account of normativity may not be judged relevant by those who would argue that certain beliefs about hell, other faiths or the real presence (or whatever) are to be considered orthodox or heretical on the basis of the *other criteria* of orthodoxy, such as unambiguous endorsement or rejection by scripture and/or tradition, and therefore that we do not need to count heads in these matters. But for those who are not convinced that these beliefs can be unambiguously endorsed or rejected on these other criteria, and who are persuaded of the existence of a more sociologically defined principle of orthodox belief, statistical data may appear more relevant. In any case, to reject as irrelevant what ordinary, faithful, practising Christians actually think may be said to imply a particular understanding of the doctrine of the church. In a whole variety of ways, then, and for a whole variety of reasons, we still need to face the serious implications of the claim that 'orthodoxy in theology is never capable of much more refined definition than that supposed by the somewhat loose consensus of the faithful' (Holmer, 1978: 198).

Our western experience of political parties, and particularly of recent developments in the British scene, may be instructive here, for it seems to me that organized religions are rather similar institutions. They are essentially living movements, embodying concrete practices and communities, rather than abstract systems of beliefs and values, although they certainly express both. They are composed of people with commitments who engage in a range of activities, but who carry along with them a rag-bag of ideology that is filled with a whole gamut of different ideological beliefs and values. Not only are these very various, but in a real sense they are often secondary to the *movement*, its practices and goals. Further, they are constantly changing.

I offer but one ecclesiastical example. The history of the Anglican Churches' determinations about the ethical acceptability of artificial contraception, as made by the Lambeth Conference of Anglican Bishops at its meetings every ten years, reveals the bishops moving from being utterly appalled by the idea in 1908 (as 'demoralising to character and hostile to national welfare'), to a grudging acceptance in 1930 (in cases where there is 'a clearly felt moral obligation to avoid parenthood'), to the 1958 endorsement of any family planning methods that are acceptable to the husband and wife. (I imagine that the present view would be something like, 'For goodness sake, yes, wonderful idea.') In Britain, 'New' Labour has changed like that, and the Conservative Party is currently engaged in something similar. Are these scenarios wholly shameful? As long as certain core reference points (including core values and beliefs) are retained, is it not inevitable that much of the rest of the institutional beast will be fairly amoeboid or protean? It will need to change as it explores and seeks to live in a changing society. Separated from the rest of society it would die.

Even academic and official ecclesiastical theology are driven by changes that go on in mass society among the great unwashed – in which honourable category I am content to include myself. Our values, assumptions, beliefs and ways of thinking change very markedly over time, and our churches and theologies, as much as our political parties, must eventually catch up with many of these changes. In Christianity it is the lay people, the ordinary theologians, who often change first – despite the clergy's continual grumbling about their conservative nature.

'The Church of England is like the Tory party', Bishop Richard Holloway recently complained, 'a long-running institution that can't cope with dramatic change' (Grove, 2001: 3). But no institution is good at change, especially those that have succeeded in the past in insulating themselves from the engines of change of the broader society, and from the context and territory that that society provides and inhabits. Institutions do not need to be quite so unresponsive, however. Ironically enough, it is established churches like the Church of England that have the least excuse. In ministering to a wider parish, understood as a geographical area embracing a mixed community, and not just to a gathered congregation, such churches *must* be pastorally open to the changing society outside their doors. In practice, this means not just an honest recognition of the way changes in society can, and often should, impact on the church. It also demands a more pastorally sensitive recognition of the 'toe-curling embarrassment' of the church 'beginner' as well as of the needs of the 'honest searcher' (cf. Hay and Hunt, 2000: 33–4).

Ordinary theology, even among the 'linguistically competent', is particularly open to change because it is particularly open to outside influence. Jean Bouteiller has described those at the edge of church life as *threshold Christians*. He argues that the church is still 'visited, frequented, questioned, explored, loved, criticized by a crowd of people who call themselves more or less Christians. . . . Many encamped at the Church's doors are willing to be recognized as being of the Church and to be linked to it, but they are very hesitant about being recognized as being integrally *within* the Church.' Such people enable, encourage, demand and sometimes force the church to be open. Bouteiller's account moves us, therefore, towards a more open ecclesiology.

> When one speaks of threshold Christians, one pictures the Church as a building or as an open space, places arranged more or less for entering or leaving, coming and going. These are the building's entrances, the doors. One can easily imagine the many activities that can take place on these thresholds: meetings, movement, mixing of people, waiting, initiation, revelation, discussion, ceremonies, and so on. Moreover, the threshold is an integral part of the building; it is neither an accessory nor an appendix.
>
> (Bouteiller, 1979: 67–8)

In the light of this account of ecclesiological *liminality*, one could argue that it is not helpful to model the church as an ark of salvation whose sailors pluck the saved from the turbulent currents of worldliness, in order to protect them on a journey away from this dangerous ocean to a safe haven far away. Alternative metaphors, such as the dominical ones of the leaven in the lump, the salt in the stew and even the candle on the candlestick (Matthew 5: 13–16; 13: 33) image an ecclesiology that recognizes no impermeable, rigid, protective barriers between the church-belongers and those who are outside the walls. Under these circumstances, in many areas of belief and practice, churchgoers will change much as the society changes.

Ecclesiology *can* cope with this situation, while retaining even 'holiness' as among the marks of the church. The doctrine of the church's holiness implies that it is 'called out' and set apart, and therefore is the community of *hoi hagioi*, the saints (who are of course still sinners – 'both holy and sinful'). Such holiness comes from obedience; and an obedient response to the call of God rarely results in escaping the world, but allowing Christ to be formed in them where they are, as Mary did. Perhaps it is significant that the words 'holiness/holy' and the word 'whole' are etymologically related in their Old English ('halignes/halig' and 'hal') and Germanic roots. Wholeness is about completeness, entirety, an undiminished state with no parts removed. The church, again like Mary, is called 'warts and all'. There is a comforting unsaintliness about the biblical accounts of saints, so unlike the later spruced up half-truths of traditional hagiography. The truth about sanctity enables us to see God working through people who are in some ways extraordinarily ordinary. All that is required is the response to God's call. (Not even that is needed in the case of sacraments: those very ordinary objects and actions that are set apart to symbolize and convey God's grace, quite apart from their ordinariness and the unworthiness of their ministers.)

Further, as Barth insists, the church's holiness is not a species of self-concern:

> The Church can never be satisfied with what it can be and do as such. As His community it points beyond itself. At bottom it can never consider its own security, let alone its appearance. As His community it is always free from itself. In its deepest and most proper tendency it is not churchly, but worldly – the Church with open doors and great windows, behind which it does better not to close itself in upon itself again by putting in pious stained-glass windows. It is holy in its openness to the street and even the alley, in its turning to the profanity of all human life – the holiness which, according to Rom. 12:5, does not scorn to rejoice with them that do rejoice and to weep with them that weep. Its mission is not additional to its being. It is, as it is sent and active in its mission.
>
> (Barth, 1956: 724–5)

This 'openness to the street', and the broader human existence that others have called 'the church outside the church' (Dorothy Sölle) or 'anonymous Christianity' (Karl Rahner), allows the possibility of an open ecclesiology that can acknowledge, honour and take seriously its own thresholds, and some of the very ordinary beliefs that visit, rest and flourish there. Is it too fanciful to claim a parallel here with – and perhaps a moral for – the doing of theology and the study of theology? For the church's openness to ordinary life should entail an *openness to ordinary theology*, and an acceptance of ordinary theology's openness to change, both with respect to the theology of churchgoers and of those beyond the church's more conspicuous portals. Ordinary theology is truly a warts and all theology, open to the alley.

It is this openness, above all other influences, that renders the church a body that is vulnerable to change. While a great deal of the change that society is subject to must be resisted, there is much too that should surely be welcomed. Ecclesial institutions too often, implicitly or explicitly, resist changes in values, practices and beliefs that should be embraced: especially the changes that relate to increased ecclesial plurality, gender- and class-equality, and the development of non-judgemental attitudes (at least to some extent and in certain contexts). But this resistance is not to be explained on the grounds that churches are resistant to change as such, for patently many of them simultaneously embrace other changes that *should* be resisted, such as the commodification of caring and educational services, the introduction of brain-dead managerial practices that destroy professional respect and collegial trust, and the culture of status. Admittedly, these criticisms express my own personal and particular (and jaundiced?) views; many doubtless see these things very differently. But there are others who have voiced similar criticisms (see Drane, 2000: 75). Where we might all agree is over the claim that all Christians have a responsibility to make Christian moral and spiritual judgements about the beliefs, attitudes, values and practices that exist within a society, and to decide on the basis of such judgements whether we should welcome or resist their growing influence in the church. What none of us can do is to pretend that such things are not already flourishing inside our church walls. They are, and it is inevitable that they will, since being the church in the world involves being open to the world's changes. Ordinary theology is the species of Christian theology most likely to reflect them and best placed to respond to them. *It is the church's front line.*

Clearly these discussions raise profound questions for ecclesiology and the theology of Christian identity. In particular, they bring us back to the question of the *locus of authority* for the beliefs of the church. Most churches distinguish different roles and offices within the church, and locate authority differently ('appropriately') for different roles. But most will now allow the lay baptized *some* say in the debate about and definition of doctrine, if only by recognizing the importance of the exercise of reason in the pursuit of truth (in principle something that is not limited to particular roles, or even to academic theologians) and of the 'primacy' or 'authority' of the conscience of the ordinary believer. A proper recognition of proper authority and hard-won freedom of belief are constituents of the practices that shape all Christian believers, not just those of academic theologians. And 'embodying true freedom can be a result of authentic obedience – a freedom and obedience that is no respecter of rank or order in the community' (Tilley, 2000: 184).

In principle, then, our attitude to ordinary theology must intimately relate to our understanding of the nature of God's church. And whatever we make of it theologically, speaking statistically ordinary theology *is* the theology of God's church.

Epilogue

I am very conscious that the position that I have tried to defend in this book is open to many misunderstandings. In particular, I hope that I have said enough to nail the idea that my advocacy of ordinary theology can be reduced to the endorsement of an uncritical, popular theology in which 'anything goes'. There are always choices to be made in theology, with some theologies and theologians being properly preferred over others. On the whole, ordinary believers understand this very well.

To take ordinary theology more seriously – and this is all that I am asking for, *not* that we cease any longer to take academic theology seriously – is to begin where most people are, with their 'ordinary' (non-technical, non-scholarly) beliefs and language. In principle, ordinary language 'can everywhere be supplemented and improved upon and superseded'. So wrote J. L. Austin, who stands among the strongest advocates of 'ordinary language philosophy' (or 'linguistic phenomenology' – his 'less misleading' name for it). But in recognizing that 'ordinary language is *not* the last word', Austin also insisted that we remember that 'it *is* the *first* word' (Austin, 1970: 185, cf. 182).

In theology too the first word should count for more than it does, even with professional theologians and students of 'the Christian thing'. It certainly should be taken seriously by the church's ministers, preachers and educators, who are the people above all who need to be alert to the ordinary theology and theologizing of those in their care, and to recognize the significance for their congregations of the learning context of their theology.

But perhaps the main burden of this book has been that, whatever anybody else thinks, the significance of their own theology and its genesis can never be in any doubt for ordinary theologians themselves.

Bibliography

Abercrombie, Nicholas; Baker, John; Brett, Sebastian and Foster, Jane (1970), 'Superstition and Religion: The God of the Gaps', in David Martin and Michael Hill (eds), *A Sociological Yearbook of Religion in Britain: 3*, London: SCM, pp. 93–129.

Abraham, William (1997), 'Revelation Reaffirmed', in Paul Avis (ed.), *Divine Revelation*, London: Darton, Longman and Todd, pp. 201–15.

Abrams, Mark; Gerard, David and Timms, Noel (eds) (1985), *Values and Social Change in Britain*, Basingstoke: Macmillan.

Adams, Douglas (1980), *The Restaurant at the End of the Universe: The Hitch Hiker's Guide to the Galaxy 2*, London: Pan.

Adams, Robert M. (1987), *The Virtue of Faith*, New York: Oxford University Press.

Ahern, Geoffrey (1984), *The Triune God in Hackney and Enfield: 30 Trinitarian Christians and Secularisation*, London: Centre for Ecumenical Studies.

Ahern, Geoffrey and Davie, Grace (1987), *Inner City God: The Nature of Belief in the Inner City*, London: Hodder & Stoughton.

Alston, William P. (1981), 'The Christian Language-Game', in F. J. Crosson (ed.), *The Autonomy of Religious Belief*, Notre Dame, Ind.: University of Notre Dame Press, pp. 128–62.

Alston, William P. (1991), *Perceiving God: The Epistemology of Religious Experience*, Ithaca, NY: Cornell University Press.

Argyle, Michael (1983), *The Psychology of Interpersonal Behaviour*, Harmondsworth: Penguin.

Arrington, Robert L. (1989), *Rationalism, Realism, and Relativism: Perspectives in Contemporary Moral Epistemology*, Ithaca, NY: Cornell University Press.

Ary, Donald; Jacobs, Lucy Cheser and Razavieh, Asghar (1990), *Introduction to Research in Education*, Orlando, Fla.: Holt, Rinehart and Winston.

Astley, Jeffrey (1978), 'A Critical Analysis of the Religious Epistemology of Ian T. Ramsey', unpublished Ph.D. Thesis, University of Durham.

Astley, Jeff (1981), 'The "indispensability" of the incarnation', *King's Theological Review*, IV, 1: 15–21.

Astley, Jeff (1984), 'Ian Ramsey and the problem of religious knowledge', *Journal of Theological Studies*, N.S. 35, 2: 414–40.

Astley, Jeff (1992), 'Christian Worship and the Hidden Curriculum of Christian Learning', in Jeff Astley and David Day (eds), *The Contours of Christian Education*, Great Wakering: McCrimmons, pp. 141–52.

Astley, Jeff (1994a), 'The Place of Understanding in Christian Education and Education about Christianity', in Jeff Astley and Leslie J. Francis (eds), *Critical Perspectives on Christian Education: A Reader on the Aims, Principles and Philosophy of Christian Education*, Leominster: Gracewing, pp. 105–17.

Astley, Jeff (1994b), *The Philosophy of Christian Religious Education*, Birmingham, Ala.: Religious Education Press.

Astley, Jeff (1996), 'Theology for the Untheological? Theology, Philosophy and the Classroom', in Jeff Astley and Leslie J. Francis (eds) (1996), *Christian Theology and Religious Education: Connections and Contradictions*, London: SPCK, pp. 60–77.

Astley, Jeff (1999), 'Learning Moral and Spiritual Wisdom', in Stephen C. Barton (ed.), *Where Shall Wisdom be Found? Wisdom in the Bible, the Church and the Contemporary World*, Edinburgh: T. & T. Clark, pp. 321–34.

Astley, Jeff (2000a), *Choosing Life? Christianity and Moral Problems*, London: Darton, Longman and Todd.

Astley, Jeff (2000b), 'On Gaining and Losing Faith with Style: A Study of Post-Modernity and/or Confusion among College Students', in Leslie J. Francis and Jaacov J. Katz (eds), *Joining and Leaving Religion: Research Perspectives*, Leominster: Gracewing, pp. 249–68.

Astley, Jeff (2000c), 'Aims and Approaches in Christian Education', in Jeff Astley (ed.), *Learning in the Way: Research and Reflection on Adult Christian Education*, Leominster: Gracewing, pp. 1–32.

Atkinson, D. and Field, D. (eds) (1995), *A New Dictionary of Christian Ethics and Pastoral Theology*, Leicester: Inter-Varsity Press.

Augustine (1961), *Confessions*, trans. R. S. Pine-Coffin, Harmondsworth: Penguin.

Austin, J. L. (1970), 'A Plea for Excuses', *Philosophical Papers*, ed. J. O. Urmson and G. J. Warnock, second edn, Oxford: Oxford University Press, pp. 175–204.

Avis, Paul (1999), *God and the Creative Imagination: Metaphor, Symbol and Myth in Religion and Theology*, London: Routledge.

Ayer, A. J. (1956), *The Problem of Knowledge*, Harmondsworth: Penguin.

Bailey, Edward (1989), 'The Folk Religion of the English People', in Paul Badham (ed.), *Religion, State and Society in Modern Britain*, Lampeter: Edwin Mellen, pp. 145–58.

Bailey, Edward (1990), 'Implicit religion: a bibliographical introduction', *Social Compass*, 37, 4: 499–509.

Bailey, Edward (1995), 'Implicit Religion', in John Hinnells (ed.), *A New Dictionary of Religions*, Oxford: Blackwell, pp. 234–5.

Bailey, Edward (1997), *Implicit Religion in Contemporary Society*, Kampen, The Netherlands: Kok Pharos; Weinheim: Deutscher Studien Verlag.

Bailey, Edward (1998), *Implicit Religion: An Introduction*, London: Middlesex University Press.

Bailey, Kenneth D. (1994), *Methods of Social Research*, New York: The Free Press.

Bairnwick Staff (1984), *Manual for Mentors*, Sewanee, Tenn.: School of Theology, The University of the South.

Ballard, Paul (1995), 'Practical theology as an academic discipline', *Theology*, XCVIII, 782: 112–22.

Ballard, Paul and Pritchard, John (1996), *Practical Theology in Action: Christian Thinking in the Service of Church and Society*, London: SPCK.

von Balthasar, Hans Urs (1960), *Verbum Caro*, I, Einsiedeln, Switzerland: Johannesverlag (in English as *The Word Made Flesh*, trans. A. V. Littledale with Alexander Due, San Francisco: Ignatius Press, 1989).

Bambrough, Renford (1989), 'Does Philosophy "Leave Everything As It Is"? Even Theology?', in Godfrey Vesey (ed.), *The Philosophy in Christianity*, Cambridge: Cambridge University Press, pp. 225–36.

Bandura, Albert (1969), 'Social-Learning Theory of Identificatory Processes', in David A. Goslin (ed.), *Handbook of Socialization Theory and Research*, Chicago: Rand McNally, pp. 213–62.

Barr, James (1999), *The Concept of Biblical Theology: An Old Testament Perspective*, London: SCM.

Barrett, Cyril (1991), *Wittgenstein on Ethics and Religious Belief*, Oxford: Blackwell.

Barrow, Robin and Milburn, Geoffrey (1990), *A Critical Dictionary of Educational Concepts*, New York: Teachers College Press.

Barth, Karl (1956), *Church Dogmatics,* Vol. IV/1, trans. G. W. Bromiley, Edinburgh: T. & T. Clark.

Barth, Karl (1961), *Church Dogmatics*, Vol. III/4, trans. A. T. Mackay *et al.*, Edinburgh: T. & T. Clark.

Barth, Karl (1969), *How I Changed My Mind*, Edinburgh: Saint Andrew Press.

Barth, Karl (1975), *Church Dogmatics*, Vol. I/1, trans. G. W. Bromiley, Edinburgh: T. & T. Clark.

Baumer, Franklin L. (1960), *Religion and the Rise of Scepticism*, New York: Harcourt, Brace and World.

Bausch, William J. (1984), *Storytelling: Imagination and Faith*, Mystic, Conn.: Twenty-Third Publications.

Belenky, Mary Field; Clinchy, Blythe McVicker; Goldberger, Nancy Rule and Tarule, Jill Mattuck (1986), *Women's Ways of Knowing: The Development of Self, Voice and Mind*, New York: Basic Books.

Bellah, Robert N. (1970), *Beyond Belief: Essays in Religion in a Post-Traditional World*, New York: Harper & Row.

Bellah, Robert N. *et al.* (1985), *Habits of the Heart: Individualism and Commitment in American Life*, Berkeley: University of California Press.

Bem, Sandra L. (1975), 'Sex role and adaptability: one consequence of psychological androgogyny', *Journal of Personality and Social Psychology*, 3: 634–43.

Bem, Sandra L. (1981), *Bem Sex Role Inventory: Professional Manual*, Pala Alto, Calif.: Consulting Psychologists Press.

Berger, Peter L. (1973), *The Social Reality of Religion*, Harmondsworth: Penguin.

Berger, Peter L. and Luckmann, Thomas (1967), *The Social Construction of Reality: A Treatise in the Sociology of Knowledge*, Harmondsworth: Penguin.

Bernstein, Basil (1971), *Class, Codes and Control: Theoretical Studies Towards a Sociology of Language*, London: Routledge & Kegan Paul.

Berntsen, John A. (1996), 'Christian Affections and the Catechumenate', in Jeff Astley, Leslie J. Francis and Colin Crowder (eds), *Theological Perspectives on Christian Formation: A Reader in Theology and Christian Education*, Leominster: Gracewing Fowler Wright; Grand Rapids, Mich.: Eerdmans, pp. 229–43.

Bettenson, Henry (ed.) (1967), *Documents of the Christian Church*, Oxford: Oxford University Press.

Blackburn, Simon (1998), *Ruling Passions: A Theory of Practical Reasoning*, Oxford: Oxford University Press.

Blanshard, Brand (1967), 'Wisdom', in Paul Edwards (ed.), *The Encyclopedia of Philosophy*, Vol. 8, New York: Macmillan and Free Press, pp. 322–4.

Borg, Walter R. and Gall, Meredith D. (1983), *Educational Research: An Introduction*, New York: Longman.

Bouteiller, Jean (1979), 'Threshold Christians: A Challenge for the Church', in William J. Reedy (ed.), *Becoming a Catholic Christian*, New York: Sadlier, pp. 65–80.

Braaten, Carl E. (1984), 'Prolegomena to Christian Dogmatics', in Carl E. Braaten and Robert W. Jenson (eds), *Christian Dogmatics*, Vol. 1, Philadelphia: Fortress, pp. 5–78.

Braun, Willi (2000), 'Religion', in Willi Braun and Russell T. McCutcheon (eds), *Guide to the Study of Religion*, London: Cassell, pp. 3–18.

Brooke, John Hedley (1991), *Science and Religion: Some Historical Perspectives*, Cambridge: Cambridge University Press.

Brookfield, Stephen D. (1986), *Understanding and Facilitating Adult Learning: A Comprehensive Analysis of Principles and Effective Practices*, Milton Keynes: Open University Press.

Brown, Callum (2001), *The Death of Christian Britain: Understanding Secularisation 1800–2000*, London: Routledge.

Brown, David (1985), *The Divine Trinity*, London: Duckworth.

Brown, David (1999), *Revelation and Change*, Oxford: Oxford University Press.

Browning, Don S. (1991), *A Fundamental Practical Theology: Descriptive and Strategic Proposals*, Minneapolis, Minn.: Fortress.

Bruce, Steve (1995), *Religion in Modern Britain*, Oxford: Oxford University Press.

Brueggemann, Walter (1996), 'Passion and Perspective: Two Dimensions of Education in the Bible', in Jeff Astley, Leslie J. Francis and Colin Crowder (eds), *Theological Perspectives on Christian Formation: A Reader in Theology and Christian Education*, Leominster: Gracewing Fowler Wright; Grand Rapids, Mich.: Eerdmans, pp. 71–9. First published 1985.

Brümmer, Vincent (1981), *Theology and Philosophical Inquiry*, London: Macmillan.

Brümmer, Vincent (1992), *Speaking of a Personal God: An Essay in Philosophical Theology*, Cambridge: Cambridge University Press.

Bryman, A. and Cramer, D. (1992), *Quantitative Data Analysis for Social Scientists*, London: Routledge.

Buckler, Guy and Astley, Jeff (1992), 'Learning and Believing in an Urban Parish', in Jeff Astley and David Day (eds), *The Contours of Christian Education*, Great Wakering: McCrimmons, pp. 396–416.

Burke, Peter (1981), *Montaigne*, Oxford: Oxford University Press.

Buttitta, Peter K. (1995), 'Theological Reflection in Health Ministry: A Strategy for Parish Nurses', in James D. Whitehead and Evelyn Eaton Whitehead, *Method in Ministry: Theological Reflection and Christian Ministry*, Kansas City, Mo.: Steed and Ward, pp. 112–22.

Caird, G. B. (1980), *The Language and Imagery of the Bible*, London: Duckworth.

Caldwell, Zarrin T. (ed.) (2001), *Religious Education in Schools: Ideas and Experiences from Around the World*, Oxford: International Association for Religious Freedom.

Carr, David (1991), *Educating the Virtues: An Essay on the Philosophical Psychology of Moral Development and Education*, London: Routledge.

Carr, Wesley (1984), *The Priestlike Task*, London: SPCK.

de Certeau, Michel (1984), *The Practice of Everyday Life*, trans. Steven Rendall, Berkeley: University of California Press.

Clack, Brian R. (1999), *An Introduction to Wittgenstein's Philosophy of Religion*, Edinburgh: Edinburgh University Press.

Clark, David (1982), *Between Pulpit and Pew: Folk Religion in a North Yorkshire Fishing Village*, London: Cambridge University Press.

Clark, W. H. (1971), 'Intense Religious Experience', in Merton P. Strommen (ed.), *Research in Religious Development: A Comprehensive Handbook*, New York: Hawthorn, pp. 521–50.

COD (1982), *The Concise Oxford Dictionary of Current English*, ed. J. B. Sykes, seventh edn, Oxford: Oxford University Press.

COD (1995), *The Concise Oxford Dictionary*, ed. Della Thompson, ninth edn, in *The Oxford Compendium* CD version, Oxford: Oxford University Press.

COD (1999), *The Concise Oxford Dictionary*, ed. Judy Pearsall, tenth edn, Oxford: Oxford University Press.

Cohen, Louis; Manion, Lawrence and Morrison, Keith (2000), *Research Methods in Education*, London: RoutledgeFalmer.

Conn, Walter (1986), *Christian Conversion: A Developmental Interpretation of Autonomy and Surrender*, New York: Paulist.

Cottingham, John (1998), *Philosophy and the Good Life: Reason and the Passions in Greek, Cartesian and Psychoanalytic Ethics*, Cambridge: Cambridge University Press.

Cowdell, Scott (1988), *Atheist Priest? Don Cupitt and Christianity*, London: SCM.

Cox, Harvey (1965), *The Secular City: Secularization and Urbanization in Theological Perspective*, London: SCM.

Cragg, Kenneth (1981), '"According to the Scriptures"': Literacy and Revelation', in Michael Wadsworth (ed.), *Ways of Reading the Bible*, Brighton: Harvester, pp. 23–36.

Craig, Yvonne (1994), *Learning for Life: A Handbook of Adult Religious Education*, London: Mowbray.

Cranton, Patricia (2001), *Becoming an Authentic Teacher in Higher Education*, Malabar, Fla.: Krieger.

Crites, Stephen (1971), 'The narrative quality of experience', *Journal of the American Academy of Religion*, XXXIX, 3: 291–311.

Cross, K. Patricia (1981), *Adults as Learners*, London: Jossey-Bass.

Crowder, Colin (ed.) (1997), *God and Reality: Essays on Christian Non-Realism*, London: Mowbray.

Cunliffe-Jones, Hubert (ed.) (1978), *A History of Christian Doctrine*, assisted by Benjamin Drewery, Edinburgh: T. & T. Clark.

Cupitt, Don (1980), *Taking Leave of God*, London: SCM.
Cupitt, Don (1989), *Radicals and the Future of the Church*, London: SCM.
Cupitt, Don (1997), *After God: The Future of Religion*, London: Weidenfeld and Nicolson.
Cupitt, Don (1998a), *The Religion of Being*, London: SCM.
Cupitt, Don (1998b), *The Revelation of Being*, London: SCM.
Cupitt, Don (1999a), *The New Religion of Life in Everyday Speech*, London: SCM.
Cupitt, Don (1999b), *The Meaning of It All in Everyday Speech*, London: SCM.
Cupitt, Don (2000a), *Kingdom Come in Everyday Speech*, London: SCM.
Cupitt, Don (2000b), *Philosophy's Own Religion*, London: SCM.
Cupitt, Don (2001), *Reforming Christianity*, Santa Rosa, Calif.: Polebridge.
Daloz, L. (1986), *Effective Teaching and Mentoring*, San Francisco: Jossey Bass.
Davie, Donald (1988), *To Scorch or Freeze: Poems about the Sacred*, Chicago: University of Chicago Press.
Davie, Grace (1994), *Religion in Britain Since 1945: Believing Without Belonging*, Oxford: Blackwell.
Davis, Caroline Frank (1989), *The Evidential Force of Religious Experience*, Oxford: Oxford University Press.
Day, James M. (1999), 'The Primacy of Relationship: A Meditation on Education, Faith and the Dialogical Self', in James C. Conroy (ed.), *Catholic Education: Inside-Out/Outside-In*, Dublin: Veritas, pp. 263–84.
Dewey, John (1963), *Experience and Education: The Kappa Delta Pi Lecture Series*, London: Collier.
Dhavamony, Mariasusai (1973), *Phenomenology of Religion*, Rome: Gregorian University Press.
Dickinson, Emily (1970), *The Complete Poems*, ed. Thomas H. Johnson, London: Faber and Faber.
Drane, John (2000), *The McDonaldization of the Church: Spirituality, Creativity, and the Future of the Church*, London: Darton, Longman and Todd.
Drury, John (1972), *Angels and Dirt: An Enquiry into Theology and Prayer*, London: Darton, Longman and Todd.
Dulles, Avery (1983), *Models of Revelation*, Dublin: Gill and Macmillan.
Dunn, James D. G. (1977), *Unity and Diversity in the New Testament*, London: SCM.
Durston, D. (1989), 'Theological reflection: definitions, criteria', *British Journal of Theological Education*, 3, 1: 32–9.
Dykstra, Craig (1981), *Vision and Character*, New York: Paulist.
Dykstra, Craig R. (1996), 'No Longer Strangers: The Church and Its Educational Ministry', in Jeff Astley, Leslie J. Francis and Colin Crowder (eds), *Theological Perspectives on Christian Formation: A Reader in Theology and Christian Education*, Leominster: Gracewing Fowler Wright; Grand Rapids, Mich.: Eerdmans, pp. 106–18. First published 1985.
Edgley, Roy (1969), *Reason in Theory and Practice*, London: Hutchinson.
Edwards, Jonathan (1961), *Select Works, Volume III: Treatise Concerning the Religious Affections*, London: Banner of Truth. First published 1746.

Eichrodt, Walther (1967), *Theology of the Old Testament*, trans. J. A. Baker, London: SCM.

Elias, John L. (1982), *The Foundations and Practice of Adult Religious Education*, Malabar, Fla.: Krieger.

Elias, John L. and Merriam, Sharan (1980), *Philosophical Foundations of Adult Education*, Malabar, Fla.: Kreiger.

Ely, Margot *et al.* (1991), *Doing Qualitative Research: Circles within Circles*, London: Falmer.

Erricker, Clive (1999), 'Phenomenological Approaches', in Peter Connolly (ed.), *Approaches to the Study of Religion*, London: Cassell, pp. 73–104.

Evans, Donald D. (1963), *The Logic of Self-Involvement: A Theological Study of Everyday Language with Special Reference to the Christian Use of Language about God as Creator*, London: SCM.

Evans, Donald D. (1968), 'Differences between Scientific and Religious Assertions', in Ian G. Barbour (ed.), *Science and Religion: New Perspectives in the Dialogue*, London: SCM, pp. 101–33.

Evans, Donald (1979), *Struggle and Fulfillment: The Inner Dynamics of Religion and Morality*, Cleveland: Collins.

Farley, Edward (1983), *Theologia: The Fragmentation and Unity of Theological Education*, Philadelphia: Fortress.

Farley, Edward (1988), *The Fragility of Knowledge: Theological Education in the Church and the University*, Philadelphia: Fortress.

Farrer, Austin (1967), *Faith and Speculation: An Essay in Philosophical Theology*, London: A. & C. Black.

Ferré, Frederick (1967), *Basic Modern Philosophy of Religion*, London: Allen & Unwin.

Feyerabend, Paul (1987), *Farewell to Reason*, London: Verso.

Fiorenza, Francis Schüssler (1996), 'Thinking Theologically about Theological Education', in Jeff Astley, Leslie J. Francis and Colin Crowder (eds), *Theological Perspectives on Christian Formation: A Reader in Theology and Christian Education*, Leominster: Gracewing Fowler Wright; Grand Rapids, Mich.: Eerdmans, pp. 318–41. First published 1988.

Fisher, Elizabeth; Astley, Jeff and Wilcox, Carolyn (1992), 'A Survey of Bible Reading Practice and Attitudes to the Bible Among Anglican Congregations', in Jeff Astley and David Day (eds), *The Contours of Christian Education*, Great Wakering: McCrimmons, pp. 382–95.

Ford, David F. (1997), *The Shape of Living*, London: HarperCollins.

Ford, David F. (1999), *Theology: A Very Short Introduction*, Oxford: Oxford University Press.

Fowler, Jim (1978), 'Life/Faith Patterns: Structures of Trust and Loyalty', in Jim Fowler and Sam Keen, *Life Maps: Conversations on the Journey of Faith*, ed. Jerome Berryman, Waco, Texas: Word Books, pp. 14–101.

Fowler, James W. (1981), *Stages of Faith: The Psychology of Human Development and the Quest for Meaning*, San Francisco: Harper & Row.

Fowler, James W. (1983), 'Practical Theology and the Shaping of Christian Lives', in Don S. Browning (ed.), *Practical Theology*, San Francisco: Harper & Row, pp. 148–66.

Fowler, James W. (1990), 'Reconstituting *Paideia* in Public Education', in Parker J. Palmer, Barbara G. Wheeler and James W. Fowler (eds), *Caring for the Commonweal: Education for Religious and Public Life*, Macon, Ga.: Mercer University Press, pp. 63–89.

Fowler, James W. (1992), 'The Enlightenment and Faith Development Theory', in Jeff Astley and Leslie J. Francis (eds), *Christian Perspectives on Faith Development: A Reader*, Leominster: Gracewing; Grand Rapids, Mich.: Eerdmans, pp. 15–28. First published 1988.

Fowler, James W. (1996), *Faithful Change: The Personal and Public Challenges of Postmodern Life*, Nashville: Abingdon.

Fowler, James W. (2001), 'Faith development theory and the postmodern challenges', *The International Journal for the Psychology of Religion*, 11, 3: 159–72.

Francis, Leslie J. (1997), 'The psychology of gender differences in religion: a review of empirical research', *Religion*, 27: 81–96.

Francis, Leslie J. (2000), 'The Pews Talk Back: The Church Congregation Survey', in Jeff Astley (ed.), *Learning in the Way: Research and Reflection on Adult Christian Education*, Leominster: Gracewing, pp. 161–86.

Francis, Leslie J. (2001), *The Values Debate: A Voice from the Pupils*, London: Woburn.

Francis, Leslie J. and Wilcox, Carolyn (1998), 'Religiosity and femininity: do women really hold a more positive attitude toward Christianity?', *Journal for the Scientific Study of Religion*, 37: 462–9.

Frankfurt, Harry G. (1988), *The Importance of What We Care About*, Cambridge: Cambridge University Press.

Frazer, James George (1922), *The Golden Bough: A Study in Magic and Religion*, London: Macmillan.

Frei, Hans (1992), *Types of Christian Theology*, ed. George Hunsinger and William C. Placher, New Haven: Yale University Press.

Frei, Hans W. (1975), *The Identity of Jesus Christ: The Hermeneutical Bases of Dogmatic Theology*, Philadelphia: Fortress.

Frost, Robert (1951), *Complete Poems of Robert Frost*, London: Jonathan Cape.

Gadamer, Hans-Georg (1982), *Truth and Method*, trans. and ed. Garrett Barden and John Cumming, New York: Crossroad.

Gage, N. L. (1978), *The Scientific Basis of the Art of Teaching*, New York: Teachers College Press.

Gagné, Robert M. (1972), 'Domains of learning', *Interchange*, 3, 1: 1–8.

Gagné, Robert M. (1977), *The Conditions of Learning*, New York: Holt, Rinehart and Winston.

Gardiner, Patrick (1988), *Kierkegaard*, Oxford: Oxford University Press.

Gardner, Howard (1993), *Frames of Mind: The Theory of Multiple Intelligences*, London: HarperCollins.

Geertz, Clifford (1993), *The Interpretation of Culture*, London: HarperCollins.

Gibbard, Allan (1990), *Wise Choices, Apt Feelings: A Theory of Normative Judgment*, Oxford: Oxford University Press.

Gibbs, Mark and Morton, T. Ralph (1964), *God's Frozen People: A Book for – and about – Ordinary Christians*, London: Collins.

Gibbs, Mark and Morton, T. Ralph (1971), *God's Lively People: Christians in Tomorrow's World*, London: Collins.

Gill, Robin (1999), *Churchgoing and Christian Ethics*, Cambridge: Cambridge University Press.

Gillespie, V. Bailey (1979), *Religious Conversion and Personal Identity*, Birmingham, Ala.: Religious Education Press.

Gillham, Bill (2000), *The Research Interview*, London: Continuum.

Glaser, B. D. and Strauss, A. K. (1967), *The Discovery of Grounded Theory*, Chicago: Aldine.

Goleman, Daniel (1995), *Emotional Intelligence*, New York: Basic Books.

Gordon, Peter and Lawton, Denis (1984), *A Guide to English Educational Terms*, London: Batsford.

Graham, Elaine L. (1996), *Transforming Practice: Pastoral Theology in an Age of Uncertainty*, London: Mowbray.

Graham, Robert (1998), *Taking Each Other Seriously: Experiences in Learning and Teaching*, Durham: Fieldhouse Press/University of Durham School of Education.

Green, Joel B. (2001), 'Crucifixion', in Marcus Bockmuehl (ed.), *The Cambridge Companion to Jesus*, Cambridge: Cambridge University Press, pp. 87–101.

Green, Laurie (1990), *Let's Do Theology: A Pastoral Cycle Resource Book*, London: Mowbray.

Greenwood, Robin (1994), *Transforming Priesthood: A New Theology of Mission and Ministry*, London: SPCK.

Grey, Mary (1996), 'Sapiential Yearnings: The Challenge of Feminist Theology to Religious Education', in Jeff Astley and Leslie J. Francis (eds), *Christian Theology and Religious Education: Connections and Contradictions*, London: SPCK, pp. 78–94.

Groome, Thomas H. (1978), 'Christian Education for Freedom: A "Shared Praxis" Approach', in Padraic O'Hare (ed.), *Foundations of Religious Education*, New York: Paulist, pp. 8–39.

Groome, Thomas H. (1980), *Christian Religious Education: Sharing Our Story and Vision*, San Francisco: Harper & Row.

Groome, Thomas H. (1991), *Sharing Faith: A Comprehensive Approach to Religious Education and Pastoral Ministry*, San Francisco: HarperSanFrancisco.

Groome, Thomas (1998), *Educating for Life: A Spiritual Vision for Every Teacher and Parent*, Allen, Texas: Thomas More.

Grove, Valerie (2001), 'The bishop and the actress', *The Times: Feature*, Saturday, 18 August.

Habermas, Jürgen (1970), 'Knowledge and Interest', in Dorothy Emmet and Alasdair MacIntyre (eds), *Sociological Theory and Philosophical Analysis*, London: Macmillan, pp. 36–54.

Habermas, Jürgen (1979), *Communication and the Evolution of Society*, London: Heinemann.

Habgood, John (1983), *Church and Nation in a Secular Age*, London: Darton, Longman and Todd.

Hamilton, Malcolm (2001), 'Implicit religion and related concepts: seeking precision', *Implicit Religion,* 4, 1: 5–13.

Hamlyn, David W. (1978), *Experience and the Growth of Understanding*, London: Routledge & Kegan Paul.

Hamlyn, David (1989), 'Education and Wittgenstein's philosophy', *Journal of Philosophy of Education*, 23, 2: 213–22.

Hamm, Cornell M. (1989), *Philosophical Issues in Education: An Introduction*, Lewes: Falmer.

Hammersley, Martin (1998), *Reading Ethnographic Research: A Critical Guide*, London: Longman.

Hanson, R. P. C. (1973), *The Attractiveness of God: Essays in Christian Doctrine*, London: SPCK.

Harding, Stephen; Phillips, David and Fogarty, Michael (eds) (1986), *Contrasting Values in Western Europe*, London: Macmillan.

Hardy, Daniel W. (1989), 'Theology through Philosophy', in David F. Ford (ed.), *The Modern Theologians: An Introduction to Christian Theology in the Twentieth Century*, Vol. II, Oxford: Blackwell, pp. 30–71.

Harris, Maria (1991), *Teaching and Religious Imagination: An Essay in the Theology of Teaching*, San Francisco: HarperSanFrancisco.

Hastings, Adrian (2000a), 'Orthodoxy', in Adrian Hastings, Alistair Mason and Hugh Pyper (eds), *The Oxford Companion to Christian Thought*, Oxford: Oxford University Press, pp. 504–5.

Hastings, Adrian (2000b), 'Theology', in Adrian Hastings, Alistair Mason and Hugh Pyper (eds), *The Oxford Companion to Christian Thought*, Oxford: Oxford University Press, pp. 700–702.

Hauerwas, Stanley and Jones, L. Gregory (eds) (1989), *Why Narrative? Readings in Narrative Theology*, Grand Rapids, Mich.: Eerdmans.

Hay, David and Hunt, Kate (2000), *Understanding the Spirituality of People Who Don't Go to Church: A Report of the Findings of the Adults' Spirituality Project at the University of Nottingham*, Nottingham: University of Nottingham.

Heitink, Gerben (1999), *Practical Theology: History, Theory, Action Domains*, Grand Rapids, Mich.: Eerdmans.

Hempton, David (1988), '"Popular Religion" 1800–1986', in Terence Thomas (ed.), *The British: Their Religious Beliefs and Practices 1800–1986*, London: Routledge, pp. 181–210.

Hick, John (1969), 'Religious Faith as Experiencing-As', in G. N. A. Vesey (ed.), *Talk of God*, London: Macmillan, pp. 20–35.

Hick, John (1973), *God and the Universe of Faiths*, London: Macmillan.

Hick, John (1980), *God Has Many Names: Britain's New Religious Pluralism*, London: Macmillan.

Hick, John (1983a), 'Prayer, Providence and Miracle', in Michael Goulder and John Hick, *Why Believe in God?*, London: SCM, pp. 64–80.

Hick, John (1983b), *Philosophy of Religion*, Englewood Cliffs, NJ: Prentice-Hall.

Hick, John (1983c), *The Second Christianity*, London: SCM.

Hick, John (1985), *Problems of Religious Pluralism*, London: Macmillan.

Higgins, Gregory C. (1996), 'The Significance of Postliberalism for Religious Education', in Jeff Astley, Leslie J. Francis and Colin Crowder (eds), *Theological Perspectives on Christian Formation: A Reader in Theology and Christian Education*, Leominster: Gracewing Fowler Wright; Grand Rapids, Mich.: Eerdmans, pp. 135–45. First published 1989.

Hill, Peter C. and Hood, Ralph W. (eds) (1999), *Measures of Religiosity*, Birmingham, Ala.: Religious Education Press.

Hobson, Peter R. and Edwards, John S. (1999), *Religious Education in a Pluralist Society: The Key Philosophical Issues*, London: Woburn.

Hodgson, Peter C. (1994), *Winds of the Spirit: A Constructive Christian Theology*, London: SCM.

Hodgson, Peter C. (1999), *God's Wisdom: Toward a Theology of Education*, Louisville, Ky.: Westminster John Knox Press.

Hoggart, Richard (1958), *The Uses of Literacy*, Harmondsworth: Penguin.

Holmer, Paul L. (1978), *The Grammar of Faith*, San Francisco: Harper & Row.

Holmer, Paul L. (1984), *Making Christian Sense*, Philadelphia: Westminster.

Hopewell, James F. (1987), *Congregation: Stories and Structures*, ed. Barbara G. Wheeler, London: SCM.

Hornsby-Smith, Michael P. (1991), *Roman Catholic Beliefs in England: Customary Catholicism and Transformations of Religious Authority*, Cambridge: Cambridge University Press.

Hornsby-Smith, Michael P.; Lee, Raymond M. and Reilly, Peter A. (1985), 'Common religion and customary religion: a critique and a proposal', *Review of Religious Research*, 26, 3: 244–52.

Hospers, John (1967), *An Introduction to Philosophical Analysis*, London: Routledge & Kegan Paul.

Hudson, W. Donald (1980), 'The Rational System of Beliefs', in David Martin, John Orme Mills and W. S. F. Pickering (eds), *Sociology and Theology: Alliance and Conflict*, Brighton: Harvester, pp. 80–101.

Hull, John M. (1984), *Studies in Religion and Education*, Lewes: Falmer.

Hull, John M. (1985), *What Prevents Christian Adults from Learning?*, London: SCM.

Hull, John M. (1991), *God-talk with Young Children*, Derby: CEM.

Hyman, Gavin (2001), 'Religious thought in everyday language: a response to Don Cupitt', *Modern Believing*, 42, 4: 24–30.

Inbody, Tyron (1992), 'History of Empirical Theology', in Randolph Crump Miller (ed.), *Empirical Theology: A Handbook*, Birmingham, Ala.: Religious Education Press, pp. 11–35.

Jackson, Philip W.; Boostrom, Robert E. and Hansen, David T. (1993), *The Moral Life of Schools*, San Francisco: Jossey-Bass.

Jackson, Robert (1993), 'Religious Education and the Arts of Interpretation', in Dennis Starkings (ed.), *Religion and the Arts in Education: Dimensions of Spirituality*, London: Hodder & Stoughton, pp. 148–58.

Jackson, Robert (1997), *Religious Education: An Interpretive Approach*, London: Hodder & Stoughton.

Jacobs, Eric and Worcester, Robert (1990), *We British: Britain under the MORIscope*, London: Weidenfeld and Nicolson.

Jacobs, Michael (1982), *Still Small Voice: A Practical Introduction to Counselling for Pastors and Other Helpers*, London: SPCK.

Jahoda, Gustav (1969), *The Psychology of Superstition*, Harmondsworth: Penguin.

James, William (1960), *The Varieties of Religious Experience: A Study in Human Nature*, London: Collins. Lectures delivered 1901–1902.

Jarvis, Peter (1995), *Adult and Continuing Education: Theory and Practice*, London: Routledge.

Jarvis, Peter; Holford, John and Griffin, Colin (1998), *The Theory and Practice of Learning*, London: Kogan Page.

Jeanrod, Werner G. (1994), *Theological Hermeneutics: Development and Significance*, London: SCM.

Jeffner, Anders (1972), *The Study of Religious Language*, London: SCM.

Jenkins, Timothy (1999), *Religion in English Everyday Life: An Ethnographic Approach*, New York and Oxford: Berghahn Books.

Jones, Susan H. (2001), 'The Personality Profile of Anglican Clergy: 1992–1996', unpublished Ph.D. thesis, University of Wales, Bangor.

Judge, E. A. (1996), 'The Reaction Against Classical Education in the New Testament', in Jeff Astley, Leslie J. Francis and Colin Crowder (eds), *Theological Perspectives on Christian Formation: A Reader in Theology and Christian Education*, Leominster: Gracewing Fowler Wright; Grand Rapids, Mich.: Eerdmans, pp. 80–87. First published 1983.

Jung, Carl Gustav (1977), *The Symbolic Life: Collected Works*, Vol. 18, trans. R. F. C. Hull, London: Routledge & Kegan Paul.

Kaufman, Gordon D. (1972), *God the Problem*, Cambridge, Mass.: Harvard University Press.

Kay, William K. (1997), 'Belief in God in Great Britain 1945–1996: Moving the scenery behind classroom RE', *British Journal of Religious Education*, 20, 1: 28–41.

Kay, William K. (forthcoming), 'Empirical theology: a natural development?'

Kay, William K. and Francis, Leslie J. (1985), 'The seamless robe: interdisciplinary enquiry in religious education', *British Journal of Religious Education*, 7, 2: 64–7.

Kay, William K. and Francis, Leslie J. (1996), *Drift from the Churches: Attitude toward Christianity during Childhood and Adolescence*, Cardiff: University of Wales Press.

Keen, Sam (1971), *To A Dancing God*, Glasgow: Collins.

Kellenberger, James (1972), *Religious Discovery, Faith, and Knowledge*, Englewood Cliffs, NJ: Prentice-Hall.

Kellenberger, J. (1985), *The Cognitivity of Religion: Three Perspectives*, London: Macmillan.

Kelsey, David H. (1975), *The Uses of Scripture in Recent Theology*, London: SCM.

Kelsey, D. H. (1983), 'Method, Theological', in Alan Richardson and John Bowden (eds), *A New Dictionary of Christian Theology*, London: SCM, pp. 363–68.

Kelsey, David H. (1992), *To Understand God Truly: What's Theological about a Theological School*, Louisville, Ky.: Westminster/John Knox.

Kelsey, David H. (1993), *Between Athens and Berlin: The Theological Education Debate*, Grand Rapids, Mich.: Eerdmans.

Kerr, Fergus (1986), *Theology After Wittgenstein*, Oxford: Blackwell.

Kerr, Fergus (1997), *Immortal Longings: Versions of Transcending Humanity*, London: SPCK.

Kerr, Fergus (1998), 'Truth in Religion: Wittgensteinian Considerations', in David Carr (ed.), *Education, Knowledge and Truth: Beyond the Postmodern Impasse*, London: Routledge, pp. 68–79.

Keynes, G. (1961), *Poetry and Prose of William Blake*, London: Nonesuch.

Kierkegaard, Søren (1941a), *Concluding Unscientific Postscript*, trans. David F. Swenson and Walter Lowrie, Princeton: Princeton University Press.

Kierkegaard, Søren (1941b), *Training in Christianity*, trans. Walter Lowrie, Princeton: Princeton University Press.

Kierkegaard, Søren (1967), *Søren Kierkegaard's Journals and Papers*, trans. H. V. Hong and E. H. Hong, Bloomington, Ind.: Indiana University Press.

Kierkegaard, Søren (1968), *Kierkegaard: Attack Upon 'Christendom': 1854–1855*, trans. Walter Lowrie, Princeton: Princeton University Press.

Killen, Patricia O'Connell and De Beer, John (1995), *The Art of Theological Reflection*, New York: Crossroad.

Kilpatrick, William Heard (1963), *Philosophy of Education*, New York: Macmillan.

Kinast, Robert L. (2000), *What Are They Saying About Theological Reflection?*, Mahwah, NJ: Paulist.

Knowles, Malcolm (1975), *Self-Directed Learning: A Guide for Learners and Teachers*, Englewood Cliffs, NJ:Prentice Hall Regents.

Knowles, Malcolm (1990) *The Adult Learner: A Neglected Species*, Houston: Gulf.

Kolb, David A. (1984), *Experiential Learning: Experience as the Source of Learning and Development*, Englewood Cliffs, NJ: Prentice-Hall.

Kraemer, Heindrich (1958), *A Theology of the Laity*, London: Lutterworth.

Krailsheimer, A. J. (1980), *Conversion*, London: SCM.

Krarup, Helen (n.d.), *'Conventional Religion and Common Religion in Leeds' Interview Schedule: Basic Frequencies by Question*, Leeds: Department of Sociology, University of Leeds.

Küng, Hans (1971), *The Church*, trans. Ray and Rosaleen Ockenden, London: Search.

Küng, Hans (1976), *On Being a Christian*, trans. Edward Quinn, London: Collins.

Kuschel, Karl-Joseph (1994), *Laughter: A Theological Reflection*, trans. John Bowden, London: SCM.

Lang, L. Wyatt (1931), *A Study of Conversion: An Enquiry into the Development of Christian Personality*, London: George Allen & Unwin.

Langford, Glenn (1985), *Education, Persons and Society*, London: Macmillan.

Langford, Michael (1981), *Providence*, London: SCM.

Lash, Nicholas (1986), *Easter in Ordinary: Reflections on Human Experience and the Knowledge of God*, Charlottesville: University Press of Virginia.

Lash, Nicholas (1996), *The Beginning and the End of 'Religion'*, Cambridge: Cambridge University Press.

Lave, J. and Wenger, E. (1999), 'Legitimate Peripheral Participation in Communities of Practice', in Robert McCormick and Carrie Paechter (eds), *Learning and Knowledge*, London: Paul Chapman, pp. 21–35.

Lawson, Kenneth (1974), 'Learning situations or educational situations', *Adult Education*, 47: 88–92.

Lee, James Michael (1971), *The Shape of Religious Instruction: A Social Science Approach*, Birmingham, Ala.: Religious Education Press.

Lee, James Michael (1973), *The Flow of Religious Instruction: A Social Science Approach*, Birmingham, Ala.: Religious Education Press.

Lee, James Michael (1982), 'The Authentic Source of Religious Instruction', in Norma H. Thompson (ed.), *Religious Education and Theology*, Birmingham, Ala.: Religious Education Press, pp. 100–197.

Lee, James Michael (1985), *The Content of Religious Instruction: A Social Science Approach*, Birmingham, Ala.: Religious Education Press.

van der Leeuw, Gerardus (1938), *Religion in Essence and Manifestation: A Study in Phenomenology*, Vol. 2, London: Allen & Unwin.

Le Guin, Ursula K. (1989), *Dancing at the Edge of the World: Thoughts on Words, Women, Places*, New York: Grove.

Leith, John H. (ed.) (1971), *Creeds of the Churches: A Reader in Christian Doctrine from the Bible to the Present*, Oxford: Blackwell.

Lindbeck, George A. (1984), *The Nature of Doctrine: Religion and Theology in a Postliberal Age*, London: SPCK.

Lindbeck, George A. (1996), 'Spiritual Formation and Theological Education', in Jeff Astley, Leslie J. Francis and Colin Crowder (eds), *Theological Perspectives on Christian Formation: A Reader in Theology and Christian Education*, Leominster: Gracewing Fowler Wright; Grand Rapids, Mich.: Eerdmans, pp. 289–302. First published 1988.

Louth, Andrew (1983), *Discerning the Mystery: An Essay on the Nature of Theology*, Oxford: Oxford University Press.

Lovell, R. Bernard (1984), *Adult Learning*, London: Croom Helm.

Luckmann, Thomas (1967), *The Invisible Religion: The Problem of Religion in Modern Society*, New York, Macmillan.

Lyon, David (1994), *Postmodernity*, Buckingham: Open University Press.

Lyons, William (1980), *Emotion*, Cambridge: Cambridge University Press.

Lyotard, Jean François (1984), *The Postmodern Condition: A Report on Knowledge*, Manchester: Manchester University Press.

van Maanen, John (1988), *Tales from the Field: On Writing Ethnography*, Chicago: University of Chicago Press.

McClendon, James Wm. (1974), *Biography as Theology: How Life Stories Can Remake Today's Theology*, Nashville: Abingdon.

McClendon, James Wm. and Smith, James M. (1975), *Understanding Religious Convictions*, Notre Dame, Ind.: University of Notre Dame Press.

McCourt, Frank (1997), *Angela's Ashes: A Memoir of a Childhood*, London: HarperCollins.

McFague, Sallie (1982), 'An Epilogue: The Christian Paradigm', in Peter C. Hodgson and Robert H. King (eds), *Christian Theology: An Introduction to Its Traditions and Tasks*, Philadelphia: Fortress, pp. 323–6.

McFague, Sallie (1983), *Metaphorical Theology: Models of God in Religious Language*, London: SCM.

McGhee, Michael (1992), 'Moral Truths: Ethics and the Spiritual Life', in Michael McGhee (ed.), *Philosophy, Religion and the Spiritual Life*, Cambridge: Cambridge University Press, pp. 229–46.

McGhee, Michael (2000), *Transformations of Mind: Philosophy as Spiritual Practice*, Cambridge: Cambridge University Press.

McGrath, Alister E. (1993), 'Doctrine and Dogma', in Alister E. McGrath (ed.), *The Blackwell Encyclopaedia of Modern Christian Thought*, Oxford: Blackwell, pp. 112–19.

McGrath, Alister E. (1997), *The Genesis of Doctrine: A Study in the Foundations of Doctrinal Criticism*, Grand Rapids, Mich.: Eerdmans; Vancouver: Regent College.

MacIntyre, Alasdair (1994), 'Relativism, Power and Philosophy', in Jeff Astley and Leslie J. Francis (eds), *Critical Perspectives on Christian Education: A Reader on the Aims, Principles and Philosophy of Christian Education*, Leominster: Gracewing, pp. 463–83. First published 1985.

McLeod, John (1994), *Doing Counselling Research*, London: Sage.

McLuhan, Marshall (1964), *Understanding Media: The Extensions of Man*, New York: Mentor.

McPherson, Ian (2001), 'Kierkegaard as an educational thinker: communication through and across ways of being', *Journal of Philosophy of Education*, 35, 2: 157–74.

Macquarrie, John (1960), *The Scope of Demythologizing: Bultmann and His Critics*, London: SCM.

Macquarrie, John (1967), *God-Talk: An Examination of the Language and Logic of Theology*, London: SCM.

Macquarrie, John (1975), *Thinking about God*, London: SCM.

Macquarrie, John (1977), *Principles of Christian Theology*, revised edn, London, SCM.

Madge, John (1953), *The Tools of Social Science*, London: Longmans Green.

Malcolm, Norman (1967), 'Knowledge and Belief', in A. Philip Griffiths (ed.), *Knowledge and Belief*, Oxford: Oxford University Press, pp. 69–81.

Malcolm, Norman (1977), 'The Groundlessness of Belief', in Stuart C. Brown (ed.), *Reason and Religion*, Ithaca, NY: Cornell University Press, pp. 143–57.

Manheimer, Ronald J. (1977), *Kierkegaard as Educator*, Berkeley: University of California Press.

Marchand, Philip (1989), *Marshall McLuhan: The Medium and the Messenger*, New York: Ticknor and Fields.

Marples, Roger (1978), 'Is religious education possible?', *Journal of Philosophy of Education*, 12: 81–91.

Marsh, Catherine (1988), *Exploring Data: An Introduction to Data Analysis for Social Scientists*, Cambridge: Polity.

Martin, Bernice and Pluck, Ronald (1976), *Young People's Beliefs: An Exploratory Study Commissioned by the General Synod Board of Education of the Views and Behavioural Patterns of Young People Related to their Beliefs*, London: General Synod Board of Education.

Martin, David (1967), *A Sociology of English Religion*, London, Heinemann.

Martin, David (1969), *The Religious and the Secular*, London: Routledge & Kegan Paul.

Martin, David (1980), *The Breaking of the Image: A Sociology of Christian Theory and Practice*, Oxford: Blackwell.

Martin, Dean M. (1994), 'Learning to Become a Christian', in Jeff Astley and Leslie J. Francis (eds), *Critical Perspectives on Christian Education: A Reader on the Aims, Principles and Philosophy of Christian Education*, Leominster: Gracewing, pp. 184–201. First published 1987.

Martin, Robert K. (1998), *The Incarnate Ground of Christian Faith: Toward a Christian Theological Epistemology for the Educational Ministry of the Church*, Lanham, Md.: University Press of America.

Mason, David R. (1989), 'Faith, religion, and theology', *Journal of Religious Studies*, 15: 1–15.

Maurer, Ernstpeter (2000), 'Reading the Bible Theologically', in Gerhard Sauter and John Barton (eds), *Revelation and Story: Narrative Theology and the Centrality of Story*, Aldershot: Ashgate, pp. 61–78.

Melanchthon, Philip (1969), *Loci Communes Theologici*, ed. Wilhelm Pauch, trans. Lowell J. Satre and Wilhelm Pauch, *Melanchthon and Bucer*, London: SCM, pp. 18–152.

Melchert, Charles F. (1998), *Wise Teaching: Biblical Wisdom and Educational Ministry*, Harrisburg, Pa.: Trinity Press International.

Meye, Robert P. (1988), 'Theological education as character formation', *Theological Education*, XXIV, Supplement 1: 'Theological Education as the Formation of Character': 96–126.

Migliore, Daniel L. (1991), *Faith Seeking Understanding: An Introduction to Christian Theology*, Grand Rapids, Mich.: Eerdmans.

Milbank, John (1993), *Theology and Social Theory: Beyond Secular Reason*, Oxford: Blackwell.

Mitchell, Basil (1973), *The Justification of Religious Belief*, London: Macmillan.

Mitchell, Basil (1980), *Morality: Religious and Secular – The Dilemma of Traditional Conscience*, Oxford: Oxford University Press.

Mitchell, Basil (1991), 'Philosophy and Theology', in Ann Loades and Loyal D. Rue (eds), *Contemporary Classics in Philosophy of Religion*, La Salle, Ill.: Open Court, pp. 7–20. First published 1987.

Mol, Hans (1976), *Identity and the Sacred: A Sketch for a New Social-Scientific Theory of Religion*, Oxford: Blackwell.

Moltmann, Jürgen (1997), *The Source of Life: The Holy Spirit and the Theology of Life*, trans. Margaret Kohl, London: SCM.

Moltmann-Wendel, Elisabeth (1994), *I am My Body: New Ways of Embodiment*, London: SCM.

de Montaigne, Michel (1958), *Essays*, trans. J. M. Cohen, London: Penguin.

de Montaigne, Michel (1991), *The Essays of Michel de Montaigne*, trans. and ed. M. A. Screech, London: Allen Lane.

Moore, Gareth (1988), *Believing in God: A Philosophical Essay*, Edinburgh: T. & T. Clark.

Moran, Gabriel (1997), *Showing How: The Act of Teaching*, Valley Forge, Pa.: Trinity Press International.

Morris, Charles R. (1997), *American Catholic: The Saints and Sinners Who Built America's Most Powerful Church*, New York: Random House.

Moseley, Romney M.; Jarvis, David and Fowler, James W. (1986), *Manual for Faith Development Research*, Atlanta, Ga.: Emory University.

Moustakas, Clark (1994), *Phenomenological Research Methods*, Thousand Oaks, Calif.: Sage.

Newman, John Henry (1913), *A Grammar of Assent*, London: Longmans, Green.

Niebuhr, H. Richard (1941), *The Meaning of Revelation*, New York: Macmillan.

Nipkow, Karl Ernst (1985), 'Can Theology Have an Educational Role?', in M. C. Felderhof (ed.), *Religious Education in a Pluralistic Society*, London: Hodder & Stoughton, pp. 23–38.

Nipkow, Karl Ernst (1996), 'Pluralism, Theology and Education: A German Perspective', in Jeff Astley and Leslie J. Francis (eds), *Christian Theology and Religious Education: Connections and Contradictions*, London: SPCK, pp. 38–59.

Nowell-Smith, Patrick (1999), 'Morality: Religious and Secular', in Eleonore Stump and Michael J. Murray (eds), *Philosophy of Religion: The Big Questions*, Oxford: Blackwell, pp. 403–11.

NSOED (1996), *New Shorter Oxford English Dictionary*, ed. Lesley Brown, CD version 1.0.03/02.10.96s, Oxford: Oxford University Press.

Obelkevich, Jim (1976), *Religion and Rural Society: South Lindsey, 1825–1875*, Oxford: Oxford University Press.

Oppenheim, A. N. (1992), *Questionnaire Design, Interviewing and Attitude Measurement*, London: Pinter.

Orr, Meg (2000), 'The Role of the Teacher in the Theological Education of the Laity', in Jeff Astley (ed.), *Learning in the Way: Research and Reflection on Adult Christian Education*, Leominster: Gracewing, pp. 72–89.

Osmer, Richard (1990a), *A Teachable Spirit: Recovering the Teaching Office in the Church*, Louisville, Ky.: Westminster/John Knox Press.

Osmer, Richard, R. (1990b), 'Teaching as Practical Theology', in Jack L. Seymour and Donald E. Miller (eds), *Theological Approaches to Christian Education*, Nashville: Abingdon, pp. 216–38.

Osmond, Rosalie (1993), *Changing Perspectives: Christian Culture and Morals in England Today*, London: Darton, Longman and Todd.

Pailin, David (1992), *A Gentle Touch: From a Theology of Handicap to a Theology of Human Being*, London: SPCK.

Paton, H. J. (ed.) (1948), *The Moral Law*, London: Hutchinson.

Pattison, George (1995), unpublished paper given at Artists and Theologians Colloquium, University College, Durham, 5 September.

Pattison, George (1997), *Kierkegaard and the Crisis of Faith: An Introduction to His Thought*, London: SPCK.

Pattison, George (1998), *The End of Theology – And the Task of Thinking about God*, London: SCM.

Pattison, George (2001), *A Short Course in the Philosophy of Religion*, London: SCM.

Pattison, Stephen and Woodward, James (2000), 'An Introduction to Pastoral and Practical Theology', in James Woodward and Stephen Pattison (eds), *The Blackwell Reader in Pastoral and Practical Theology*, Oxford: Blackwell, pp. 1–19.

Patton, Michael Quinn (1987), *How to Use Qualitative Methods in Evaluation*, Newbury Park, Calif.: Sage.

Pelikan, Jaroslav (1971–89), *The Christian Tradition: A History of the Development of Doctrine*, 5 vols, Chicago: University of Chicago Press.

Pepper, Stephen C. (1935), 'The root metaphor theory of metaphysics', *Journal of Philosophy*, XXXII, 14: 365–74.

Phillips, D. Z. (1965), *The Concept of Prayer*, London: Routledge & Kegan Paul.

Phillips, D. Z. (1970a), *Death and Immortality*, London: Macmillan.

Phillips, D. Z. (1970b), *Faith and Philosophical Enquiry*, London: Routledge & Kegan Paul.

Phillips, D. Z. (1976), *Religion Without Explanation*, Oxford: Blackwell.

Phillips, D. Z. (1986), *Belief, Change and Forms of Life*, London: Macmillan.

Phillips, D. Z. (1988), *Faith After Foundationalism*, London: Routledge.

Phillips, D. Z. (1993), *Wittgenstein and Religion*, Basingstoke: Macmillan.

Polanyi, Michael (1962), *Personal Knowledge: Towards A Post-Critical Philosophy*, London: Routledge & Kegan Paul.

Polanyi, Michael (1967), *The Tacit Dimension*, New York: Doubleday.

Price, Henry H. (1969), *Belief*, London: George Allen & Unwin.

Pring, Richard (2000), *Philosophy of Educational Research*, London: Continuum.

Pruyser, Paul (1974), *Between Belief and Unbelief*, London: Sheldon.

Putnam, Hilary (1992), *Renewing Philosophy*, Cambridge, Mass.: Harvard University Press.

Quinton, Anthony (1973), *The Nature of Things*, London: Routledge & Kegan Paul.

Rahner, Karl (1975), 'Theology', in Karl Rahner (ed.), *Encyclopaedia of Theology: A Concise Sacramentum Mundi*, London: Burns & Oates, pp. 1686–1701.

Rambo, Lewis R. (1980), 'Psychological perspectives on conversion', *Pacific Theological Review*, 13: 21–6.

Ramsey, Ian T. (1957), *Religious Language*, London: SCM.

Ramsey, Ian T. (1962), 'Logical empiricism and patristics', *Studia Patristica*, 5, 3: 541–6.

Ramsey, Ian T. (1963), *On Being Sure in Religion*, London: Athlone.

Ramsey, Ian T. (1964a), 'History and the Gospels: some philosophical reflections, *Studia Evangelica*, III, 6: 201–17.
Ramsey, Ian T. (1964b), *Models and Mystery*, Oxford: Oxford University Press.
Ramsey, Ian T. (1965a), 'Contemporary philosophy and the Christian faith', *Religious Studies*, 1, 1: 47–61.
Ramsey, Ian T. (1965b), *Christian Discourse: Some Logical Explorations*, Oxford: Oxford University Press.
Ramsey, Ian T. (1966), 'Talking About God: Models, Ancient and Modern', in F. W. Dillistone (ed.), *Myth and Symbol*, London: SPCK, pp. 76–97.
Ramsey, Ian T. (1967), 'Models and Mystery', a reply to Braithwaite, Miller and Barton, *Theoria to Theory*, 1, 3: 263–9.
Ramsey, Ian T. (1969), 'Fullness of Life', in T. Wilson (ed.), *All One Body*, London: Darton, Longman and Todd, pp. 35–58.
Ramsey, Ian T. (1973), *Models for Divine Activity*, London: SCM.
Reed, Bruce D. (1978), *The Dynamics of Religion: Process and Movement in Christian Churches*, London: Darton, Longman and Todd.
Rhees, Rush (1969), *Without Answers*, London: Routledge & Kegan Paul.
Richter, Philip and Francis, Leslie J. (1998), *Gone But Not Forgotten: Church Leaving and Returning*, London: Darton, Longman and Todd.
Ricoeur, Paul (1970), *Freud and Philosophy: An Essay on Interpretation*, trans. Denis Savage, New Haven: Yale University Press.
Ritschl, Dietrich (1984), *The Logic of Theology: A Brief Account of the Relationship Between Basic Concepts in Theology*, London: SCM.
Robbins, Mandy and Francis, Leslie J. (2000), 'Religion, personality and well-being: the relationship between church attendance and purpose in life', *Journal of Research on Christian Education*, 9, 2: 223–38.
Robertson, Roland (1970), *The Sociological Interpretation of Religion*, Oxford: Blackwell.
Rogers, Alan (1986), *Teaching Adults*, Milton Keynes: Open University Press.
Rogers, Carl R. and Freiberg, H. Jerome (1994), *Freedom to Learn*, Upper Saddle River, NJ: Prentice-Hall.
Rose, Tim (2001), *Kierkegaard's Christocentric Theology*, Aldershot: Ashgate.
Runzo, Joseph (1986), *Reason, Relativism and God*, London: Macmillan.
Ryan, Alan (1970), *The Philosophy of the Social Sciences*, London: Macmillan.
Saddington, James Anthony (1992), 'Learner Experience: A Rich Resource for Learning', in John Mulligan and Colin Griffin (eds), *Empowerment through Experiential Learning: Explorations of Good Practice*, London: Kogan Page, pp. 37–49.
Sauter, Gerhard and Barton, John (eds) (2000), *Revelation and Story: Narrative Theology and the Centrality of Story*, Aldershot: Ashgate.
Schools Council (1971), *Religious Education in Secondary Schools*, London: Evans/Methuen.
Schreiner, Peter (ed.) (2000), *Religious Education in Europe: A Collection of Basic Information about RE in European Countries*, Münster: Comenius-Institut.
Schreiter, Robert J. (1985), *Constructing Local Theologies*, Maryknoll, NY: Orbis.

Scruton, Roger (1994), *Modern Philosophy: A Survey*, London: Sinclair-Stevenson.
Scruton, Roger (1998), *An Intelligent Person's Guide to Modern Culture*, London: Duckworth.
Scruton, Roger (2000), *England: An Elegy*, London: Chatto & Windus.
Sexson, Lynda (1982), *Ordinarily Sacred*, New York: Crossroad.
Sheldrake, Philip (1998), *Spirituality and Theology: Christian Living and the Doctrine of God*, London: Darton, Longman and Todd.
Simmons, Henry C. (n.d.), 'Human Development: Some Conditions for Adult Faith at Age Thirty', in John L. Elias (ed.), *Religious Education in Adulthood*, New Haven: The Religious Education Association, pp. 10–19. First published 1976.
Slee, Nicola Mary (1999), 'The Patterns and Processes of Women's Faith Development: A Qualitative Study', unpublished Ph.D. Thesis, University of Birmingham.
Slee, Nicola (2001), 'Apophatic faithing in women's spirituality', *British Journal of Theological Education*, 11, 2: 23–37.
Smart, Ninian (1968), *Secular Education and the Logic of Religion*, London: Faber and Faber.
Smart, Ninian (1973a), *The Phenomenon of Religion*, London: Macmillan.
Smart, Ninian (1973b), *The Science of Religion and the Sociology of Knowledge*, Princeton, : Princeton University Press.
Smart, Ninian (1979), *The Phenomenon of Christianity*, London: Collins.
Smart, Ninian (1996), *Dimensions of the Sacred*, London: HarperCollins.
Solomon, Robert C. (1973), 'Emotions and choice', *Review of Metaphysics*, 27, 1: 20–41.
Soskice, Janet Martin (1985), *Metaphor and Religious Language*, Oxford: Oxford University Press.
Soskice, Janet Martin (1992), 'Love and Attention', in Michael McGhee (ed.), *Philosophy, Religion and the Spiritual Life*, Cambridge: Cambridge University Press, pp. 59–72.
Spohn, William C. (1999), *Go and Do Likewise: Jesus and Ethics*, New York: Continuum.
Sprigge, T. L. S. (1988), *The Rational Foundations of Ethics*, London: Routledge & Kegan Paul.
Stiver, Dan R. (1996), *The Philosophy of Religious Language: Sign, Symbol, and Story*, Oxford: Blackwell.
Sutherland, Stewart (1984), *God, Jesus and Belief*, Oxford: Blackwell.
Sutherland, Stewart R. (1985), 'Concluding Remarks', in M. C. Felderhof (ed.), *Religious Education in a Pluralistic Society*, London: Hodder & Stoughton, pp. 137–42.
Sutherland, Stewart R. (1986a), 'Theology and Humour', in Alistair Kee and Eugene Thomas Long (eds), *Being and Truth: Essays in Honour of John Macquarrie*, London: SCM, pp. 123–35.
Sutherland, Stewart R. (1986b), 'Education and Theology', in Joanna Yates (ed.), *Faith for the Future*, London: National Society and Church House Publishing, pp. 35–41.
Swinburne, Richard (1979), *The Existence of God*, Oxford: Oxford University Press.
Swinburne, Richard (1981), *Faith and Reason*, Oxford: Clarendon.

Sykes, Stephen W. (1979), 'The Incarnation as the Foundation of the Church', in Michael Goulder (ed.), *Incarnation and Myth: The Debate Continues*, London: SCM, pp. 115–27.

Sykes, S. W. (1983), 'Theology', in Alan Richardson and John Bowden (eds), *A New Dictionary of Christian Theology*, London: SCM, pp. 566–67.

Sykes, Stephen (1984), *The Identity of Christianity*, London: SPCK.

Tannen, Deborah (1990), *You Just Don't Understand: Women and Men in Conversation*, London: Virago.

Tannen, Deborah (1995), *Talking from 9 to 5: How Women's and Men's Conversational Styles Affect Who Gets Heard, Who Gets Credit, and What Gets Done at Work*, London: Virago.

Taylor, Charles (1960), 'Clericalism', *The Downside Review*, LXXVIII, 252: 167–80.

Taylor, Charles (1989), *Sources of the Self: The Making of the Modern Identity*, Cambridge: Cambridge University Press.

TeSelle, Sallie McFague (1975), *Speaking in Parables: A Study in Metaphor and Theology*, London: SCM.

Thiessen, Elmer J. (1993), *Teaching for Commitment: Liberal Education, Indoctrination and Christian Nurture*, Montreal and Kingston: McGill-Queen's University Press; Leominster: Gracewing.

Thiselton, Anthony C. (1980), *The Two Horizons: New Testament Hermeneutics and Philosophical Description with Special Reference to Heidegger, Bultmann, Gadamer and Wittgenstein*, Exeter: Paternoster.

Thiselton, Anthony C. (1992), *New Horizons in Hermeneutics*, London: HarperCollins.

Thomas, Owen C. (1983), *Introduction to Theology*, Wilton, Conn.: Morehouse.

Tight, Malcolm (1996), *Key Concepts in Adult Education and Training*, London: Routledge.

Tilley, Terrence W. (1985), *Story Theology*, Wilmington, Del.: Michael Glazier.

Tilley, Terrence W. (2000), *Inventing Catholic Tradition*, Maryknoll, NY: Orbis.

Tilley, Terrence W. *et al.* (1995), *Postmodern Theologies: The Challenge of Religious Diversity*, Maryknoll, NY: Orbis.

Tinsley, John (1996), 'Tell it Slant', in Jeff Astley, Leslie J. Francis and Colin Crowder (eds), *Theological Perspectives on Christian Formation: A Reader in Theology and Christian Education*, Leominster: Gracewing Fowler Wright; Grand Rapids, Mich.: Eerdmans, pp. 88–94. First published 1979.

Titelman, P. (1979), 'Some Implications of Ricoeur's Conception of Hermeneutics for Phenomenological Psychology', in A. Georgia *et al.* (eds), *Duquesne Studies in Phenomenological Psychology*, Vol. 3, Pittsburgh: Duquesne University Press, pp. 182–92.

Toon, Richard (n.d.), *Methodological Problems in the Study of Implicit Religion*, Leeds: Department of Sociology, University of Leeds.

Towler, Robert (1974), *Homo Religiosus*, London: Constable.

Towler, Robert (1984), *The Need for Certainty: A Sociological Study of Conventional Religion*, London: Routledge & Kegan Paul.

Towler, Robert (n.d.), *Conventional Religion and Common Religion in Great Britain*, Leeds: Department of Sociology, University of Leeds.

Tracy, David (1975), *Blessed Rage for Order: The New Pluralism in Theology*, New York: Seabury.

Tracy, David (1981), *The Analogical Imagination: Christian Theology and the Culture of Pluralism*, London: SCM.

Tracy, David (1983), 'The Foundations of Practical Theology', in Don S. Browning (ed.), *Practical Theology*, San Francisco: Harper & Row, pp. 61–82.

Tracy, David (1994), *On Naming the Present: God, Hermeneutics and the Church*, Maryknoll, NY: Orbis; London, SCM.

van der Ven, Johannes (1993), *Practical Theology: An Empirical Approach*, Kampen, Netherlands: Kok Pharos.

Wainwright, Geoffrey (1993), 'Method in Theology', in Alister E. McGrath (ed.), *The Blackwell Encyclopaedia of Modern Christian Thought*, Oxford: Blackwell, pp. 369–73.

Wakefield, Gordon S. (1983), 'Spirituality', in Alan Richardson and John Bowden (eds), *A New Dictionary of Christian Theology*, London: SCM, pp. 549–50.

Walker, Andrew (1996), *Telling the Story: Gospel, Mission and Culture*, London: SPCK.

Ward, Keith (1994), *Religion and Revelation: A Theology of Revelation in the World's Religions*, Oxford: Oxford University Press.

Warnke, G. (1987), *Gadamer: Hermeneutics, Tradition and Reason*, Stanford, Calif.: University of Stanford Press.

Weber, Max (1949), *The Methodology of the Social Sciences*, trans. Edward A. Shils and Henry A. Finch, New York: Free Press.

Weiser, Artur (1962), *The Psalms: A Commentary*, trans. Herbert Hartwell, London: SCM.

Wellington, Jerry (2000), *Educational Research: Contemporary Issues and Practical Approaches*, London: Continuum.

West, Michael; Noble, Graham and Todd, Andrew (1999), *Living Theology*, London: Darton, Longman and Todd.

Westerhoff, John (1978), 'A necessary paradox: catechesis and evangelism, nurture and conversion', *Religious Education*, LXXIII: 409–16.

White, Stephen Ross (1994), *Don Cupitt and the Future of Christian Doctrine*, London: SCM.

Whitehead, James D. and Whitehead, Evelyn Eaton (1995), *Method in Ministry: Theological Reflection and Christian Ministry*, Kansas City: Sheed and Ward.

Wiles, Maurice F. (1986), *God's Action in the World*, London: SCM.

Williams, Bernard (1985), *Ethics and the Limits of Philosophy*, London: Collins.

Williams, Michael (1985), 'Theology versus faith, academic versus pastoral theology: a dichotomy?', *Anvil*, 2, 2: 153–70.

Williams, Rowan (2000a), *Lost Icons: Reflections on Cultural Bereavement*, Edinburgh: T. & T. Clark.

Williams, Rowan (2000b), *On Christian Theology*, Oxford: Blackwell.

Williams, S. C. (1999), *Religious Belief and Popular Culture in Southwark, c.1880–1939*, Oxford: Oxford University Press.

Winch, P. G. (1958), *The Idea of a Social Science*, London: Routledge & Kegan Paul.

Wingeier, Douglas E. (1994), 'Christian Education as Faith Translation', in Jeff Astley and Leslie J. Francis (eds), *Critical Perspectives on Christian Education: A Reader on the Aims, Principles and Philosophy of Christian Education*, Leominster: Gracewing, pp. 238–50. First published 1977.

Wittgenstein, Ludwig (1966), *Lectures and Conversations in Aesthetics, Psychology and Religious Belief*, ed. Cyril Barrett, Oxford: Blackwell.

Wittgenstein, Ludwig (1968), *Philosophical Investigations*, trans. G. E. M. Anscombe, Oxford: Blackwell.

Wittgenstein, Ludwig (1974), *On Certainty*, ed. G. E. M. Anscombe and G. H. von Wright, trans. Denis Paul and G. E. M. Anscombe, Oxford: Blackwell.

Wittgenstein, Ludwig (1980), *Culture and Value*, ed. G. H. von Wright, trans. Peter Winch, Oxford: Blackwell.

Wood, Charles M. (1985), *Vision and Discernment: An Orientation in Theological Study*, Atlanta, Ga.: Scholars Press.

Wood, Charles M. (1993), *The Formation of Christian Understanding*, Valley Forge, Pa.: Trinity Press International.

Wood, Charles (1996a), 'Theological Education and Education for Church Leadership', in Jeff Astley, Leslie J. Francis and Colin Crowder (eds), *Theological Perspectives on Christian Formation: A Reader in Theology and Christian Education*, Leominster: Gracewing Fowler Wright; Grand Rapids, Mich.: Eerdmans, pp. 303–14. First published 1990.

Wood, Charles (1996b), 'Theological Inquiry and Theological Education', in Jeff Astley, Leslie J. Francis and Colin Crowder (eds), *Theological Perspectives on Christian Formation: A Reader in Theology and Christian Education*, Leominster: Gracewing Fowler Wright; Grand Rapids, Mich.: Eerdmans, pp. 342–58. First published 1985.

Woodhead, Linda (1997), 'Christianity according to its interpreters', *Reviews in Religion and Theology*, 4: 7–12.

Zuidberg, Gerard (2001), *The God of the Pastor: The Spirituality of Roman Catholic Pastors in the Netherlands*, Leiden: Brill.

Name Index

Subject Index